12.11.05

To MATthew, I value our
friendship and Admire
your work.

David R Woodward

Field Marshal
Sir William Robertson

Field Marshal Sir William Robertson

FIELD MARSHAL
SIR WILLIAM ROBERTSON

Chief of the
Imperial General Staff
in the Great War

David R. Woodward

Westport, Connecticut
London

Library of Congress Cataloging-in-Publication Data

Woodward, David R., 1939–
    Field Marshal Sir William Robertson : Chief of the Imperial
General Staff in the Great War / David R. Woodward.
        p.   cm.
    Includes bibliographical references and index.
    ISBN 0–275–95422–6 (alk. paper)
    1. Robertson, William Robert, Sir, 1860–1933. 2. World War,
1914–1918—Great Britain. 3. Marshals—Great Britain—Biography.
I. Title.
D546.W59   1998
940.3′092
[B]—DC21   97–24549

British Library Cataloguing in Publication Data is available.

Library of Congress Catalog Card Number: 97–24549
ISBN: 0–275–95422–6

First published in 1998

Praeger Publishers, 88 Post Road West, Westport, CT 06881
An imprint of Greenwood Publishing Group, Inc.

Printed in the United States of America

The paper used in this book complies with the
Permanent Paper Standard issued by the National
Information Standards Organization (Z39.48–1984).

10 9 8 7 6 5 4 3 2 1

Contents

Illustrations

Acknowledgments

I am very much in the debt of a number of individuals who have assisted me in the preparation of this volume. My wife, Martha, and good friend and colleague, Dr. Robert F. Maddox, read various versions of the manuscript and offered helpful suggestions. Michael McCarthy provided computer expertise. Marshall University granted me a sabbatical during the fall term of 1995 and provided financial assistance in the form of a summer research grant. This book also owes much to the staff members of the British archives in which I have worked. R.W.A. Suddaby, the Keeper of the Department of Documents at the Imperial War Museum, and Patricia J. Methven of the Liddell Hart Centre for Military Archives deserve special recognition in this regard.

I have made every effort to avoid infringing upon the copyrights of any individuals or institutions. I am very much obliged to the following individuals and institutions for granting me access to and when possible permission to quote documents in their possession: the Trustees of the Liddell Hart Centre for Military Archives; the Trustees of the Imperial War Museum; the Masters and Fellows of Churchill College; the Clerk of the Records on behalf of the Beaverbrook Foundation Trustees; the Trustees of the National Library of Scotland; Bodleian Library, Oxford; Adrian Fitzgerald; Richard Kirke; Belinda Bell; Lord Shelborne; Lord Haig; the Earl of Derby; Lord Robertson; Alisdair Murray; Andrew Rawlinson; and Jane Bonham-Carter. Unpublished Crown-copyright material in the Public Record Office and the collections of the British Library are reproduced by permission of the controller of Her Majesty's Stationery Office. The gracious permission of Her Majesty Queen Elizabeth II for the use of material from the Royal Archives is also acknowledged. The Special Collections Branch of the U.S. Army Military History Institute provided me photographs from its collection.

Prologue

Field Marshal Sir William Robertson's career is a truly remarkable story. He was the first to demonstrate that a private in the British army could have a marshal's baton in his knapsack. He also was the first ranker to qualify for the Staff College at Camberley and the first to become its commandant. The zenith of his career was his service as Chief of the Imperial General Staff (CIGS). From December 1915 to February 1918 he served as the government's military adviser and as the professional head of the army. He and Sir Douglas Haig, the commander in chief of the British Expeditionary Force (BEF), constituted what is arguably the most important military partnership in British history. Their dominating influence helped ensure that Britain concentrated its military resources against the main body of the German army.

This book is not a biography of Robertson. Rather it focuses on his controversial role in the higher direction of the war, when he supervised the operational commands in France, Egypt, Mesopotamia, Salonika, and East Africa, and briefly, in Italy and Gallipoli as well.

No conflict in British history has provoked or continues to provoke so much controversy. The BEF's great battles in France and Flanders are frequently portrayed as "senseless slaughter," sanctioned by myopic politicians, and conducted by hidebound soldiers for little or no purpose. British casualties were certainly unprecedented. Excluding Indian and dominion forces, roughly one in eight who served in the British army was killed and one in three was wounded. The odds of a British soldier surviving the war without being killed, wounded, or captured were only one in two.[1] These heart-rending casualties (2,471,152) best explain the passion when Britain's politicians and especially her military leaders are discussed. Sadly, an appreciation of the extraordinarily difficult and limited choices confronting the British war leaders in their coalition war has become another casualty of the war.

It is best to state one's sympathies before beginning the precarious journey across the treacherous literary terrain of the Great War. Few simple answers can be found in this conflict of unprecedented scope, complexity, and violence. "Because it was the first, all-out, mass industrialized coalition war of this century," Paul Kennedy has written, "it tested effectiveness at all levels—political, strategic, operational, and tactical—and usually found things wanting."[2] Having been a student of World War I for over thirty years, this writer says amen to that.

The war's disappointing outcome also led many to believe that there were no real winners, or, in fact, anything worth fighting for. My view, however, is that German expansionism had to be resisted. Frustration over the increasing flow of British soldiers to the killing fields of the western front is understandable. "Are we really bound to hand over the ordering of our troops to France," David Lloyd George exclaimed in 1915, "as if we were her vassal?"[3] But Britain couldn't fight this war to the last Russian or Frenchman. The British couldn't pursue a policy of limited liability on the western front if German expansionism was to be thwarted. The price of victory proved tragically high but was still preferable to a disastrous peace.

Prior to 1918 the Allies didn't have the technical means to end the stalemate, and the formula for success proved to be more tactical than strategical. Robertson understood the essentials of victory, destroying the German army rather than conquering territory. His advocacy of skillfully applied attrition versus Haig's attempts at a strategic breakthrough constitutes an important theme in this study.

NOTES

1. J. M. Winter, *The Great War and the British People* (Cambridge, 1986), 72–73.

2. Paul Kennedy, "Military Effectiveness in the First World War," in *Military Effectiveness*, vol. 1: *The First World War*, ed. Allan R. Millett and Williamson Murray (Boston, 1989), 329.

3. Martin Gilbert, ed., *Winston S. Churchill, Vol. 3 Companion Part 1 Documents July 1914–April 1915* (London, 1972), 472.

Chapter 1

"The Cleverest Man in the Army"

William Robert Robertson was born of humble parents on January 29, 1860, in the Lincolnshire village of Welbourn, some twelve miles south of Lincoln. Educated in the village Anglican school, he entered domestic service at age thirteen. In 1877 he enlisted for twelve years in the 16th (Queen's) Lancers to the dismay of his mother, who wrote, "I would rather Bury you than see you in a red coat."[1] Robertson's choice of a career in the Victorian army seemed a particularly bad one. Although the purchase of most commissions had recently been abolished, British officers were almost exclusively selected from the middle and upper classes and were usually products of public schools. Robertson had none of the advantages of wealth, education, or social standing. But Robertson was by no means typical of the other troopers in the 16th Lancers. Possessing grit, raw ability, and especially a dogged perseverance, he let no obstacle thwart his advancement. Strong and athletic, he excelled in sword, lance, and shooting, winning first prizes in all three in troop competitions. He ran ten miles every Saturday. It was his brain rather than his brawn, however, that was the key to his advancement. Dedicated to his profession, he sought to remedy his rudimentary education, reading everything available to him on past wars, strategy, and tactics. Passing the required written and oral examinations, he was gazetted in 1888 second lieutenant and posted to the 3rd Dragoon Guards.

With only four or five rankers being commissioned each year in the 1880s, Robertson was apprehensive about the reaction of his "social superiors." "Its all amongst strangers—strangers in more ways than one.... The officers who now know me are very nice, but its a difficult business because you see I feel that I am acting under a false flag if they do not know my previous life," he confided to his mother.[2]

Virtually penniless, he couldn't afford the life-style of a cavalry subaltern. His father, a tailor, made his clothes when he was commissioned. He drank water instead of alcohol and didn't smoke following meals because a pipe, for which he could afford tobacco, was not allowed in mess. A posting to India, where pay was higher and expenses lower, helped him survive on the economic margin. Because cash awards were given by the Indian government to officers who learned native languages, Robertson mastered Urdu, Hindi, Persian, Pashto, Punjabi, and Gurkhali.

His remarkable success as a linguist, which could only be achieved through hard study and discipline, made him stand out from most of his fellow officers who seemed primarily interested in polo and brandy. While others slept through the oppressive midday heat, Robertson worked with native tutors. This intellectual work prepared him for a greater hurdle, passing the entrance exam for the Staff College at Camberley, for which he was nominated by the commander in chief in India. To join Britain's military elite, he needed to master mathematics and either German or French. He mastered German and later qualified at Camberley as an interpreter in French. "By rising regularly every morning between four and five o'clock, in winter as in summer, I was able to get through a large amount of spade work, crude and ill-directed though it might be, before going to office for the day,"[3] he writes in his memoirs. Tutors and an educated and polished wife, Mildred Adelaide, the second daughter of Lieutenant-General Charles Thomas Palin of the India Army, also helped.

Blessed with a remarkable memory and a sharp mind, Captain Robertson distinguished himself at Camberley. A quick study, one of his favorite expressions was, "Yes, yes. I have got that, get on to the next point."[4] Britain's leading military theorist, George F. R. Henderson, became his intellectual mentor. In "Hender's" classes on strategy and tactics, many of the future leaders of the British army in World War I, including Sir Douglas Haig, learned an amalgam of the thought of the military writers of the nineteenth century: Baron de Jomini, Carl von Clausewitz, and Sir Edward Hamley, the author of The Operations of War (1866), among others.[5] Emphasis was on principles of war, such as the destruction of the main body of the enemy's forces, and concentrating superior strength, physical and moral, on the battlefield. Clausewitz, with his emphasis on battle over maneuver and mass over skill, seemed especially suited to the Great War. Robertson was conversant with Clausewitz's writings for his papers contain notes taken from *On War* for lectures he delivered at the Staff College.[6] But the belief that overwhelming forces should be concentrated on the primary front was not uniquely Clausewitzian. It dominated the military theory of the day.[7]

The maxims that Robertson absorbed at Camberley, in his words, seemed "as old as the hills" when the Great War began.[8] He and Haig were in complete agreement about concentrating British forces in the theater that attracted the main body of the enemy, which throughout the war was France and Flanders. As Robertson writes in his memoirs, "There was never, so far as I know, any material difference of opinion between us in regard to the main principles to be observed in order to win the war."[9]

Following Staff College, Robertson briefly did intelligence work on Lord Roberts's staff during the South African War. Returning to London, he gained an important assignment, head of the Foreign Military Intelligence Section, 1901–1907. The Intelligence Division in the War Office had recently been subdivided into three sections: Imperial, Foreign, and Special. From being a staff captain, the junior of two officers in the Colonial (now Imperial) Section, Robertson became the chief of a staff with nine officers. In 1903 he was promoted to colonel. In India, he had been one of the oldest lieutenants in the army; now he was one of the youngest colonels. Heads turned in the War Office. Merit was the explanation for his rapid rise, but he also had support in high places. An authority in intelligence work, General Sir Henry Brackenbury, strongly recommended him.[10]

As always, Robertson took advantage of opportunities afforded him. His energy, organizational ability, and vision firmly established his reputation. In the view of a contemporary in the War Office, "he became rated as a superman, and only key appointments were considered good enough for him." He seemed "always to be in deep thought, both inside and outside the office." He walked the halls of the War Office "with a slow measured tread and spoke with a masterful drawl which sometimes sounded gruff, but kind withal; his approbation was expressed by a pleasant grunt." His blunt manner, not so apparent previously, was perhaps his way of letting people "see he was boss."[11]

In assessing the military potential of foreign powers, Robertson perceived Germany, with its embryonic navy, booming economy, and thirst for overseas territory, as Britain's "most persistent, deliberate, and formidable rival."[12]

Robertson's intelligence work coincided with the quickening pace of the modernization of the army that followed the South African War. The office of the commander in chief of the army was abolished and replaced as the supreme military authority by the Army Council, composed of four military members—the Chief of the General Staff, Adjutant-General, Quartermaster-General, and Master-General of Ordnance—and three civil members: the secretary of state for war, who served as chair; the Parliamentary under-secretary; and the financial secretary to the War Office.

A general staff was an essential though controversial part of the reform program. There was unease and jealousy among many officers over the creation of an "elite" to act as the "brains" of the army. Lord Kitchener was among the critics, referring to that "miserable lot. . . the soldiers of the so-called General Staff."[13] For their part, civilians feared that Parliament might be undermined and civilian control of the military put in jeopardy by an institution that resembled the great German general staff. One concern was that contingency planning might make more likely British participation in a European land war.

The growing international threat to British security and the obvious need for greater military efficiency, however, overrode these concerns; and the general staff was installed in the new War Office at Whitehall at the beginning of 1907. Its responsibilities had been clearly defined in the special army order of September 12, 1906: "to advise on the strategical distribution of the Army, to supervise the education of officers, and the training and preparation of the Army for war, to study military schemes, offensive and defensive, to collect and collate military intelligence, to direct the General policy in Army matters, and to secure continuity of action in the execution of that policy."[14]

Its "chief " was thus expected to advise the Secretary of State for War in areas such as intelligence, operations, training, and war planning. But the Imperial General Staff, as it was renamed in 1910, did not replace the Master General of the Ordnance, Adjutant-General, and Quartermaster-General, War Office institutions of long standing. As the professional head of the army, the CIGS, however, was first among equals with the heads of these ancient offices on the Army Council.

Despite the reform of Britain's war machinery, the role the "chief " would play in a great war remained an open question. Much depended on the willingness of the civilian leadership to accept his guidance. Just as crucial perhaps was the personality and vision of the CIGS. As John Gooch has noted, "events were to prove that a structure which needed a Moltke would not necesssarily get one."[15]

In 1910 Robertson's career took another important turn when he was chosen commandant of the Staff College. He took a practical and common sense approach for which he would forever after be identified. His training exercises, for example, included withdrawals as well as advances. Officers were taught to understand and appreciate not just theory but how to apply doctrine under battlefield conditions. "Training manuals do not pretend to be exhaustive tactical treatises," he told his students. "They lay down certain principles, but they do not pretend to show how these principles must be treated or modified under conditions which are so infinitely diversified."[16]

"As a lecturer," according to Sir James Edmonds, the compiler of the official British history of war, "he was in a higher class, with a style, diction, clearness and compactness of statement of the highest order, which was not surpassed by such masters of the art as the late Colonel Lonsdale Hale and the late Colonel G.F.R. ('Stonewall') Henderson."[17]

Robertson returned in 1913 to the War Office as Director of Military Training. There he became peripherally involved in the Curragh Incident. Many officers opposed military coercion to force home rule on Ulster. Robertson contemplated resignation and gave his support to the Gough brothers, who were leading opponents of the Liberal government's approach to Ireland.[18] This divisive incident gave a sharper edge to partisan politics in Parliament and provoked suspicion and even hatred between army officers and Liberal politicians. Robertson, however, emerged from this controversy without a blot on his scutcheon.

When war erupted in 1914, Robertson was expected to head the home defense forces as Director of Military Training. However, when Archibald Murray was chosen to head the expeditionary force's general staff, Robertson was selected to replace him as Quartermaster-General of the BEF. Fearing disaster because prewar plans had placed the BEF in a precarious forward position, Robertson made preparations to supply the army from the Atlantic rather than the Belgian coast. "From what I knew of the French and of Sir John French's Staff," he later said, "I feared we should begin with a retreat."[19] The BEF was consequently well supplied both during and after its headlong retreat from Mons. "Old Any-Complaints" became his nickname; when he visited troops eating their meals, he usually asked, "Any complaints, men?"[20]

Robertson, or "Wully" as he was affectionately known, was fifty-five years old in 1914, with a physical presence to match his forceful personality. Powerfully built with a prominent jaw and chin, he emanated strength. Every inch a professional soldier, he seemed to represent the best example of the prewar efforts to modernize the army. Many thought him the "cleverest man in the army."

Robertson's humble origins, perhaps even his dropping of his aitches, worked to his advantage. He was praised in high places for his simple and blunt ways, his contempt for the false and artificial. If Britain were to triumph in this total war, immense sacrifices must be demanded from the nation. Wully, this rugged son of Lincolnshire, became the embodiment of the common man for many of Britain's elite, including the king, who became an important ally. George V had attended the Royal Naval College and held the rank of commander. As the titular head of the armed services, he took very seriously his duties, frequently visiting the Grand Fleet and the western front during the Great War. At times to the obvious discomfort of prime ministers Asquith and Lloyd George, he insisted that he be consulted on the vital military and naval questions of the day.

Robertson's background also helps explain the acceptance of his crusty and extraordinarily blunt ways. He did not gladly suffer fools. After listening to an Italian officer give a long dissertation on the possibility of a Swiss invasion of his country, Robertson told a colleague: "I'd like to have kicked him in the stomach."[21] A conversation stopper was "I've heard different." He could be equally direct when he took up the pen. His papers, even when written for the eyes of his political superiors, could be wounding. Fortunately his bluntness was softened by an attractive personality. He had a quick smile, loved a good joke, and was known for his *bons mots*. When untroubled, he was lively and amusing company.

As Robertson's star rose, Murray's fell. As noted earlier, Robertson had been unimpressed with the BEF's staff work before August 1914. Murray, whose instructions have been described as "miracles of opacity, devoid of context, and a source of consternation and confusion to those who received them,"[22] was not the man to reform BEF staff work. On January 25, 1915, Robertson replaced him.

NOTES

1. Victor Bonham-Carter, *Soldier True: The Life and Times of Field-Marshal Sir William Robertson* (London, 1963), 5.

2. Ibid., 32.

3. Sir William Robertson, *From Private to Field-Marshal* (London, 1921), 79.

4. I am grateful to John Hussey for pointing out the following article to me. Sir James Edmonds, "Field-Marshal Sir William Robertson: Reminiscences and an Appreciation," *The Army Quarterly* 26 (April 1933): 16.

5. See Michael Howard, *Studies in War and Peace* (New York, 1970), 21–36; Carl von Clausewitz, *On War*, ed. Anatol Rapoport (Middlesex, England, 1968); Baron de Jomini, *The Art of War* (Westport, Conn., 1862); Tim Travers, *The*

Killing Ground: The British Army, the Western Front and the Emergence of Modern Warfare 1900–1918 (London, 1987), 85–100; and Christopher Bassford, *Clausewitz in English: The Reception of Clausewitz in Britain and America 1815–1945* (New York and Oxford, 1994).

6. See "Clausewitz, vol. 1." n.d., Robertson MSS I/3/6.

7. Sir F. Maurice, *British Strategy: A Study of the Application of the Principles of War* (London, 1929), 39.

8. Robertson, *Private to Field-Marshal*, 248.

9. Ibid., 90.

10. W.R.V. Isaac, "Field-Marshal Sir William Robertson When Head of the Foreign Military Intelligence Section, War Office" January 1960, WO Lib. AO11.14.

11. Ibid.

12. Memorandum by Robertson, November 10, 1902, Robertson MSS I/2/4.

13. John Gooch, *The Plans of War: The General Staff and British Military Strategy c. 1900–1916* (New York, 1974), 100.

14. Ibid., 107. For the General Staff's development, see also General Sir William Jackson and Field Marshal Lord Bramall, *The Chiefs: The Story of the United Kingdom Chiefs of Staff* (London, 1992), 3–52, and Dominick Graham and Shelford Bidwell, *Coalitions, Politicians and Generals: Some Aspects of Command in Two World Wars* (London, 1993), 9–23.

15. Gooch, *Plans of War*, 56.

16. Robertson, "Remarks on visit to battlefield. 1912," Robertson MSS I/2/12.

17. Edmonds, "Robertson," 17.

18. Ian F. W. Beckett, ed., *The Army and the Curragh Incident* (London, 1986), 22–23, 69–70, 277–78.

19. Edmonds, "Robertson," 19.

20. G. A. Leask, *Sir William Robertson: The Life Story of the Chief of the Imperial General Staff* (London, 1917), 116–17.

21. Diary entry of March 12, 1916, Clive MSS, CAB 45/201.

22. J.M. Bourne, *Britain and the Great War 1914–1918* (London, 1989), 27.

Chapter 2

Chief of the General Staff, BEF

The gigantic proportions of the war and the stalemated battlefield had not been anticipated by Europe's military elite, who had believed that future wars would be won quickly through offensive action. Plans involving the mobilization and movement by rail of millions were devised, and the war began with great armies on the move to deliver knockout blows. The most promising war plan, Germany's Schlieffen Plan, which sought to outflank the French army by marching across neutral Belgium, came to grief at the First Battle of the Marne in September 1914. When the opposing armies reached the sea, there were no more flanks to turn. From the Belgian coast to the Swiss Alps, soldiers began to dig.

"What we call our first line is a zone in some places as much as five or six miles in depth," Robertson informed Major Clive Wigram, George V's equerry. "In it there may be as many as six rows of trenches and every house, wood, and topographical feature is placed in a state of defence. . . . Every man in the Army, including the Cavalry Corps, digs practically every day where digging can be done during daylight."[1]

Britain's small army of volunteers was dwarfed by the large Continental conscript armies. The six divisions and one cavalry division committed in August and the reinforcements that followed were decimated in the first hundred days. Casualties were larger than the BEF's original strength. Given its resources, the BEF's role was bound to be limited. The decision to build a mass volunteer army might enable Britain eventually to fight on equal terms with Germany, but for the present the flow of reinforcements to the BEF was clouded in uncertainty, and the munitions industry was incapable of meeting the ever-expanding need for guns and shells.

In 1915 Germany shifted her attention to the eastern front and sent the Tsarist army reeling. Meanwhile in the west, the French commander in chief, Joseph Joffre, pursued an aggressive policy to expel the Germans from northern France. In a supporting role, the British First Army, commanded by Haig, launched four offensives in 1915: Neuve Chapelle (March 10–12), Aubers Ridge (May 9), Festubert (May 15–27), and Loos (September 25–October 8).

Appalled by the enormous casualties and limited results of trench warfare, Lloyd George believed that a "war of attrition" was being substituted for a "war of intelligence." In his purple prose, the generals expected to "'break through' and drive the Germans back across the Rhine, a routed and broken mob, chased by cavalry."[2] The "westerner" Robertson, in particular, became a focus of his attack on British generalship in his memoirs. By implication Wully was blamed for unnecessarily expending tens of thousands of British soldiers in futile offensives.

It is true that Robertson believed in the offensive. "Go for your man," he had told his students at Camberley. "There is no necessity to come to the Staff College in order to learn that only by the offensive can you win. That is obvious to everybody."[3] If the British stayed in their trenches, the strategical initiative would be forfeited to the Germans. With interior lines, an excellent system of rail transportation, and domination of the strategy of the Central Powers, Germany could concentrate its reserves, east or west, and attack Britain's allies on its own timetable.

But did the poorly equipped and undermanned BEF in 1915 have the ability to influence German actions? Neuve Chapelle, Aubers Ridge, and Festubert were comparatively small operations of limited duration; only Loos, with its some sixty thousand British casualties, was a major British offensive. Why not, as many civilians advocated, husband limited British manpower by resorting to an "active" defense in the west? New allies such as Greece and Romania might be found through the judicious use of British power in the eastern Mediterranean at either the Dardanelles or the Balkans. If France insisted on trying to rupture the German defenses, grant it the dubious honor of taking on the main body of the German army single-handedly.

To those who saw a passive policy as a way of saving British lives, Robertson sarcastically noted, "The attitude of the British mind at home appears to be that any loss in defence may be joyfully accepted as a sign of true bulldog tenacity against odds, but that losses incurred in attack are lamentable and unjustifiable unless the attack ends in the complete and decisive defeat of the enemy."[4] The heavy losses inflicted on British defenders in April during the German offensive, the Second Battle of Ypres, gave force to these words.

Robertson also emphasized that Britain was in a coalition war with the French and Russians, which made considerable sacrifice unavoidable. When the Cabinet mulled over a defensive policy and possible lines of retreat following the Second Battle of Ypres, Robertson pointed out some home truths. A withdrawal to the Channel ports, Britain's exit route from the Continental war, would be catastrophic. "Once we are hemmed in with our backs to the sea we become helpless spectators while the fate of the war is decided elsewhere by the defeat of the French."[5] It would be almost as dangerous, he argued, if the British on their section of the common front refused to fight. France would be discouraged; and Russia, if left to take on Germany, Austria-Hungary, and the Ottoman Empire without strong support from her western allies, might drop out of the war.[6]

As for peripheral operations to gain Balkan allies, Robertson maintained that the Balkan peoples would ultimately act in their own best interests, not Britain's.[7] "We are looking all round the world for people to pull the chestnuts out of the fire for us,"[8] he lamented. Nor could the British escape trench warfare through operations in the eastern Mediterranean. "Has our success against entrenchments in the Gallipoli peninsula," he asked, "been greater than in Flanders?" As least the BEF's effort offered the possibility of defeating the main enemy.[9]

Robertson's skepticism about "eastern" operations and his rejection of a defensive posture in France didn't make him the unimaginative and inflexible general, as caricatured by Lloyd George. He and his handpicked Director of Military Operations, Frederick B. Maurice, recognized early that the face of war had been radically changed by mass conscript armies and the new military technology. Robertson had become close to Maurice at Camberley when the latter had served under him as an instructor of military history. Tall and fair, with a round face and a boxer's nose, Maurice had one of the better minds in the British army; he later became a distinguished military theorist, serving as a Professor of Military Studies at London University and for a time as a military correspondent to the *Daily Chronicle* and *Daily News*. He and Robertson were as one on tactics and strategy, and tended to reinforce the thinking of the other.

Prior to the first atom bomb, no period in warfare had experienced a greater technological revolution.[10] Machine guns, clip-fed, breech-loading rifles, and advances in artillery dramatically increased firepower. Germany's introduction of poison gas warfare in April 1915 was yet another reflection of how applied science and technology affected warfare.

Following Joffre's costly failures in 1915 to rupture the German line, many French politicians were inclined to agree with British skeptics of the offensive. The siege battles seemed to prove the prewar theories of the Polish military visionary, Ivan Bloch, who suggested that the great increase in firepower made trench warfare inevitable, with the advantage going to the defense. Bloch didn't argue that the trenches were impenetrable, but he believed that soldiers, confronted by a firestorm of metal, "would not have the courage and endurance to assault trenches."[11] Hence it is not surprising that Robertson and other officers emphasized the moral qualities of the attacker to overcome the awesome firepower and strength of the defense.[12] Robertson spoke of "stout hearts" and "fortitude"; and believed that a pessimistic general, which he likened to "cowardice," should not be tolerated, even when that pessimism might be justified.[13] But Robertson equally condemned "foolish optimism."[14]

Forced to make unprecedented adjustments to the art of war, many officers were slow to change their nineteenth-century image of warfare, emphasizing the individual soldier over the new technology. But this wasn't true of Robertson, who grasped early the major elements in achieving a tactical success. Prior to the BEF's first offensive in 1915, he emphasized that the replacement of "field warfare" by "fortress warfare" required new methods. Ambitious strategical objectives with emphasis on a quick rupture of the line were rejected. Rather, a battlefield should be chosen that conferred the tactical advantage to the British, and then a cautious approach pursued that killed Germans through the employment of massive artillery. In Robertson's words, "If the Germans are to be defeated they must be beaten by a process of slow attrition, by a slow and gradual advance on our part, each step being prepared by a predominant artillery fire and great expenditure of ammunition."[15] Robertson also stressed the importance of counter-battery work.[16] To his credit, he thus recognized early the formula that ultimately allowed the BEF to defeat the German army in 1918: artillery, methodical preparation, and limited objectives.[17]

Robertson wanted any large-scale offensive predicated on the prospect of reasonable success, which was not necessarily the capture of important strategical objectives or a breakthrough; having the better manpower policy was also viewed as a success. When the French wanted the British to attack the strong enemy front at Loos, Robertson preferred a cautious "wearing" attack by the Second Army on the northern flank to gain the Messines-Wytschaete ridge. "We should not be helping the French by throwing away thousands of lives in knocking our heads against a brick wall," he told a fellow officer.[18] In other papers, Robertson stressed the element of surprise, experimenting with new methods, and realistic objectives to prevent elements of the "attacking force getting out of touch with the remainder, to a ragged line which has facilitated counterattack, and to the infantry advancing further and faster than was expected, with the result that they have sometimes been hit by our own guns."[19]

The attacking Allied forces lacked the technical means to win a decisive victory prior to 1918 over the powerful German army. But this didn't mean that Robertson, an advocate of the offensive, was guilty of substituting "attrition" for "intelligence." "Attrition," or the gradual process of wearing down the enemy, has been defined in a variety of ways.[20] To Robertson, it meant an approach to trench warfare that emphasized killing Germans over conquering territory. Offensives with distant strategic objectives that promised a rapid breakthrough by rushing the series of defensive lines in one bound led to unnecessary loss of life. Equally, Robertson deprecated a policy of pinprick attacks or "active defense" that might prolong the war indefinitely. As he told Joffre's chief of staff, General Pélli, if it were indeed "hopeless" to attack on the western front, then the Allies had no choice but to seek peace unless the Central Powers could be exhausted by blockade.[21]

Robertson and Maurice viewed the extensive system of earthworks as being stronger than permanent fortifications because they had the characteristic of an "elastic band." Their preference was to resort to "the usual methods of siege warfare to which all nations have resorted when their attempts to capture fortifications by assault have failed; mining must be used to supplement bombardment and efforts must be concentrated on a slow but sure advance from one locality to another carried out with the maximum of persistence combined with a minimum of casualties."[22]

The elasticity of the front, however, made it difficult to wage a successful "wearing" campaign against the enemy's reserves. If the enemy had no vital stake in defending his original trench system, he might inflict heavy casualties on the attacker while gradually giving way, while new defenses were being established to his rear. Maurice's solution was to attack where German troops were nailed to their trenches in defense of vital political or strategical interests. "In that case," he noted, "a slow advance by siege methods would probably meet with determined resistance on the part of the defender and if carried on without intermission, and on a considerable scale, might well draw in a large number of reserves to meet it without involving very heavy losses on the attacking side."[23]

After becoming CIGS, Robertson needed to sell the offensive to skeptical civilians. His task would have been made easier if he had been confident that the German army could be defeated in 1916. Such an achievement would be commensurate with the required sacrifices of going on the offensive. But Robertson, although he didn't rule out a rupture of a section of the enemy's front, deprecated the idea of a win-the-war breakthrough. On a front of millions rather than hundreds of thousands of soldiers, it was possible with the new weaponry, especially gas and the improved artillery, to overwhelm a section of the enemy's front, but under the circumstance of siege warfare, this was but a "prelude to a fresh battle with the reserves which the enemy has quartered behind his trench lines." His sober assessment was that "it is highly improbable that the enemy will be completely defeated as the result of a single great effort. On the contrary, we must anticipate prolonged fighting, a great expenditure of ammunition and heavy losses, even when his defensive lines have been penetrated."[24]

Although he desired the prudent employment of British personnel in the offensive, Robertson was brutally frank about the high casualties that would result from fighting the main body of the German army.[25]

On the other hand, Robertson encouraged the civilians to believe in dramatically better results in 1916 because the "Allies would have more men, more ammunition, more big guns" and the offensive for the first time would take place on "a very wide front, say of 20 miles, and made in great depth," which would protect the attackers from enfilade artillery fire on the flanks. Even if a decisive victory was not won, attrition would work in favor of the Allies because "the Germans are approaching the limit of their resources."[26]

As Robertson adjusted to modern, industrialized warfare, he came to realize that much more than methods was involved. The entire higher conduct of the war must be changed. First, the government must commit to total mobilization of the country, including conscription; second, the general staff must be revived and placed in control of strategy; and, third, a common war plan must be formulated between the French and British.[27]

Horrified by the prospect of massive casualties, some British politicians hoped to avoid taking on the main body of the German army. In Robertson's view, Lord Kitchener was much to blame for the influence that amateurs such as Winston Churchill, the First Lord of the Admiralty, and Lloyd George enjoyed. Attending a cabinet meeting, he was shocked to discover that "all the talking was done by the people least competent to discuss the subject. The Lord Chancellor delivered an exceptionally long harangue on strategy. The Secretary of State for War said nothing."[28]

Kitchener, assuming the role of supreme war lord, hoped to avoid an open-ended commitment to the Continental war. Acutely aware of Britain's limited military resources, ("I am put here to conduct a great war and I have no army"[29]), he sought to maintain strategic flexibility. His plan was to use his emerging New Armies as the Entente's strategic reserve, deploying it to exploit opportunities in the outer theaters such as Gallipoli. By limiting involvement on the western front, Kitchener hoped to preserve British manpower until 1917 when both Britain's allies and opponents would have spent themselves with "colossal losses without corresponding advantages." The BEF could then play the decisive role in both defeating the Central Powers and making peace.[30]

Britain's small army shaped Kitchener's initial orders to the BEF's commander in chief. Sir John French's instructions have been described as being "so hedged about by warnings and qualifications as to be unworkable if interpreted either in the letter or the spirit." On the one hand, Sir John was told "to support and cooperate" with Joffre. Conversely, Kitchener implied that the BEF should "cooperate without actually fighting, or fight without incurring casualties and avoid provoking his opponent by 'forward movements' lest he struck back."[31]

A strategy so favorable to British self-interest had no chance of being implemented in a coalition war against a powerful adversary such as Germany. The necessity of supporting France and Russia, as Kitchener himself came to realize, gave Britain little or no freedom of action. As he told the Dardanelles Committee on August 20, 1915: "There could be no doubt that the main theatre of operations was in France, and that it was out of the question to risk losing the whole campaign for the sake of the Dardanelles." If the British continued a policy of limited liability on the western front, they ran the very serious risk of breaking up the anti-German coalition. "Unfortunately we had to make war as we must," Kitchener admitted, "and not as we should like."[32]

Kitchener thus accepted the necessity of supporting Britain's allies "*even though, by so doing, we suffered very heavy losses indeed.*"[33] One result of his earlier attempts to hoard British manpower was to sow confusion and intensify the debate over strategic questions in the councils of war in London. At different times, both the "westerners" and "easterners," who favored an indirect strategy, were given encouragement by his actions. The result was that Britain's limited military resources were stretched too thin to be effective on any front.

If Kitchener's grand design of conserving British manpower, faulty though it proved to be, had been made clear to the political leadership,

British strategy would at least have had a coherence it lacked. But Kitchener's temperament and life of isolation made him ill-fitted to deal with politicians. Autocratic and secretive, he was at his worst at cabinet meetings. It was, he noted, "repugnant and unnatural to have to discuss military secrets with a large number of gentlemen with some of whom he was but barely acquainted."[34] He either lapsed into "obstinacy and silence," Lord Esher has noted, or he would ramble incoherently. "He would seem to be thinking aloud, his mind tossing in a flood of difficulties."[35] A straight answer was seldom forthcoming. A "slippery fish"[36] was Lord Milner's acid assessment.

H. H. Asquith's coalition government, which has been characterized as a "ramshackle, quarrelsome and irresolute confederation,"[37] came close to disintegration during the last half of 1915. Division and confusion over the best approach to victory also became prominent in Paris. France had insisted on concentrating on the main body of the enemy, but the depressing results of the autumn campaign and German successes in Southeastern Europe created support in Paris for opening a major campaign in the Balkans.

Pressured by the French, the British agreed to the dispatch of a small Anglo-French force to Salonika, Greece, even though the intent of this military intervention was fuzzy. "Were we simply going to make a demonstration or to open up a great campaign," Sir Edward Carson, a member of the Dardanelles Committee, wanted to know. "Quixotic chivalry" was Lord Curzon's equally damning assessment.[38] An earlier alternative to concentrating on the German army had been the unsuccessful effort to defeat Turkey by naval and land operations at the Dardanelles, which had been sold on its political advantages and the belief that British losses would be small. This venture had been characterized by much loose thinking about Turkish weakness and the technical difficulties of both forcing the Turkish Straits with warships and employing troops on the Gallipoli Peninsula.

Another campaign was being opened haphazardly in Mesopotamia. Concern that a Holy War might develop in Persia, Afghanistan and the northwest frontier of India had contributed to an ill-planned and ultimately disastrous advance up the Tigris toward Baghdad. On another Turkish front, Egyptian authorities expressed alarm about the prospect of a large-scale Turkish assault on the Suez Canal and requested massive reinforcements. From his vantage point at GHQ, Robertson was distressed by "the daily fever and loss of all balance when a telegram came from Mesopotamia asking for more troops, or from Egypt saying 15 divisions were wanted at once."[39]

An important factor in the chaotic deployment of the limited British military resources was Kitchener's refusal to ask the general staff for technical advice on the feasibility of the schemes being advocated. The CIGS, Sir James Wolfe Murray, was, in Hankey's words, "a feeble old man."[40] Cowed by Kitchener, Sir James initiated nothing as campaigns were being advocated and launched in the outlying theaters of war.[41]

In close touch with the thinking of the general staff through correspondence with Sir Charles E. Callwell, who had been recalled from retirement to serve as Director of Military Operations, Robertson began to fill the strategic void in London. His appreciations on the military situation made him the most effective counter to Kitchener's policy of limited liability. He ridiculed attempts to escape coming to grips with the German army and called the naval attempt to force the Dardanelles a "ridiculous farce." He was willing to bet Callwell at any odds that it would not succeed.[42]

Robertson believed that the government's indecision created an impossible situation for the BEF regarding the planning and execution of joint operations with the French. "We must know the military policy of the Government," he wrote his commander in chief. "Until recently it was thought that the policy of the Government was the reconquest of Belgium and the defeat of the German Armies in this theatre. . . . We can obtain no information as to when the New Armies are to come out, nor even if they are to come out at all." If London withheld reinforcements and made France a secondary theater, the BEF had no choice but to so inform the French and go on the defensive.[43]

After Kitchener wired Sir John French on May 16 that he would send no more reinforcements until certain that the German defenses could be broken,[44] Robertson wrote Wigram: "So long as we pay attention to Italy, the Balkan States and all such rubbish we shall never have contented minds. What we have got to do is to organize ourselves properly and realise that we have got to finish the job by our own exertions, in conjunction with Russia and France. . . . Our chief trouble lies in England and with the War Office."[45] In his opinion, the strength of the alliance would "increase only to the extent to which the British Army is increased" and concentrated in France.[46]

Robertson hoped to diminish Kitchener's influence by revitalizing the moribund general staff. "The S. of S. for War has not the time to study matters & formulate advice, in addition to his other work," he wrote the king's private secretary and trusted adviser, Lord Stamfordham. "The General Staff, with a trusted & competent head, should be allowed to function & do the work for which it was designed, & which it alone can do. It has been obliterated. . . . The present method of the higher conduct of the war can only lead to disaster."[47]

Field Marshal Sir John French

The king's backing contributed to Robertson's voice being heard in London. The uncertainty and confusion over the higher direction of the war that paralyzed the government, however, played a greater part in Robertson's growing influence. Attending a council of war in early July, Robertson was asked if he had any comments. Indeed he did; a map was found, and Robertson launched into a forty-five minute lecture. There was none of Kitchener's indecisiveness. When Wully was interrupted, he stood silent, staring at the minister under his dark and bushy eyebrows. According to one secondhand account, the impression he made was extraordinary: The ministers "realised that here was a man who really knew what he was talking about, who really based his deductions on unanswerable facts."[48]

In early November, he submitted a paper on the "Conduct of the War," which argued that "the war may end either in the defeat of the Central Powers, in the defeat of the Entente, or in mutual exhaustion. The object of the Entente Powers is to bring about the first of these results, which can only be attained by the defeat or exhaustion of the predominant partner in the Central Alliance—Germany. Every plan of operation must therefore be examined from the point of view of its bearing on this result. If it is not, it will have a false basis, and will accordingly lead to false conclusions."[49] This memorandum, which probably played an essential role in Robertson's elevation to CIGS, also stressed that the British had four distinct campaigns under way with large reserves not designated for any particular theater. "It is essential in these circumstances," he wrote, "that there should be one military authority responsible for advising His Majesty's Government regarding military policy in all theatres."[50]

Although signed by Robertson, this and many future memoranda were written by his alter ego "Freddy" Maurice.[51] Maurice's authorship of appreciations bearing Robertson's signature was certainly not due to any lack of fluency by Robertson but was largely a result of the demands on his time. It may safely be assumed that the ideas expressed by Maurice were also held by Robertson.

Robertson received valuable support from Haig in redirecting Britain's war effort. Haig's and Robertson's attempts to revive the general staff led to James Wolfe Murray's removal. But his replacement, Archibald Murray, who was promoted from Deputy CIGS to CIGS, did not satisfy them. Despite trips to London to assist him, Robertson was unsuccessful in getting him to stand up to Kitchener. "It is of course no use laying down these excellent principles and expressing such entire conviction of their soundness," he wrote on October 21, "unless we are prepared to carry them to their logical conclusion and stand or fall by them."[52]

Widespread opposition within the government to Kitchener finally forced Asquith to act. Fearing the public's reaction to Kitchener's removal from office, Asquith sent him on a fact-finding mission to the Mediterranean at the beginning of November with the hope that he would remain there to direct operations. In his absence Asquith took over the War Office.

With Kitchener away from the War Office, Murray and Robertson submitted memoranda to the cabinet advocating the concentration of British resources in the west, but Kitchener, who had cleverly taken the official seals of the Secretary of State for War with him,[53] continued to exercise his authority. A frustrated Robertson told Haig: "I think K. is the chief trouble. He ought to be moved on. . . . Thanks to K.'s absence the General Staff have recently made a certain position for themselves and for Murray but the latter is as wobbly as ever."[54]

Matters came to a head when Kitchener, after visiting Rome and Athens, announced that he was returning. When Murray reported Kitchener's imminent return and warned that he probably intended the diversion of troops to Egypt, Robertson told him to stand firm, but he now saw no way to redirect British strategy but to become CIGS himself, a move that had been discussed in some quarters since early October. Kitchener had long since lost his credibility with most of the ministers. He now was abandoned by Asquith, who told Robertson that Kitchener was "an impossible colleague" and that his "veracity left much to be desired."[55] But would there be enough room in the War Office for both Robertson and Kitchener, especially because they were not close? As Wully wrote years later, "I was not particularly a Kitchener man, never having served with him anywhere except on Lord Roberts's staff in South Africa."[56]

It quickly developed that Kitchener's return forced Asquith's hand and gave Robertson the opportunity to become CIGS on his own terms. To solve the crisis of Britain's high command, more was needed than limiting Kitchener's authority. The direction of the Battle of Loos highlighted Sir John French's failures as commander in chief. His lack of Staff College training and high-strung temperament made it increasingly obvious that he was not up to commanding a force destined to be the largest British army in history. "These sudden moods are weird and marvelous but we never now even have explanations"[57] was the way his private secretary described his mercurial personality.

Lord Kitchener and Sir William Robertson on Anzac Day, 1916

Office of the Chief of the Imperial General Staff

When Murray had been recalled from France, French had wanted his bosom friend, Sir Henry Wilson, Robertson's predecessor as commandant of the Staff College, as his chief of general staff. When Wilson had been rejected by Kitchener and the political leadership, he had accepted Robertson. Yet Wilson, who now served as the chief liaison officer with the French, assumed the role of an unofficial adviser and was Sir John's constant companion. Robertson took his meals in a separate mess.[58]

One anecdote in particular is revealing of Robertson's relationship with Sir John. In early August, when Wully had prepared a memorandum that argued against withholding the New Armies from the western theater, French refused to forward or even to read it. He explained that he was already "fully acquainted with the situation" and that the home authorities knew his views. Robertson's appreciation eventually found its way to Kitchener anyway—through a roundabout way: the king's equerry, Wigram.[59] Wully was used to being ignored. When French visited London to talk to Kitchener and others, he left his chief of staff behind. "I don't think any good would be done by my going with him," Robertson informed Wigram. "We totally disagree on all important points & I could hardly do that in public."[60] Robertson thought that French's "mind was never the same for two consecutive minutes" and accused him of contemplating "reckless and impossible things."[61]

Sir John was also frequently at odds with Marshal Joffre, making Anglo-French unity on military policy difficult. "Joffre and he have never yet been a mile within the heart of each other," Robertson once wrote Stamfordham.[62] Conversely, Robertson, who had good relations with Joffre, lobbied for the formulation of a "definite Anglo-French plan" apart from any general Entente campaign plan. After a plan was adopted, he suggested that neither government could change it without the support of the other.[63]

If anything, Haig had an even lower opinion of Sir John's leadership, and he joined Robertson in lobbying the king and the political leadership to shake up the high command. Haig wanted the forceful north countryman as CIGS, but Robertson, who had acted in French's place when the latter was sick in early September,[64] was also in the running for the greater prize, commander in chief of the BEF. In his resignation letter, French designated him as his successor, and Kitchener told Lord Esher on December 4 that he believed the "government intend to appoint Robertson Commander-in-Chief."[65] But in the end Haig was chosen. "It does not look as if dear old R would get the succession to the Chief," Esher wrote Sir John's private secretary. "The Army will grieve all the more at the Chief's departure."[66]

Robertson was willing to relinquish any claim to the leadership of the BEF if Haig, his senior in rank and a commander of troops since the beginning of hostilities, got the command. Though suited for either position, Wully was known best to the ministers for providing with decisiveness and clarity his views on military questions. Haig, on the other hand, was thought to be a poor choice as CIGS. The last thing the government needed was another incoherent military adviser. The influential journalist Charles à Court Repington warned Bonar Law that Haig "is incapable of conveying his views to subordinates by word of mouth, as you can judge if you get him before the War Council and examine him yourself."[67]

On December 6, Asquith wrote Lord Stamfordham: "He [French] suggests Robertson as his successor, but I assume that we shall have to take Haig. K & I both agree that Robertson should become C.I.G.S. here."[68]

When Kitchener had approached Robertson on December 4 about becoming CIGS, Robertson told him "No, not if he continued to be his own C.I.G.S."[69] Robertson expressed what he wanted through an analogy of the way that Germany had conducted its wars of unification: "The War Council becomes a sort of Commander-in-Chief, he becomes Chief of the Staff to that Council. Thus the War Office is separate, and C.G.S. does not deal through him [Kitchener], but consults any department of the W.O. for such information as he requires. In short, W.R.'s office is the 'Great General Staff,' the War Council is the Kaiser, W.R. is Moltke [chief of general staff], K. is von Roon [minister of war]."[70]

Asquith left it to these two stubborn and proud men to formulate a working relationship. Negotiations lasting three days took place at the Hotel Crillon in Paris. Robertson was firm, but he hoped not to force Kitchener's resignation with his humiliating terms. "I am an unknown man in the country," he wrote Wigram. "K. with me would be a great help. Without him I would be nobody in the eyes of the public."[71] Many documents were drafted and exchanged before Robertson got what he considered non-negotiable: independence from the secretary of state for war. He wanted the government to receive its advice on military operations through one authoritative channel—the CIGS. Initially Robertson had also demanded that all operations orders go under his authority. This Kitchener (and previous military practice) would not accept, so it was slightly modified. Robertson issued orders to the armies, but he did so under the secretary of state for war's authority.

When the exchange of papers concluded, Kitchener's authority was limited to the feeding and clothing of the army. On his way back to his hotel room, with Kitchener's capitulation safely in hand, Robertson "popped in on a pal in one of the rooms, saying the 'b____r's signed' popped out again with a grin."[72] He had reason to smile. Robertson's powers as CIGS, given the full force of law by an order in council issued by the king in January, remain unprecedented in British history. Robertson's trump card had been George V, who applied behind-the-scenes pressure on Asquith and Kitchener every step of the way.

Robertson had gained his dominant position because of Kitchener's unsteady and contradictory direction of the British war effort. British strategy, the creation of committees of civilians with little grasp of military reality, had led to disasters at the Dardanelles and on the Tigris. A controversial campaign, with little consideration being given to ends and means, had also been launched in the Balkans. All of these peripheral ventures were undertaken without their feasibility being examined by the general staff.

To emasculate Kitchener, the architect of limited liability for British manpower, Asquith's government accepted Robertson, the most influential advocate for concentrating maximum British resources on the western front. With France and Russia flagging, Robertson wanted the civilians to face facts: Britain couldn't defeat her chief strategic rival by shifting the fighting to other nations. The government's willingness to grant him unprecedented authority was an admission that the war machinery had broken down. In a sense the civilians wanted Robertson to save them from themselves. If left to their own devices, no consensus seemed possible on how best to fight the war.

Robertson's contention that "the whole conduct of the war wants getting in hand, firstly by our Government, secondly by . . . the General Staff, and thirdly as between these two and the French"[73] helped make him CIGS. But would his inflated powers as CIGS solve the crisis in the higher direction of the war or would it exacerbate tension between the military and civil authorities? His future standing depended very much on how the civilians perceived that his approach to winning the war was working.

NOTES

1. Robertson to Wigram, July 13, 1915, RA Geo. V Q. 2522/3/185.
2. David Lloyd George, *War Memoirs of David Lloyd George* (London, 1938), vol. 1, 259.
3. Leask, *Robertson*, 109.
4. "The Offensive under Present Conditions," June 15, 1915, WO 158/17. This general staff memorandum was unsigned, but its language was certainly Robertson's.

5. Robertson to French, June 25, 1915, WO 158/17.

6. Robertson, "General Staff Note on the General Military Situation," August 5, 1915, WO 158/17.

7. Robertson to Callwell, February 22, 1915, Robertson MSS I/8/9.

8. Ibid.

9. Robertson, Notes on Winston Churchill's Memorandum, June 26, 1915, Robertson MSS I/5/6.

10. James S. Corum, *The Roots of Blitzkrieg: Hans Von Seeckt and German Military Reform* (Lawrence, Kans., 1992), 18.

11. See Maurice, *British Strategy*, 10–13.

12. Travers, *Killing Ground*, 62–82.

13. John Charteris, *At G.H.Q.* (London, 1931), 22; Robertson to Curzon, March 2, 1916, David R. Woodward, ed., *The Military Correspondence of Field-Marshal Sir William Robertson, Chief of the Imperial General Staff, December 1915–February 1918* [hereafter cited as MCWR], (London, 1989), 37–38.

14. Charteris, *At G.H.Q.*, 22.

15. Robertson, "Memorandum on the Possibility of Undertaking Offensive Operations," February 8, 1915, WO 158/17.

16. Robertson, "General Staff Note on the General Military Situation," August 5, 1915, WO 158/17.

17. On the importance of artillery, see Jonathan Bailey, "British Artillery in the Great War," in *British Fighting Methods in the Great War*, ed. Paddy Griffith (London, 1996), 23–49; Robin Prior and Trevor Wilson, *Command on the Western Front: The Military Career of Sir Henry Rawlinson 1914–1918* (Oxford, 1992), 393–94; Paddy Griffith, *Battle Tactics of the Western Front: The British Army's Art of Attack 1916–18* (New Haven, 1994), 135–58; and Shelford Bidwell and Dominick Graham, *Fire-Power: British Army Weapons and Theories of War 1904–1945* (Boston, 1985), 46–146.

18. Diary entry of July 26, 1915, Clive MSS, Cab 45/201; and Robertson, "Note on prospective offensive operation," July 20, 1915, WO 158/17.

19. Note, n.d. WO 158/17. Although unsigned, this note seems to be Robertson's.

20. See the perceptive comments by David French in "The Meaning of Attrition, 1914–1916," *English Historical Review* 103 (April 1988): 385–405.

21. Robertson, "General Staff Note on the Situation, 2nd December 1915," minuted by Robertson, "Handed to General Pélli as an unofficial statement of our views." WO 158/18.

22. Maurice, "Co-operation with the French in the Offensive," June 19, 1915, WO 158/17.

23. Ibid.

24. Robertson, "Note Prepared for the War Committee by the Chief of the Imperial General Staff on the Question of Offensive Operations on the Western Front," January 1, 1916, WO 106/310.

25. See Hankey, "The General Review of the War," October 31, 1916, CAB 42/22/14.

26. War Committee, December 28, 1915, Cab 42/6/14; and Robertson, "Note Prepared for the War Committee by the Chief of the Imperial General Staff on the Question of Offensive Operations on the Western Front, January 1, 1916, WO 106/310.

27. Robertson to Callwell, October 26, 1915, Robertson MSS I/8/33.

28. Reginald Viscount Esher, *The Tragedy of Lord Kitchener* (London, 1921), 149.

29. Ibid., 35.

30. See French, "Meaning of Attrition," 387–89; Keith Neilson, "Kitchener: A Reputation Refurbished?" *Canadian Journal of History* 15 (August 1980): 207–27; the quotes are from Hankey's interview with Kitchener, May 29, 1915, Hankey MSS, CAB 63/5.

31. Graham and Bidwell, *Coalitions, Politicians and Generals*, 66.

32. Dardanelles Committee, August 20, 1915, CAB 42/3/16.

33. Diary entry of August 19, 1915, Haig MSS No. 102.

34. Philip Magnus, *Kitchener: Portrait of an Imperialist* (London, 1958), 284.

35. Esher, *Tragedy of Lord Kitchener*, 150.

36. Milner to Gwynne, August 18, 1915, Keith Wilson, ed., *The Rasp of War: The Letters of H. A. Gwynne to the Countess Bathurst 1914–1918* (London, 1988), 116.

37. Cassar blames Asquith's lack of support for Kitchener for this state of affairs. But it is more likely that Kitchener's unworkable policy of limited liability and his personality were more to blame. George H. Cassar, *Asquith as War Leader* (London and Rio Grande, 1994), 131.

38. Dardanelles Committee, October 4 and 25, 1915, CAB 42/4/2 & 17.

39. Diary entry of November 29, 1915, Clive MSS, CAB 45/201.

40. Diary entry of May 18, 1915, Hankey MSS, 1/1.

41. For a fuller development of this point, see Gooch, *Plans of War*, 299–326.

42. Robertson to Callwell, March 19 and 31, 1915, Robertson MSS I/8/15 & 17.

43. Robertson, "Government Military Policy," April 2, 1915, WO 158/17.

44. Kitchener to French, May 16, 1915, WO 159/4.

45. Robertson to Wigram, May 16, 1915, RA Geo. V Q. 2522/3/175.

46. Robertson, "General Staff Note on the General Military Situation," August 5, 1915, WO 158/17.

47. Robertson to Stamfordham, n.d., but probably written in June or early July 1915, Robertson MSS I/12/3.

48. Diary entry of July 5, 1915, Clive MSS, CAB 45/201.

49. Memorandum by Robertson, November 8, 1915, CAB 42/5/6.

50. Ibid.

51. See, for example, Maurice to his wife, November 4, 1915, Maurice MSS 3/1/4.

52. Robertson to Murray, October 21, 1915, Robertson MSS I/15/1.

53. "Extracts from an account by Major General Sir Arthur Lynden-Bell," n.d., Lynden-Bell MSS 90/1/1.

54. Robertson to Haig, November 17, 1915, Haig MSS No. 103.

55. George H. Cassar, *Kitchener: Architect of Victory* (London, 1977), 427.

56. Robertson to Selborne, March 24, 1927, Selborne MSS 95, fols. 22–23.

57. Diary entry of October 5, 1915, Fitzgerald MSS PP/MCR/118.

58. See Charteris, *At G.H.Q.*, 87; and diary entry of November 12, 1915, Clive MSS, CAB 45/201. It should be noted that Robertson believed separate messes served both men best. Robertson, *Private to Field-Marshal*, 222.

59. See Robertson's minute on his "General Staff Note on the General Military Situation," August 5, 1915, WO 158/17. This same memorandum, dated August 3, is in the Kitchener MSS, WO 159/4; see also Bonham-Carter, *Soldier True*, 124–25.

60. Robertson to Wigram, June 23, 1915, RA Geo. V Q. 2522/3/183.

61. Lord Hankey, *The Supreme Command 1914–1918* (London, 1962), vol. 1, 339; and diary entry of October 24, 1915, Haig MSS No. 103.

62. William James Philpott, "British Military Strategy on the Western Front: Independence or Alliance, 1904–1918," D. Phil thesis, Oxford, 1991, 258.

63. Notes of Robertson's conversation with Kitchener, October 31, 1915, WO 159/4; Robertson's Note, December 2, 1915, minuted "Handed by C.G.S. to General Pélli as an unofficial statement of our views." WO 158/18; and diary entries of October 19 and November 12, 1915, Clive MSS, CAB 45/201.

64. Diary entry of September 1, 1915, Fitzgerald MSS PP/MCR/118.

65. Diary entry of December 4, 1915, Esher MSS 2/15.

66. Esher to Fitzgerald, December 11, 1915, Fitzgerald MSS 3/29.

67. Repington to Bonar Law, November 16, 1915, Bonar Law MSS 51/5/27.

68. Asquith to Stamfordham, December 6, 1915, RA Geo. V Q. 838/52.

69. Robertson to Wigram, December 5, 1915, RA Geo. V Q. 838/50.

70. Diary entry of December 6, 1915, Clive MSS, CAB 45/201.

71. Robertson to Wigram, December 11, 1915, RA Geo. V Q. 838/61.

72. Gwynne to Sir Henry Wilson, January 16, 1916, Keith Wilson, *Rasp of War*, 158.

73. Robertson to Callwell, October 26, 1915, Robertson MSS I/8/33.

Chapter 3

Prelude to the Somme

When Robertson assumed his new duties on December 23, 1915, he found the War Office "in a greater state of muddle and chaos"[1] than anticipated. To end the "K and chaos" era, he brought three men from GHQ who were known for their competence and loyalty. Robert Dundas Whigham, who had served under Robertson at Camberley and was his sub-chief at GHQ, became Deputy-CIGS. Maurice, who had headed operations at GHQ, came to the War Office as Director of Military Operations. Sir George M. W. Macdonogh, Robertson's chief of military intelligence at GHQ, assumed the same role in London. Robertson's confidence in this shy, taciturn, and secretive intelligence officer was repaid many times over. He "seemed to have a sort of pigeon-hole memory in which he could store things away, and bring them out whenever he wanted to, as from a card index."[2] In addition to providing Robertson with accurate intelligence, Macdonogh, who kept in close contact with the Foreign Office, drafted general staff memoranda on war aims and peace negotiations that bore Robertson's signature. One unfortunate aspect of Robertson's taking Maurice and Macdonogh to London with him was that their replacements, especially John Charteris for Macdonogh, were not as able. Sir Launcelot Kiggell, the new CGS, was certainly no Robertson either. This "brain drain" had serious consequences for the future conduct of BEF operations.

Robertson became CIGS because he believed that "the whole conduct of the war wants getting in hand."[3] He had achieved his first goal with his compact with Kitchener that revived the general staff and gained its "chief" unprecedented influence. But his powers were far from absolute, and unless he had the confidence of the political leadership, he would ultimately fail.

Robertson hoped to be a British von Moltke while the War Committee acted as Kaiser. But Asquith's quarrelsome coalition spoke with many contradictory voices. A recent commentator suggests that "it suffered from a form of pernicious anaemia: because its members were forever wrangling about some great or small issue they rarely had time to make sensible decisions in good time about mundane subjects."[4] On one occasion Robertson wondered aloud if he had been "attending a Cabinet or a committee of lunatics."[5] Like many other senior officers, Robertson was contemptuous of the inevitable maneuvers, indecision, and muddle that characterized the deliberations of the Cabinet and the smaller committees established to direct the war effort—the latest being the War Committee, initially composed of the Prime Minister; Lloyd George, minister of munitions; Bonar Law, leader of the Unionists; Arthur Balfour, First Lord of the Admiralty; and Reginald McKenna, chancellor of the exchequer.

Robertson carefully avoided one pitfall: being drawn into taking sides with either the Liberals or Unionists. On the eve of Asquith's fall from power, Robertson told a newspaper editor who was intriguing to involve him in the 1916 December crisis, "I feel that I ought to keep clear of any particular sect or movement. They are all bad. The only difference is that some are worse than others. In any case, I need to keep on a straight and unbiassed road."[6]

Despite Robertson's lack of empathy with civilians and his impatience with a parliamentary system of government, he was remarkably successful in getting his way, in part, because the higher direction of the war had broken down, and a clear and firm course was desired. This Robertson, a great simplifier, provided. "He knew what he wanted," Hankey has written, "and he nearly always got his way,"[7] but not without a struggle, and not without considerable cunning and sophistication on his part.

Described as an "ambulating refrigerator,"[8] Robertson was just as deliberate when he discussed military questions with civilians. Kitchener self-destructed when he argued strategy with Churchill and Lloyd George, two of the most brilliant debaters of their era. If you engaged politicians in debate, Robertson once told a fellow officer, they would "gently push and shoulder you" until you found yourself on "a road with a dead end, then you are done." Robertson believed that he should give his best professional advice and then refuse to debate. To illustrate his point, he picked up a geranium. When the politician says, "'It looks to me like a camellia' or 'I think it's a carnation,' or 'It smells like a rose,' or 'It might be a hibiscus,' you don't try to prove that it is not a camellia, or a carnation, or a rose, or hibiscus; you simply repeat 'It's a geranium.'"9

Wully, of course, provided technical advice on the feasibility of military operations. But he argued that if his professional judgment were rejected, then someone who had the government's confidence should replace him. This, however, was a very dangerous option for the government because of two obstacles, both of which Robertson helped erect: the press's support of the soldiers and the united front presented by Robertson and his commanders in chief abroad.

Robertson's account of the war omits any reference to either his close relationship with journalists or the pivotal role played by the press. Yet no general, not even the mischief-maker Sir Henry Wilson, understood or made better use of the national press. Fleet Street came dangerously close to supplanting Parliament. Never in British history have newspapers had greater significance in a war, with the national newspapers, all of them in London except for the *Manchester Guardian*, decisively shaping popular perceptions.

Until late 1917, the dominant view expressed in the newspapers was that Robertson was a necessary barrier to amateur forays into the strategy and conduct of the war. Wully's door was open to journalists, editors, and owners of newspapers. He dined and corresponded with them, passing along inside information if it furthered his position.[10] He was particularly close to the extremely influential and right-wing *Morning Post*, receiving its editor, H. A. Gwynne, almost as a fellow comrade in arms. Gwynne had been Reuter's chief war correspondent around the turn of the century, covering among other conflicts Kitchener's expeditions in the Sudan in 1896 and the South African War. Robertson was even closer to the leading war correspondent of the day, a former officer, Colonel Charles à Court Repington, who refers to Wully in his memoirs as one "of my oldest and most valued soldier friends."[11] Lord Northcliffe, the powerful press magnate, who employed Repington on the *Times*, also initially supported the general staff, limiting Lloyd George's intrusions into Robertson's bailiwick and sustaining public support for the prolonged and bloody Battle of the Somme.

Although Haig despised journalists, he reluctantly accepted Robertson's advice to invite some leading newspaper proprietors to the front. GHQ quickly came to recognize the value of the Fourth Estate, so much so, that Robertson was soon cautioning Haig's staff not to raise public expectations by claiming too much for the Somme offensive.[12]

Having witnessed the breakdown of relations between Kitchener's War Office and Sir John French, which had encouraged the civilians to become involved in war policy, Robertson was determined that he and Haig stand as one. Lloyd George has written that Robertson was "terrified," "over-awed," and "dominated" by Haig, his senior in the army.[13] This was not a fair characterization, for Robertson feared no man. He supported Haig, even when it was ill advised, to prevent the civilians from undermining Britain's commitment to the land war in France and Flanders. Standing apart, Robertson and Haig were vulnerable. Together they seemed invincible because of the political risks of removing them both. An extreme expression of Robertson's conception of a monolithic military leadership came on March 8, 1916, when he wrote Haig: "I am writing this with the object of saying that practically anything may happen to our boasted British Constitution before this war ends, & that the great asset is the army—whose value will be fixed largely by the extent to which we at the top stick together and stand firm."[14]

The Robertson-Haig combination in some respects was an anomaly. There was the wide social gulf. Haig, the personification of the gentleman-officer, was born into wealth and prominent lineage. After Oxford,[15] he entered Sandhurst and was commissioned as a subaltern in the 7th Hussars. He married a lord's daughter in the private chapel in Buckingham Palace. Robertson, the ranker, was from another world. "How much easier, though, it is to work with a gentleman," Haig once commented to his wife about dealing with his "social inferior" Robertson.[16]

Their differing personalities also served to separate them. Robertson was at times forceful to the point of rudeness, although not to Haig, whom he treated with deference. Haig, disciplined and reserved, kept his feelings under tight control and thought Robertson guilty of self-advertisement when he talked of his battles with the civilians and the changes that he contemplated in the War Office.

Robertson expected his other commanders in chief to subordinate their theaters to Haig's front where the main body of the German army was located. He used "secret and personal" letters and "R" telegrams that were not seen by the ministers, including the secretary of state for war. His secret correspondence with Lieutenant-General G. F. Milne, the commander in chief of the British forces in the Balkan theater, serves as a good illustration of this attempt to ensure that his subordinates, no matter what the government's position, knew exactly how the general staff stood on the deployment of the War Office's resources. On October 25, 1916, he informed Milne that the "War Committee felt compelled to send the additional division and I wish you clearly to understand that I have no intention of adopting the Balkans as a main theater." Two days later Milne responded: "I fully realise the position and trust nothing I have said has led to the sending of the other division. . . . Any offensive is impracticable except on a scale which is, I realise, inconsistent with your policy on the Western Front."[17]

Although Robertson believed that he and Haig had finally got the civilians "into a corner, & finally have the upper hand,"[18] two events in May demonstrated that there were clear limits to their power. Robertson initially tried to prevent civilian involvement by limiting information. Archibald Murray had given the War Committee weekly appreciations, but Robertson provided only a "summary" that included little more than could be gained from the newspapers. Hankey viewed his comments as "really almost an insult to the intelligence of the War Committee and the Cabinet." When troops were transferred to the western front from Egypt and Britain with little or no reference to the War Committee, Hankey, as the secretary of the War Committee, conspired with Lloyd George to put the question of military information on the agenda.[19]

This attack on his secrecy came at a bad time for Robertson because the War Committee was already disturbed over his recent attempt to prevent civilian interference into the affairs of the BEF. Seeking ways to conserve shipping, the government wanted to investigate the enormous amount of grain being shipped to France to feed the BEF's horses allocated to transport and cavalry. Haig reacted angrily, telling the civilians that he "was responsible for the efficiency of the armies in France"; Robertson and the Army Council supported Haig in an uncompromising fashion on May 22.[20] The army's arrogance proved too much for the civilians, and their strong reaction served to define the limits of Robertson's power.

Haig spoke of being responsible for the BEF, but who was ultimately responsible for the British army, the ministers wanted to know. Lloyd George reminded the generals that they were responsible to the "Government, and through the Government to Parliament, and through Parliament to the people. The effect of this [Haig's] letter was to tell the War Committee 'to mind their own business' and not interfere." But the government had "a perfect right to investigate any matter connected with the war that they pleased." The government also had a right to be furnished with more-complete military information.[21] On the issue of civilian supremacy, Robertson wisely retreated.

Coalition warfare also limited Robertson's ability to control the conduct of the war. A telling argument in favor of his "western" strategy was the necessity of fighting all-out to support Britain's Continental allies. Fears that an Anglo-French rupture would be catastrophic, however, undercut Robertson's strategic views on the Balkans.[22] Allied intervention at Salonika in 1915 failed to save Serbia and created serious political difficulties with Greece. Robertson hoped to liquidate this venture when the Allied generals gathered at Chantilly on December 6–8, 1915. France, Russia, and Italy were designated the "principal" fronts, and all other theaters were declared "subsidiary." Yet the French, Russians, and Italians refused to abandon the failed Balkan campaign. Robertson viewed as "nonsense" the argument that an Allied presence at Salonika might bring in Greece and Romania. It "makes one use bad language," he wrote Callwell. "The fact is it is all political."[23]

French interest in the Balkans had indeed been intensified by domestic politics. In July 1915, Joffre had sacked General Maurice Paul Emmanuel Sarrail, the commander of the Third Army. The removal of Sarrail, who was considered the leading Republican general in an army dominated by clerical and monarchist officers, sparked outrage from the Radical-Socialists. Another place had to be found for him to maintain political unity, and he was sent to command the French forces at Salonika. His presence in the Balkans attracted political support for his campaign.

Although the government sympathized with Robertson's Balkan views, it hesitated to confront Paris because of the political consequences.[24] As Bonar Law had earlier remarked, if there were "any breach in the Alliance the war would be lost."[25] Stymied by political considerations from withdrawing, Robertson focused on limiting British operations in Macedonia. His intentions were made crystal clear to Lieutenant-General Sir B. T. Mahon, who first commanded the British forces at Salonika. "Until you hear from me you can take it that I am not out for any offensive operations in the Balkans," he wrote. "Such operations would be unsound from every point of view, and the day they are sanctioned I shall leave the War Office. . . . I do not intend to have anything to do with British soldiers being engaged in killing Bulgars and getting killed themselves in return."[26]

Robertson expressed himself just as strongly when he argued with Joffre in front of Asquith and Aristide Briand, the French premier, at an Anglo-French conference in late March. Joffre responded in kind, thumped the table, and called Robertson "un homme terrible."[27] To Wully's chagrin nothing would sway the French, not even the support he got from the War Committee. What he called the "hideous nightmare"[28] continued, with political concerns overriding military considerations.

Robertson agreed with Clausewitz that civilians determined the object of war. This was in fact the starting point for any effective prosecution of war. In a paper prepared in mid-1915, "Notes on the Machinery of the Government for Conducting the War," he argued that it was necessary for the government "to recognise that war after all is nothing but an instrument of policy, and that its conduct, while conforming to strategical principles, should also conform to the political object of the Government. The Government must, therefore, know its mind and what it is trying to accomplish before its naval and military advisers can give the necessary advice."[29]

Asquith's government had begun the war with two basic war aims: the restoration of Belgian independence and the destruction of German "militarism." The first might be obtained through a negotiated peace; the latter depended on Germany's defeat. When Robertson became CIGS, the government's definition of war aims had evolved little beyond some secret treaties designed primarily to gain new allies (Italy and the sharif of Mecca) or keep old ones (Russia). The promise of Constantinople and the Straits to Russia if she saw the war through represented Britain's most important concession to coalition politics. Fearing that comprehensive discussions of the postwar settlement would divide the alliance, the Foreign Secretary Sir Edward Grey and Asquith held their hand.[30]

As the government's military adviser, Robertson was soon involved with questions such as war aims and peace discussions that blurred the line between being a soldier and a statesman. Britain would soon have an army to match her industrial, financial, and naval resources, and Robertson wanted London to assert itself with her allies. On February 12, he wrote a paper for the War Committee on "The Assistance that Diplomacy might Render to Naval and Military Operations," suggesting that a separate peace was possible with Turkey if the Russians were pressured to relinquish their claim to the Straits. If Turkey could not be detached, he wanted to use Turkish territory as bait to detach Bulgaria.[31]

Foreign Secretary Sir Edward Grey was quick to point out a blind spot in Robertson's reasoning. "We are dependent for our very existence upon success in the war," Grey emphasized, "or at any rate upon continuing the war till Germany is comparatively exhausted, for in no other way can we get terms that will save us." Russia, France, and Italy might get "tolerable" terms without insisting that Germany give up her navy and colonies. Britain thus needed her European allies more than they needed her.[32] Robertson admitted the difficulty of pressuring Russia to give up the Straits, but he drew the line on Allied unity when Paris continued to lobby for diverting Allied, especially British, resources to a Balkan campaign. He interpreted this interest in the Balkans as a weakening of French resolve for trench warfare.[33]

Although Robertson didn't hesitate to suggest peace negotiations with Turkey or Bulgaria, countries that by themselves posed no serious strategic threat to the British Empire, he deemed a peace with an unhumbled Berlin unthinkable. Such a compromise peace would make Britain's "subsequent existence intolerable" because a "large and ruinous army in readiness" would have to be maintained "for the next struggle."[34] Robertson was especially contemptuous of President Woodrow Wilson's peace efforts at the beginning of 1916, the so-called House-Grey Memorandum, which provided for American mediation of the war. Although more favorable to Allied than German interests, the American peace program left Germany a great world power. When Wilson renewed his peace efforts in May 1916, the War Committee excused Hankey and Robertson at the beginning of their meeting on the 24th. No records were kept of the civilians' discussion, but Reginald McKenna, the chancellor of the exchequer, told Hankey later that "he, the P.M., Grey, and Balfour had been in favor of accepting President Wilson's good offices owing to the black financial outlook, while Bonar Law and Ll. George were averse, as they did not admit of the seriousness of the financial situation." When Robertson learned that a majority of the War Committee was leaning toward American mediation, he and the other members of the Army Council, which included Kitchener, threatened resignation. The matter ended there.[35]

In truth the hysteria generated by total war made it likely that the war would continue until one side gained a clear advantage over the other. In the disillusionment that followed the flawed peace settlement, many came to believe that the sacrifices were not worth the results and that the war aims of the European belligerents differed little. Modern scholarship, however, gives a clearer picture of what a German victory would have meant. Berlin's war aims were outlined in 1914 in the so-called "September Program," which held the field until Russia collapsed and German imperialists were given further opportunities for expansion. Germany planned to occupy the ports along the Channel and eliminate France as a major power. In the east, Russia was to be crippled through the loss of her borderlands to the west. Politically dominant in Europe, Germany then planned to gain economic ascendancy through a Continental bloc called "Mitteleuropa."[36] British independence, as in World War II, was truly at risk in the event of a German peace.

His government's continued reluctance to develop comprehensive war aims began to concern Robertson.[37] With Allied offensives on all primary fronts, the war was going well in August 1916, and it seemed possible that Germany might crack. Peace negotiations, Robertson wrote Lloyd George, "may arise any day in some form or another though by no means in a definite form, and I fear that we may be caught unprepared, and find that we have mobilised for Peace as we did for War—inadequately and subordinate to France." Collusion between Russia and France, allies since the 1890s, might deny Britain the "fruits of victory" and create an "intolerable future."[38] Robertson was specifically worried that British imperial interests might be sacrificed.[39]

Prior to the war, Robertson in his intelligence work had assessed the potential threat posed to British interests by the Russians and French as well as the Germans; and he was naturally concerned with future as well as present enemies. When Asquith on August 30 finally asked his colleagues to consider peace negotiations, Robertson, assisted by Macdonogh, responded with a memorandum that based a durable peace on three principles: maintaining the European balance of power, continuing British maritime supremacy, and keeping the Low Countries free from domination by a great power.

Robertson's definition of the "destruction of German militarism" did not include a demand for Germany's unconditional surrender, which he thought unlikely under present military conditions. Taking the long view, he argued that Europe's equilibrium depended upon the existence of a strong German Central European power, "as a Slav nation, the only other alternative, would always lean towards Russia." He foresaw Germany losing territory in the west, Alsace-Lorraine to France for example. In return Berlin could be compensated through either "the incorporation of Austria proper, or by a close union with a much diminished Austria-Hungary." Robertson's views towards any German-Polish settlement is especially interesting in light of later events. He recognized that a revived Poland would want access to the Baltic Sea, but he did not think it feasible for Poland to receive Danzig and West Prussia. The reader need not be reminded that the Second World War began with a German attack on Poland to end the Polish Corridor, which separated East Prussia from the rest of Germany.

Whereas Robertson wanted Germany "reasonably strong on land," he wanted "to weaken her at sea" by detaching the Kiel Canal (which he thought could be internationalized) and "various districts on the North Sea and Baltic which are of great maritime importance." He also anticipated Germany's loss of her overseas territories in Africa and elsewhere. Any future German overland advance in the Near and Middle East would be blocked by the Russians (at the Straits) and the British (Mesopotamia) and France (Syria.)[40]

Robertson's views, prepared when the Allies were pressing forward on all fronts, were moderate and statesmanlike. Germany had to be beaten on the battlefield, but he didn't argue that a good peace depended upon her humiliation. Lloyd George later claimed that "after a week's reflection on his own temerity he withdrew the memorandum and cancelled it."[41] This, however, was not the case.

To Robertson's dismay, the government continued to "dawdle along week after week and do nothing but talk and write."[42] Rather than a clear definition of war aims, Britain's position was superficially and indirectly stated in Lloyd George's famous rebuke to Wilson's continued efforts to mediate the war. In an interview with the American journalist Roy. W. Howard in late September, Lloyd George asserted, "the fight must be to a finish—to a knockout."[43] Robertson heartily agreed with the Welshman's muscular sentiment that the war must continue until "Prussian military despotism is broken beyond repair." His job as the government's strategical adviser, however, would have been easier if the civilians had given him clearer guidance on the nature of the "victory" that they envisaged.

On becoming CIGS, Wully had sought the War Committee's approval of the following position: "Our efforts are to be directed to carrying out offensive operations next spring in the main theater of war in close co-operation with the Allies and in the greatest possible strength."[44] Such an offensive would dwarf all previous British efforts. In prior Continental wars, Britain had often employed its maritime and economic power, deploying forces on the periphery, and leaving the bulk of the fighting and dying to her European allies—the so called "British way in warfare."[45] Robertson told the ministers that the BEF (which would number fifty-seven divisions by mid-1916) would have to attack in the "greatest possible strength." The casualties would be enormous, and there was no guarantee that the German lines would be broken, although Robertson suggested that the chances were improved because the Allies planned to pursue a common strategy and deploy more men, ammunition, and guns.

Lloyd George and Arthur Balfour immediately raised objections. "The defensive positions [in the west] had never been broken, and they were increasing in strength every day," Balfour insisted. Lloyd George agreed: "General Joffre had always favoured this idea of a great offensive on the West: he had always been confident, and he had always been wrong." As an alternative to the western front, Balfour—to Robertson's amazement— proposed that Britain should focus on the Russian front, where he thought a breakthrough more likely.

Bonar Law quickly pointed out the logistical impossibility of such a transfer of British troops and supplies, and Kitchener warned the civilians that there might be dire consequences if Britain refused to cooperate with the Allied plan of simultaneous offensives in the primary theaters. Although accepting the western front as the primary theater, the War Committee hedged, agreeing only to "prepare to carry out the offensive."[46]

The War Committee's equivocation gave Balfour hope that Britain might still be able to limit its casualties in France. With the advantage apparently belonging to the defender, he advocated waiting for the Germans to attack. "Do not German theories of war," he asked the War Committee, "as well as German internal necessities compel them, rightly or wrongly, to attempt the offensive?" While the Germans exhausted themselves in futile attacks, the British could engage in peripheral operations in the Turkish theater to further the security of the British Empire. "Our prestige in the East has a military value, and irrespective of political interests or national pride, it may therefore be worth while sending soldiers away from the 'main theatre of war' in order to support it," he noted. Balfour also opposed withdrawal from the Balkans, arguing that the Allied forces at Salonika would force the Germans to divert troops to that theater or admit that they were "not master of the Balkans."[47]

On January 13, the War Committee resumed its debate about the offensive with no consensus emerging. Robertson said little except to remind the government of the Allied plan for simultaneous offensives in the primary theaters. Bonar Law supported the CIGS and tried to bring the discussion into focus. If the CIGS's advice was rejected, what was the alternative? Asquith equivocated as usual, suggesting that any decision should be delayed. The War Committee then gave itself the option to veto an offensive by revising its earlier conclusion to read as follows: "Every effort is to be made to prepare for carrying out offensive operations next spring in the main theatre of the war in close co-operation with the Allies, and in the greatest possible strength, although it must not be assumed that such offensive operations are finally decided on."[48]

Grey, who attended the War Committee meetings when foreign affairs was on the agenda, was shocked by this muddled and confused debate. If it continued, he told his colleagues, the result would be "paralysis of all plan & action." Grey rejected the notion that the war could be won by going on the defensive on the western front in the hope that Germany would exhaust itself. Echoing Robertson's argument, he said that Britain's "only chance of victory is to hammer the Germans hard in the first eight months of this year. If this is impossible, we had better make up our minds to an inconclusive peace."[49]

Robertson had more than the indecision of the civilians to concern him. The Allied plan of simultaneous offensives was in trouble, with Joffre and Haig at sixes and sevens over the timing, location, and nature of the British offensive effort. There was strong sentiment at GHQ for a major British effort on the northern flank with the object of capturing the Belgian ports. The French, however, favored a common offensive on the Somme on either side of the juncture of the two armies, and feared that a British attack on the northern flank would seriously weaken any joint effort. On February 14, Haig and Joffre reached an accommodation. The British would attack with twenty-five divisions north of the Somme River on a fourteen mile front, the French with forty divisions on a twenty-five mile front to the south. Although this agreement placed the BEF's primary emphasis on the Somme, Haig refused to avert his glance from Flanders. GHQ prepared two distinct operations, one in cooperation with the French and another on the northern flank against Roulers and Thourout that included amphibious operations to capture Ostend.[50]

A source of concern for Robertson was the transparent and certainly understandable French effort to shift more of the burden of fighting Germans to the BEF. Robertson saw "seeds of friction" in Joffre's request that Haig engage in "a wearing down system on a rather extensive scale" prior to any joint Anglo-French blow.[51] The War Committee opposed (as he himself did) a large-scale British attack unconnected with the main offensive.

On February 21, Anglo-French plans were further complicated when Germany launched a powerful offensive against Verdun designed to destroy the spirit of the French army by "bleeding it white." According to the thinking of some British ministers, such as Balfour and Kitchener,[52] the Germans were playing into Allied hands by exhausting their reserves in attack.

The day after the ten-month Battle of Verdun began, the War Committee addressed the respective strengths of the opposing alliances. A long and fruitless discussion ensued, with Lloyd George insisting that "if we had no facts to go upon, he did not understand how we could decide on offensive action." Robertson responded by suggesting that these questions would be taken up by the commanders in chief at their meeting scheduled for the beginning of March. He also promised that no offensive would be launched until the French and British "were absolutely ready."[53]

What Robertson discovered from a visit to Joffre prior to a meeting of the Allied commanders in March was not reassuring. "Apparently he [Joffre] has no idea of ever taking the offensive if he can get other people to take it for him," Robertson wrote Haig. "After my visit last week to French General Headquarters, I am more convinced than ever it is we who will have to finish this war, and therefore in every way we possibly can we must take the lead or at any rate refuse to be led against our own judgment."[54]

The tenuousness of the original Allied plan of coordinated offensives was made clear to the War Committee when Robertson reported the conclusions of the Allied commanders' meeting on March 12. The Russians seemed ready to go off prematurely, the Italians not at all, and the French, absorbed with the titanic struggle over Verdun, wanted the British to bear the burden of the offensive. The date and extent of the Allied offensives were now being left to the commanders in chief concerned. So much for simultaneous and coordinated attacks. Asquith accurately characterized the present state of Allied planning as "slippery and sloppy."[55]

With a common Allied strategy in question, the military policy most favorable to British self-interest would have been to delay their offensive until the autumn or perhaps even 1917.[56] With new divisions arriving each month, the BEF was far from a well-oiled machine. "I have not got an Army in France really," Haig confessed in his diary on March 29, "but a collection of divisions untrained for the Field."[57] But was this the best policy for the anti-German coalition?

As March ended, Haig and Robertson intensified their pressure on the War Committee. First, Robertson warned the ministers that if they didn't accept the Allied policy of joint offensives, it would be "necessary to inform our Allies accordingly, and to tell them what alternative is proposed."[58] Then Haig wrote Robertson informing him that Joffre wanted "a joint attack on the largest possible scale."[59]

Joffre had suggested that he still might furnish forty divisions to the British twenty-five, but would he? Might not the British be forced into a premature offensive with inadequate French support? Robertson tried to persuade the civilians that Haig would not allow Joffre to misuse the BEF. Nor would the British attack before they were ready. Although Haig planned to attack on a large scale, he "would not make a fool of himself." The ministers "must say one way or the other," he emphasized. Robertson's persistence paid off. The War Committee at last granted permission for the offensive.[60]

Haig believed that the optimum time for his attack would be August, but circumstances beyond his control forced him to introduce his inexperienced divisions to battle earlier than that. The Austrians applied intense pressure on the Italians in the Trentino in mid-May. With the Russians planning an attack in Galicia in June, it was also necessary to tie down as many German troops in the west as possible. Of even greater urgency was the fate of France. Most of her army was being committed to Verdun. The German attack, "if allowed to continue very much longer, will exhaust her remaining resources in men,"[61] the general staff ominously reported to the War Committee.

Under intense pressure from Joffre for an attack no later than July, Haig told Robertson on May 25 that "we *must* march to the support of the French."[62] Unlike the original Anglo-French plan, however, the promised forty French divisions would not be marching with the BEF. On a front reduced from twenty-five to eight miles, the French planned to attack with five divisions, with six in reserve.[63] This is not to suggest, as is frequently the case in Anglocentric literature, that France played an insignificant role in the Somme offensive. A week before the battle ended, for example, the general staff calculated that the French had engaged the equivalent of 588 German battalions, the British 554.[64]

Robertson's visits to the front gave him a favorable impression of the BEF's preparations, and he thought that Haig had fallen in with his cautious policy of limited objectives and methodical methods. As he told Repington, Haig was "a shrewd Scot who would not do anything rash."[65] Believing, as he told Haig, that the French were determined to "go easy this year," he saw the British offensive as a means to support Britain's allies and inflict heavy losses on the enemy. A decisive victory was not in the cards.[66]

This most certainly wasn't Haig's view. Believing that he was divinely inspired to lead his country to victory,[67] Haig thought in expansive, even grandiose terms about the strategical results of his operations. Robertson emphasized artillery to kill Germans. Haig, the thruster, saw cavalry as the key to victory. In no other way could the momentum of a breakthrough be maintained and the stalemate turned into a war of movement. "It seems to me that troops & material are so imbedded in the ground in trench warfare," he wrote Robertson on May 28, "that a general retreat will be most difficult. We ought therefore to be prepared to exploit a success on the lines of 1806 [Napoleon's cavalry exploitation of the defeated Prussians at Jena]."[68]

When Robertson told the ministers on May 30 of his discussions with Joffre and Haig, he stressed that the French had been reduced to twenty-two divisions at Verdun and desperately needed assistance. Significantly Robertson said that Haig had "no idea of any attempt to break through the German lines. It would be only a move to 'degager' [to rescue] the French."[69] There is every reason to believe that Robertson was accurately describing what he thought Haig's plans were. Although Haig talked of the possibility of exploiting success, the tenor of his May 28 letter to Robertson was that his offensive was not directed toward a rupture of the German lines, just that he was prepared to exploit any German breakdown. Robertson, who left the planning of military operations to the commanders involved, was only vaguely aware of the BEF's confused tactical and strategical planning.

Haig had chosen General Sir Henry Rawlinson, the commander of the newly created Fourth Army, to lead the attack. Rawlinson based his plans on the ability of his artillery to cover the advance of the infantry. Having captured key points of the enemy's trench system, the infantry, supported by artillery, would then await German counterattacks. These tactics had the potential to economize British losses and maximize German casualties. Haig, seeking a breakthrough that would be exploited by cavalry, however, expanded Rawlinson's objectives. "I think we can do better than this [Rawlinson's limited plan to 'kill Germans'] by aiming at getting as large a combined force of French and British across the Somme and fighting the enemy in the open!"[70] Haig's distant objectives served to almost double the area to be covered by the bombardment, thereby compromising its effectiveness.[71] The resulting amalgam between Rawlinson's limited and Haig's distant objectives contributed to the disastrous first day of the Somme.

Robertson was the British leader most responsible for ending Kitchener's limited liability approach. He got the government to accept France as the primary theater. With the French imperiled at Verdun, he also ended Kitchener's policy of hoarding British manpower until Britain's Continental allies had exhausted the German reserves. France's heavy losses at Verdun and on the Somme in reality left Britain little choice but to assume more of the burden of the fighting. British casualties on the western front numbered 522,206 prior to the Somme, 2,183,930 thereafter.[72]

Britain's expanded role in the land war necessitated a different manpower policy, and Robertson played a pivotal role in getting universal conscription. One of his first acts on becoming CIGS was to press Kitchener on the army's need for soldiers, requesting an additional eighteen divisions for the BEF.[73]

The issue of compulsion had badly divided the government in 1915 and contributed to Kitchener's low standing with the pro-compulsionists. To keep his government together, Asquith resorted to half-measures. In the autumn of 1915, bowing to pressure from Lloyd George and the Unionists, he instituted the Derby plan, so named after the director of recruiting, which asked married and unmarried men to pledge their willingness to serve if called upon. Single men would be called first. This complicated system manifestly failed, and Derby admitted in January 1916 that only about half of the bachelors had actually attested. This forced Asquith to resort to another half-measure, the Compulsory Military Service Act, which applied only to bachelors. To Robertson it was obvious that married as well as single men must be conscripted if his western strategy was to be implemented. He lobbied both inside and outside the government, conducting a behind-the-scenes campaign with politicians and the press to force the government to accept conscription.[74] The contrast between his and Kitchener's approach to conscription was striking. The secretary of state for war had refused to use his great public standing to ask for conscription in 1915, and his approach to conscription remained suspect. "It was useless to have a S. of S. for War who was not determined to get the numbers," Robertson lamented to Repington.[75]

A showdown on conscription could no longer be evaded when Robertson gained the government's sanction on April 7 for a large-scale offensive on the western front. When Asquith resisted conscription despite threats of resignation from Lloyd George and the Unionists, Robertson tilted the issue in favor of the pro-compulsionists. He got the Army Council to make a strong statement in favor of the conscription of married men if an inadequate number of bachelors were taken in during the next month. His intent was to force the hand of the government. Bonar Law painted an alarming scenario of the conscription crisis leading to the collapse of the government, a Unionist victory in a general election, followed by martial law and the employment of troops to enforce subscription. This made no impression on Robertson, who rejected all personal pleas for compromise and encouraged Geoffrey Robinson, the editor of the *Times*, to make the War Office's stand on compulsion public. He also hinted that he would get the Army Council to go on record that it could no longer be responsible for the conduct of the war "unless its needs in men were supplied."[76] As he told Lieutenant-General Sir Sidney Clive, the government could either accept the Army Council's position or "squabble and break up."[77]

Lloyd George, who viewed conscription as the nation's commitment to a war to a finish, was Robertson's most important ally.[78] His no-holds-barred approach was not without irony. Hostile to fighting the main body of the German army, his support for the men that the generals needed to sustain their large-scale operations was extreme. He "would rather see old Derby with a strong General Staff conducting the war than that it should continue to be run as it now is by the present Government,"[79] he told Lord Stamfordham. Although Lloyd George characterized Robertson as "a splendid fellow,"[80] the prolonged and costly Somme offensive soon brought relations between the future prime minister and the CIGS to the boiling point.

NOTES

1. Robertson to Haig, December 26, 1915, Woodward, MCWR, 23.

2. See Walter Kirke's unpublished typescript memoir of Macdonogh (1947), Kirke MSS WMK 13.

3. Robertson to Callwell, October 26, 1915, Robertson MSS I/8/33.

4. John Turner, British Politics and the Great War: Coalition and Conflict 1915–1918 (New Haven, 1992), 101–2.

5. Charles à Court Repington, The First World War, 1914–1918 (London, 1921), vol. 1, 367.

6. Robertson to H. A. Gwynne, November 28, 1916, ibid., 115.

7. Hankey, Supreme Command, vol. 2, 446.

8. E. L. Spears, Prelude to Victory (London, 1939), 33.

9. General Sir George de S. Barrow, The Fire of Life (London, c. 1942), 164.

10. See the excellent article by J. M. McEwen, "'Brass-Hats' and the British Press during the First World War," Canadian Journal of History 18 (April 1983): 43–67.

11. Repington, First World War, vol. 1, 27.

12. Robertson to Haig, June 2, and Haig to Robertson, June 3, 1916; Robertson to Kiggell, September 29, 1916, Woodward, MCWR, 54–55, 88.

13. Lloyd George, War Memoirs, vol. 1, 468; vol. 2, 1410.

14. Robertson to Haig, March 8, 1916, Robertson MSS I/22/30.

15. Haig passed his exams, but having missed a term because of influenza, he didn't have sufficient time in residence to receive a degree.

16. Gerard J. De Groot, Douglas Haig, 1861–1928 (London, 1988), 214.

17. Woodward, MCWR, 97–99.

18. Robertson to Haig, April 26, 1916, ibid., 47.

19. See Hankey to Asquith, May 23, 1916, CAB 42/14/12; and diary entry of May 22, 1916, Hankey MSS 1/1.

20. Haig to Robertson, May 20, 1916, and Army Council (189), May 22, 1916, annexed to War Committee, May 24, 1916, CAB 42/14/10.

21. War Committee, May 24 and 30, 1916, CAB 42/14/10 & 12.

22. See David Dutton, "The 'Robertson Dictatorship' and the Balkan Campaign of 1916," *Journal of Strategic Studies* 9 (March 1986): 64–78.

23. Robertson to Callwell, December 11, 1916, Robertson MSS I/8/39.

24. Robertson, "Note for the War Committee by the Chief of the Imperial General Staff, with Reference to the General Staff Paper Dated 16th December, 1915," December 23, 1915, WO 106/310; and War Committee, December 28, 1915, CAB 42/6/14.

25. War Committee, December 6, 1915, CAB 42/6/4.

26. Robertson to Mahon, March 6, 1916, Woodward, MCWR, 38.

27. Repington, *First World War*, vol. 1, 152.

28. Sir William Robertson, *Soldiers and Statesmen 1914–1918* (London, 1926), vol. 1, 288.

29. The paper, dated June 30, 1915, is unsigned, but Robertson clearly seems to be the author. Robertson MSS I/9/6.

30. See V. H. Rothwell, *British War Aims and Peace Diplomacy, 1914–1918* (Oxford, 1971), 18–58; and Cassar, *Asquith*, 70–77.

31. Robertson, "Note Prepared by the Chief of the Imperial General Staff for the War Committee on the Assistance that Diplomacy Might Render to Naval and Military Operations," February 12, 1916, CAB 42/9/3.

32. Grey, "The Position of Great Britain with Regard to Her Allies," February 18, 1916, CAB 42/9/3.

33. War Committee, February 22, 1916, CAB 42/9/3.

34. Robertson to Wigram, January 12, 1916, Woodward, MCWR, 27.

35. Diary entry of May 24, 1916, Hankey MSS 1/1. See also David R. Woodward, *Trial by Friendship: Anglo-American Relations, 1917–1918* (Lexington, 1993), 12–16.

36. See Fritz Fischer, *Germany's Aims in the First World War* (New York, 1967); and Holger H. Herwig, *The First World War: Germany and Austria-Hungary 1914–1918* (London, 1997), 302–7, 351–52.

37. See John Gooch, "Soldiers, Strategy and War Aims in Britain 1914–1918," in *War Aims and Strategic Policy in the Great War 1914–1918*, ed. Barry Hunt and Adrian Preston (London, 1977), 21–40.

38. Robertson to Lloyd George, August 17, 1916, Macdonogh MSS, WO 106/1510.

39. He made this clear two weeks later, August 31, 1916, when he submitted a memorandum on war aims, WO 106/310.

40. Ibid. Macdonogh played a major role in producing this memorandum. See diary entry of August 23, 1916, Clive MSS, CAB 45/201; and M. V. Brett, ed., *Journals and Letters of Reginald Viscount Esher*, Vol 4: *1916–1930* (London, 1938), 54–55.

41. Lloyd George, *War Memoirs*, vol. 1, 467.

42. Robertson to Earl Crawford and Balcarres, September 28, 1916, Macdonogh MSS, WO 106/1510.

43. John Grigg, *Lloyd George from Peace to War 1912–1916* (Berkeley and Los Angeles, 1985), 425.

44. Robertson, "Note for the War Committee by the Chief of the Imperial General Staff, with reference to the General Staff Paper, Dated December 16, 1915," December 23, 1916, annexed to the War Committee, December 28, 1916, CAB 42/6/14.

45. For a good summary of the so-called "British way in warfare," see Bourne, *Britain and the Great War*, 133–35.

46. Author's italics. War Committee, December 28, 1915, CAB 42/6/14.

47. Memorandum by Balfour, December 27, 1915, WO 106/310.

48. War Committee, January 13, 1916, CAB 42/7/5.

49. Memorandum by Grey, January 14, 1916, Grey MSS, FO 800/96.

50. Philpott, "British Military Strategy on the Western Front," 331–32.

51. Robertson to Haig, January 16 and 28, 1916, Woodward, MCWR, 29, 32–33.

52. On Kitchener's position, see Cassar, *Kitchener*, 467.

53. War Committee, February 22, 1916, CAB 42/9/3.

54. Robertson to Haig, March 6, 1916, Woodward, MCWR, 40.

55. War Committee, March 21, 1916, CAB 42/11/6.

56. These were sentiments penned by Lord Esher during a visit to GHQ. Diary entry of June 1, 1916, Esher MSS 2/16.

57. Robert Blake, ed., *The Private Papers of Douglas Haig 1914–1919* (London, 1952), 137.

58. Robertson, "Future Military Operations," March 31, 1916, WO 106/310.

59. Haig to Robertson, April 4, 1916, annexed to War Committee, April 7, 1916, CAB 42/12/5.

60. War Committee, April 7, 1916, CAB 42/12/5.

61. "Summary of the Military Situation in the Various Theatres of War for the Seven Days Ending 1st June, with Comments by the General Staff," WO 106/320.

62. Blake, *Papers of Haig*, 144.

63. Tim Travers, "The Somme: July 1, 1916, The Reason Why," *MHQ: The Quarterly Journal of Military History* 7 (Summer 1995): 63.

64. German battalions that had been engaged a second time after being withdrawn and refitted were counted twice. "Summary of the Military Situation in the Various Theatres of War for the Seven Days Ending 9th November, with Comments by the General Staff," WO 106/320.

65. Repington, *First World War*, vol. 1, 196.

66. Robertson to Haig, May 28, 1916, Woodward, MCWR, 53.

67. Haig to his wife, June 22, 1916, Haig MSS No. 144.

68. Woodward, MCWR, 54.

69. War Committee, May 30, 1916, CAB 42/14/12.

70. Diary entries of April 5 and June 27, 1916, Haig MSS Nos. 105 and 106.

71. See Travers, *Killing Ground*, 127–46; and Prior and Wilson, *Command on the Western Front*, 137–53.

72. Martin Middlebrook, *The First Day on the Somme 1 July 1916* (New York, 1972), 281.

73. Robertson to Kitchener, December 27, 1915, WO 106/310.

74. See, for example, his interview with Leo Amery. John Barnes and David Nicholson, eds., *The Leo Amery Diaries:* vol. 1, *1896–1929* (London, 1980), 128.

75. Repington, *First World War*, vol. 1, 180.

76. Robinson later changed his name to Dawson. Robinson, "Notes of inter - view with Robertson," April 14, 1916, MSS Dawson 66, fols. 49–52; and "Bonar Law's conversation with Stamfordham," April 16, 1916, RA Geo. V K. 951/2.

77. Diary entry of April 17, 1916, Clive MSS, CAB 45/201.

78. For an excellent account of the conscription crisis in April, see R.J.Q. Adams and Philip P. Poirier, *The Conscription Controversy in Great Britain, 1900–18* (Columbus, 1987), 144–70.

79. Note by Lord Stamfordham, April 16, 1916, RA Geo. V K. 951.

80. George Riddell, *Lord Riddell's War Diary, 1914–1918* (London, 1933), 174.

Chapter 4

The Somme

Despite their fitness and high morale, volunteers to a man, the British soldiers poised to go "over the top" on the Somme constituted an "amateur" force when compared to the battle-tested German soldiers awaiting them in their extensively fortified positions. With the BEF more than doubling its ration strength during the previous twelve months (seventeen divisions arriving from England and Egypt since January 1), many soldiers were green. What was true of the rank and file was equally true of the commanders. Only two corps commanders on the Somme front had commanded as much as a division prior to the war; only three of the twenty-three divisional commanders had commanded as much as a brigade.[1]

After a prolonged bombardment, Haig contemplated a rapid sweep across the three lines of the German defensive system to secure the high ground between Serre and Montauban. To enable his reserve force of two infantry and three cavalry divisions to drive through the center towards Bapaume without being fired upon from the flanks, the attack took place along a broad front.

On July 1, the infantry of eleven British divisions, bayonets fixed, left their trenches in waves of successive lines. Leading the way were young officers with swagger sticks and polished Sam Browne belts. Some soldiers ran, but most walked as they navigated the shell-pocked ground and barbed wire. They were met by murderous fire from machine guns and artillery. "All along the line men could be seen throwing their arms into the air and collapsing, never to move again," writes one of the compilers of the British official history. "Badly wounded rolled about in their agony, and others less severely injured crawled to the nearest shell-holes for shelter."[2]

By nightfall only three miles of the enemy's first line of defense on the fourteen-mile front under attack had been captured. The 19,240 soldiers who were killed or died of their wounds exceeded the enemy defenders in the front-trench system.[3] Roughly one in seven British soldiers killed on the western front in 1916 was a victim of the first day of the Somme offensive.[4]

Robertson was in France, and he almost certainly was stunned when he read the report of Brigadier General H. C. Rees. The commander of the 94th Infantry Brigade, 31st Division, VIII Corps, spoke of his men advancing on the northern part of the British front

in line after line, dressed as if on parade. . . lines which advanced in such admirable order melting way under the fire. Yet not a man wavered, broke the ranks, or attempted to come back. He has never seen, indeed could never have imagined, such a magnificent display of gallantry, discipline and determination. The reports that he has had from the very few survivors of this marvelous advance bear out what he saw with his own eyes, viz: that hardly a man of ours got to the German Front Line.[5]

Haig and Robertson reacted differently to this unmitigated disaster. Haig believed that the dead, wounded, and captured (originally thought to be 40,000 instead of 57,470) were about as expected. His vision clouded by the fog of battle, he accused the VIII Corps (which included Rees' battalion) of cowardice, wrongly attributing its lack of success to troops refusing to leave their trenches.[6] Although failing to capture the village Serre, the VIII Corps suffered over 14,000 casualties.[7]

Robertson certainly didn't view the events of July 1 as a "marvelous advance." Some 60,000 casualties in a single day made a mockery of his attrition policy. It was the worst day in British military history: For example, British losses were 8,458 at Waterloo, 4,000 on D-Day.[8] Haig's infantry was doomed unless German machine guns and artillery were neutralized by artillery fire. Yet Robertson discovered from Sir A. G. Hunter-Weston, the commander of the VIII Corps, that the British had not had the necessary concentration of high-explosive shells to give the advancing Tommies a fighting chance.[9]

The preliminary artillery bombardment had commenced on June 24. Some fifty-thousand gunners spent seven days loading and firing approximately 1,500,000 shells. The results appeared devastating. "Every yard of ground had been churned up and churned again, the land being reduced

Field Marshal Sir Douglas Haig

to a desert of mud and shell-craters. Woods were uprooted and slashed to pieces, houses and cottages were razed to the ground and their ruins crushed to powder, so that whole villages were no longer recognizable."[10] But appearances were often deceiving. Fully two-thirds of the shells were shrapnel; and only nine hundred of the twelve thousand tons of high-explosive shells fired by the howitzers and heavy guns represented high-explosive. This limited explosive load and the shrapnel, though extremely effective against troops in the open, had a disappointing effect against the semipermanent German fortifications,[11] especially on the northern section of the front. German troops were terrorized but secure in tunnels twenty or more feet below the ground. "It is inadvisable to give currency to such unpleasant and dangerous facts" was Hunter-Weston's comment on the BEF's inability to silence the enemy's guns on his front.[12]

Attempts to reconcile Haig's desire to rush the three consecutive German defensive lines with Rawlinson's cautious approach of taking the first line of the German defenses and then extracting a heavy toll from the Germans when they counterattacked also contributed to the disaster. British artillery had been distributed along the entire front, making it impossible to concentrate fire. As the official history admits, "too little attention was paid by the general staff to the advice of the artillery and engineer experts, who, recalling the methods of fortress warfare, suggested the concentration of artillery fire on particular sectors rather than spreading it nearly evenly."[13] Some divisional commanders expected a rapid penetration whereas others prepared for a step-by-step advance.

On July 5, Robertson wrote his successor at GHQ, Kiggell. "The more I think of it," he noted, "the more I am convinced that at any rate until we get through the enemy's defences the road to success lies through deliberation." It was reckless to "push on too rapidly." Robertson's formula was "to plod on carefully, slowly, and deliberately until we get through and we can only do this by powerful artillery action as a preliminary, and for this we want concentration and not dispersion of artillery fire." Robertson's comments were directly critical of Haig's leadership, and Kiggell was instructed not to "show this letter to anyone."[14]

Robertson's faith in Haig had been shaken, apparently with good reason. A recent analysis by Tim Travers argues that

while Haig was committed to setting strategy and then leaving the tactics up to his army and commanders. . . there was a middle level between strategy and tactics, which might be called "grand tactics." This middle level involved key matters such as the depth of objectives in an offensive or the length of a bombardment before an offensive, or the depth of a defensive zone, and in these matters, Haig and GHQ did intervene. It can be argued that in fact Haig and GHQ got the worst of both worlds: strategy that was not tied to tactical realities, and yet sufficient intervention in the middle level area of "grand tactics" to confuse the army commanders. [15]

GHQ's failings were especially prominent in the employment of artillery. "Haig, a cavalryman," according to Shelford Bidwell and Dominick Graham, "may not have understood artillery techniques but he had successive advisers, H. S. Horne, F.D.V. Wing, H. F. Mercer, John Headlam and Noel Birch, who were all good artillerymen. Surely he took their advice? The answer is that he told them what he wanted. . . . Fortunately the science of gunnery had its own momentum and the artillery staffs directed it effectively, even if without general staff guidance."[16]

None of Robertson's doubts about Haig's leadership were shared with the government. In fact, at the same time that he was learning from Hunter-Weston that the BEF's failure to concentrate its heavy artillery had doomed the infantry at Serre and Beaumont Hamel, his initial account of the offensive for the War Committee noted that "our artillery is reported to have done its work excellently."[17] This was in fact true on the southern part of the line and in some sectors of the center where British artillery supremacy dominated the German big guns and prevented even greater British casualties.[18]

Although Robertson protected Haig with comments about Germans fighting to the last soldier and inexperienced British troops failing "to meet unexpected situations correctly,"[19] he wanted to be better informed about future operations. Prior to July 1, he had believed, as he told the War Committee, that the BEF's objectives were limited and prudent. His understanding of Haig's plans was expressed in a letter that Maurice wrote his good friend, Sir Arthur Lynden-Bell, who now headed the general staff in Egypt. "Haig is quite clear in his mind that he does not mean to knock his head against a brick wall, and if he finds he is only making a bulge and is meeting with heavy opposition he means to stop and consolidate and try somewhere else."[20]

Robertson's first letter to Haig after he returned to London offered encouragement to a commander in chief who had the difficult task of taking on the German army in its formidable defenses. But he also emphasized that he had no idea what Haig planned to do next.[21] Apparently he expected Haig to shift his emphasis to the Ypres sector in the north.

Although his initial attack had been a disaster by any measure, Haig pushed on. "Somewhat chastened, he reacted not by crawling away and licking his wounds, but rather by pushing forward with teeth bared, intent upon proving himself right"[22] is the way a recent biographer describes Haig's mood. If he maintained the pressure, he expected the Germans to crack. Another consideration was that he knew that the French would be provoked if he abandoned the joint Anglo-French offensive and focused on independent operations by his Second Army in the north.[23]

Haig's response to Robertson, dated July 8, emphasized the enemy's "heavy casualties" and "signs of serious demoralization" and argued that his forces had made progress "towards ultimate complete success." Hopeful that "demoralization [among the Germans] may spread quickly," he contemplated "a struggle lasting for several weeks" that would be "very exhausting to both sides."[24]

As inexperienced British troops and officers in July adjusted to trench warfare, with the Germans increasing their losses through counterattacks to retake lost trenches, relations remained strained between the War Office and GHQ, in part because Haig continued to keep Robertson in the dark about his operations despite the latter's urgent requests for frequent assessments of the BEF's progress and future plans. On July 14, the BEF launched another massive attack. That the Fourth Army was starting to adjust to trench warfare was demonstrated by Rawlinson's decision to attack at dawn and utilize creeping barrages, a curtain of artillery fire that preceded the advancing infantry, designed to keep German machine gunners from manning their guns until the last possible moment. By the end of the day, Rawlinson's assault had achieved many of its objectives, but once again a breakthrough proved illusive. Heavy fighting continued for the rest of the month to capture fortified positions that had not fallen in the initial attack.

Haig's limited advance and mounting losses alarmed the civilians. The casualties for the *entire* British front in July (196,081)[25] were calamitous and unsustainable. No month in the war was more costly to the BEF, not even March 1918 when the Fifth Army was destroyed by a powerful German offensive.

Not knowing Haig's mind, Robertson had a difficult time justifying the continuation of the attack, especially after the German high command suspended its all-out offensive against Verdun on July 11. As he told Clive, "I can't tell them why I consider the offensive is succeeding."[26] For his part Haig apparently viewed Robertson's requests for information as an unfair and unrealistic effort to make him accountable each week. "I cannot think that a weekly statement would be of any use to you as it would, ordinarily, only amount to 'views unchanged since last report'! The telegrams sent to 'Chief' daily really give the situation accurately,"[27] he noted with irritation.

Robertson disagreed. "The telegrams sent to me," he replied, "which as a matter of a fact do not contain daily more than is in the Press Communique, do not meet the case like a periodical review by yourself."[28]

Perhaps disturbed by Kiggell's response to his July 5th letter, which showed little inclination at GHQ to evaluate critically infantry and artillery tactics,[29] he wrote Rawlinson on July 26 cautioning him not to allow the Germans to "beat you in having the better man-power policy. . . . The general situation is now better than it has ever been before and all that is needed is the use of common-sense, careful methods, and not to be too hide-bound by the books we used to study before the war."[30]

Robertson's concern about the mounting casualty list prompted another letter on July 29, this time to Haig. "The Powers that be," he told Haig, "are beginning to get a little uneasy in regard to the situation. . . . In general, what is bothering them is the probability that we may soon have to face a bill of 2 to 300,000 casualties with no very great gains additional to the present. It is thought that the primary object—relief of pressure on Verdun—has to some extent been achieved." Haig was greatly provoked. His and Robertson's maxim of fighting the main body of the enemy's army was bound to be costly. Now Wully, who also suggested that Haig might be summoned to London to defend his offensive, seemed to have no confidence in this approach. "Not exactly the letter of a C.I.G.S.!. . . He ought to take responsibility also!" was Haig's reaction. Haig also dashed off a short note for his records that made clear that his goal remained the decisive defeat of the German army: "Objective The war must be continued until Germany is vanquished to such an extent as to be obliged to accept whatever terms the Allies may dictate to her."[31]

Having failed to rupture the German line, Haig, however, had little choice for the moment but to fall in with Robertson's limited though more realistic policy of attrition. On August 2, Kiggell told Rawlinson and Sir Hubert Gough, who commanded the reserve force designed to exploit any breakthrough, that the operations under way should now be viewed as a "'wearing out' battle."[32] The subsequent attacks in August and during the first two weeks of September were almost all on the battalion and company levels, with limited objectives. These assaults were unlikely to produce victory in 1916, or even gain positions of strategic importance. But with emphasis being placed on artillery bombardment rather than massed infantry, a greater balance between German and British losses might be obtained. Also, when considered from the broad perspective of the anti-German coalition, the BEF's steady pressure had a significance beyond the BEF's front.

Robertson concluded that he had gone as far as possible in pressing GHQ about casualties and tactics. There was the real danger that opponents of concentrating British resources on the western front would be encouraged by any breach between the War Office and GHQ. On August 1, Frederick E. Smith, the attorney general, circulated to the Cabinet a damning indictment of the Somme offensive by Winston Churchill. The former First Lord of the Admiralty predicted that the Germans would gradually give ground in the west while taking advantage of Britain's "western" preoccupation by winning important victories elsewhere. "With twenty times the shell, and five times the guns, and more than double the losses, the gains have but little exceeded those of Loos. And how was Loos viewed in retrospect?"[33]

Robertson responded on the same day with a strong defense of the British offensive by putting it in the context of the simultaneous Allied operations in the primary theaters. The success or failure of the offensive must not be measured by whether a breakthrough occurred in twenty-four hours or twenty-four days, he told the War Committee. The ministers were reminded that six weeks earlier, the French faced defeat at Verdun, the Italians were asking for help, and the Russians were still on the line they had been driven back to in 1915. Far from being a failure, the British offensive was a vital factor in the reversal of Allied fortunes. Verdun had been secured, and the Italians and Russians were advancing. Germany, which now had to contend with the British as well as the French, had quadrupled its divisions on the British Somme front since the offensive had begun, stretching German resources to the breaking point and giving the strategical initiative to the Allies.[34]

Robertson also tried to put Britain's losses into perspective. In his weekly summary of the military situation in the various theaters, he stressed that hitherto Britain's losses had been on a much smaller scale than her war partners. Total British casualties from August 1914 through July 1916 amounted to 713,748. For this same period, he estimated French casualties at 3,500,000. His conclusion was that the losses of the BEF, now a force of some 1,500,000, should not "be considered in any way excessive" when "judged by the standards of this war."[35]

Haig's appreciation, which Robertson read to the War Committee on August 5, mirrored Robertson's line of putting the Somme operations in a broad strategical perspective. Although Haig said that his attack would continue into autumn and that another great offensive would be necessary before victory was obtained, the ministers rejected Churchill's criticisms.

Robertson subsequently sent Haig a letter assuring him of the government's support.[36]

Robertson took advantage of the War Committee's expression of support to make his peace with Haig. It has been suggested that he maneuvered to dismiss Haig and take his place in July.[37] Given the differences between Robertson and GHQ over the BEF's methods, this no doubt was part of the army's rumor mill. But there is no hard evidence that Robertson sought Haig's job. In two letters, the CIGS tried to convince Haig that his actions since July 1 didn't reflect any lack of confidence. "The whole object of my recent letters in this connection has been to give you a hint as to what is happening (it always does happen unfortunately in all wars) & to show you the necessity of giving me the necessary data with which to reply to the swines."[38]

Lord Esher, whose finger was on the pulse of both the War Office and GHQ, then intervened. "If the combination of you and Robertson were to fail," he wrote Haig, "no other is possible, and we may as well hand over to Joffre or make peace. . . . No Commander-in-Chief can withstand the stabs in the back which he is bound to get from people at home, unless he has someone to interpose a shield. This, I believe (until it is conclusively proved to the contrary), Robertson will do."[39]

Although Robertson's and Esher's words served to smooth Haig's ruffled feathers, tension remained between the War Office and GHQ. There was a wide divide between Macdonogh's and Charteris's views on German morale, the latter agreeing with Haig that the Germans might crack at any moment during the Somme operations. How the war was presented to the public became an issue when GHQ began its own propaganda effort with official communiqués that were at odds with Macdonogh's more realistic assessments. In late September, Clive on a visit to GHQ, found feelings running high. "There is evidently a strong feeling between G.H.Q. and W.O. departments; the former say the W.O. are belittling the efforts of the British Army in the press, the latter consider that Charteris is not playing straight, and is gradually collecting a propaganda machinery of his own."[40] Robertson, fearing that the GHQ communiqués would raise unrealistic expectations at home, made it clear to GHQ that he took Macdonogh's side. "I think you would be well advised to be cautious how far you proceed with this rather new departure," he wrote Kiggell, "or you may lead to the impression that the enemy is beaten and that you have got a soft thing on and therefore that you will achieve more great things, which after all may not be achieved."[41]

On August 22, Lloyd George defended the results of the British offensive in Parliament. The BEF's limited though continuous operations in August, resulting in a dramatic drop in monthly casualties (75,249),[42] were in fact much easier for him to support. On July 7, the Welshman had become secretary of state for war over Robertson's opposition. Following Kitchener's shocking drowning in June when his ship, en route to Russia, hit a mine off the Orkneys, Lloyd George, as minister of munitions, was a leading candidate to head the War Office. On the day that the War Committee learned of Kitchener's death, Robertson told Hankey that "he was very anxious not to have Lloyd George."[43] To keep Lloyd George out of the War Office, he marshalled his supporters, including powerful editors and the king.

Robertson had reason to worry. Though Lloyd George had been Robertson's key ally in getting compulsion, the Welshman had initially opposed the Somme offensive and had been the leading British advocate of military involvement in the Balkans. Of immediate concern, Lloyd George obviously relished shaking up the military hierarchy. He talked with his friend C. P. Scott, the owner and editor of the *Manchester Guardian*, about the "need for a new spirit at the War Office and for rather extensive changes of personnel." If he had the power to appoint and remove officers, his strategic views would be taken seriously. "The soldiers would crawl before the man who they knew had the ultimate power over them," he told Scott, "and treat anyone who had not with contempt."[44]

When an anxious Robertson asked Asquith if he planned to appoint Lloyd George, he didn't get a straight answer. The Prime Minister would only say that "It is a difficult matter to settle." Robertson believed that he could legitimately block any of Lloyd George's amateur opinions on strategy and the conduct of the war, but it would not be so easy to prevent him from interfering in appointments, which Robertson thought "would be disastrous to the Army and indeed might have fatal results on the war."[45]

The king's support was important, but the press served as Robertson's most potent weapon. Wully told Robinson, the editor of the *Times*, that Lloyd George was a poor organizer and was primarily interested in making "a big splash in the country."[46] Gwynne's support was also enlisted, and the *Morning Post* fired a broadside on June 17: "If Mr. LLOYD GEORGE is indeed to take upon himself the great responsibility of an Office which he must know he is ill-qualified to fill we trust he will realise that his role is to provide the soldiers with what they want and allow them to run the war. . . . If he seeks petty political ends the results will be disastrous for the

Army, for the country, and for him." Other papers, including the liberal *Daily Chronicle*, took a similar line.

When Lloyd George agreed to become secretary of state for war, Asquith gave him the unenviable task of working things out with Robertson. Without the prime minister's support, Lloyd George had no chance of chipping away at the Kitchener-Robertson compact. He was reduced to scoring debating points without changing in any fundamental way Robertson's control of the War Office. His position as a figurehead was further enforced when Asquith appointed Lord Derby, known for his support of the soldiers, as War Office undersecretary.[47]

Although his victory had been total, Robertson realized that Lloyd George, even with the same powers, would never be as compliant as Kitchener had been. The Welshman was nothing if not persistent. "This d___d fellow L. G. is coming here I fear. I shall have an awful time," he wrote Kiggell.[48]

The new secretary of state for war wasted no time in disagreeing with Robertson about British policy in the Balkans. Unable to overcome the political obstacles, Wully had failed to liquidate the Salonikan venture during the first half of 1916. Although opposed by the Italians, Russians, and French, he had, however, been instrumental in thwarting plans for a large-scale offensive against Bulgaria by the Eastern Army, a coalition force of Italians, Russians, Serbs, French, and British. As he bluntly told Joffre at an Anglo-French conference held at No. 10 Downing Street on June 9: "We should consider what the Germans would most prefer us to do, to take an offensive against the Bulgarians or to send our surplus troops to the Western Front? The answer to that answered the whole question."[49] His opposition had been so vehement that his relationship with Joffre was jeopardized.[50]

The prospect that Romania might become belligerent if the Allies attacked Bulgaria, however, gave the French leverage; and they renewed their pressure on London in late June. Robertson was unimpressed. "I am convinced that if Roumania can be induced to come into the war on our side this year it will be because of the successes obtained by the Russians on the Eastern front," he informed the War Committee, "and that an offensive in the Balkans, until the conditions essential for success have been realized, will be a useless and unjustifiable sacrifice of British lives, and wasteful expenditure of war material."[51] Robertson was only prepared to accept limited British operations designed to occupy Bulgarian troops while Romania mobilized before joining the allies.[52]

The French continued to think in larger terms, and Lloyd George spoke in the War Committee in favor of a general offensive designed "to cut out Bulgaria and clear a road to Roumania." Bulgaria's defeat, the Welshman emphasized, would have profound strategical consequences for the war in both Turkey and Southeastern Europe.[53] On this point there was wide agreement. A general staff appreciation in August noted that

the supply of German munitions and personnel to Turkey would cease, and secondly, a short route would be opened up via Salonica between France and England on the one hand and Roumania and Russia on the other. The interruption of communication between Berlin and Constantinople would greatly facilitate the operations of the Russians in Armenia, and of the British, both on the Tigris and in Sinai, and would eventually lead to the setting free of large forces from these theatres for employment against German troops, either on the Western frontiers of Russia or in France. In fact, the material and moral effect of the isolation of Turkey would be immense.[54]

This paper bore Robertson's signature. Wully was no blind "westerner" who failed to appreciate Bulgaria's vital geographical position to the Central Powers. But military ends and means, when ignored, had gotten the British in difficulty in operations motivated primarily by political considerations. Without the means to fight effectively on two fronts in Europe, Robertson looked to diplomacy to eliminate Bulgaria from the war. Just as the civilians were inclined to underestimate the difficulty of the military plans they advocated, Robertson was similarly guilty of oversimplification when he strayed into the quagmire of Balkan and inter-Allied politics.

Events in late August and early September focused the government's attention once again on the Balkans. On August 20, the formidable partnership of Paul von Hindenburg and Erich Ludendorff replaced the architect of Verdun, Erich von Falkenhayn. A week later, Romania declared war on Germany and Austria-Hungary. Robertson initially thought Hindenburg a poor choice as Chief of the German General Staff, and he knew little about Ludendorff. But the "H and L" combination had made its reputation on the eastern front, and he anticipated that Germany's new military leaders "would go for Rumania," especially after Bulgaria, on September 1, declared war on Romania. Robertson rightly concluded that the Bulgarians would not open another front without strong German assurances.[55]

This was also Lloyd George's view, and he wanted the general staff to make plans with France and Italy to save Romania. On the political side,

British soldiers carrying screw-type pickets

Lloyd George demanded an aggressive policy, which included forcing the Greeks to end their neutrality. He accused his colleagues of being "too tender" and making Britain the "laughing stock of Europe." He favored sending the pro-German King Constantine a message "by a 14 gun."[56]

Not wanting British strategic priorities to be diverted, Robertson convinced the ministers on September 12 (while Lloyd George was visiting the western front) that the most realistic assistance that Britain could give Romania was to press the Germans in the west to prevent them from diverting troops to the Balkans. At best, he argued, the enemy could only throw Romania back on the defensive, not destroy her.[57]

On September 15, Haig abandoned the BEF's cautious step-by-step approach of the previous six weeks, which emphasized shells over infantry. Utilizing tanks for the first time, he launched a powerful offensive, designed to overrun all three German defensive zones in one continuous advance. Five divisions of cavalry were stationed close to the front to exploit any rupture of the German defenses. On one level the September 15 attack was more successful than July 1. Six square miles were overrun as compared to $2^3/_4$. But casualties approached twenty-nine thousand. A recent study notes that "although in absolute terms this was but half the number of casualties sustained on 1 July, as a proportion of the force engaged (approximately fifty percent of the attacking battalions) it was not substantially less than that suffered on the first day."[58] Moreover, the third line of the German defenses had not been breached. Perhaps the best explanation for the heavy losses was the poor utilization of artillery. Fearing that his tanks might be hit by their own artillery, Rawlinson had not used a creeping barrage where this new weapon was being employed, thereby leaving his infantry unprotected. Haig "virtually eliminated the possibility of gaining a substantial success at modest cost when he insisted on spreading the artillery over two defensive zones instead of one and required both infantry and cavalry to break through a third zone which was not even within range of most British guns. This was a sure prescription for an unsubdued defence and heavy casualties among the attackers."[59] The intensified fighting during the last two weeks of September made this month the second most costly (109,625) of 1916 for the BEF.[60]

The most dangerous threat within the British government to the continuation of the Somme offensive remained Lloyd George, who further provoked the soldiers on a visit to the western front in September when he told Ferdinand Foch, the commander of the Northern Army Group, that "he gave Haig all the guns and ammunition and men he could use, and nothing happened."[61] Lloyd George's suggestion that Robertson be sent to Russia to confer with his Russian counterparts was yet another element in the escalating conflict between Robertson and the Welshman. "The Eastern Generals probably concentrate their minds too exclusively on the East," Lloyd George wrote Asquith, "and I am not sure that the Western Generals are not inclined to commit a similar error by limiting their views too much to the countries where their forces are operating."[62] Lloyd George's motives were transparent to Robertson. "The idea was to let L. G. become top dog here [in the War Office] & have his wicked way,"[63] he later told Haig. With the strong backing of the king, Robertson dug in his heels, and the idea was dropped, at least for the moment.

When the Germans began their offensive against Romania on September 30, relations between the CIGS and the secretary of state for war reached the breaking point. Robertson argued that the Russians rather than the British and French were in the best position to rescue Romania.[64] On October 9, after listening to Robertson's familiar refrain that the British could best assist Romania by applying pressure in the west, Lloyd George erupted. In a long tirade, he took his colleagues in general and the general staff in particular to task for their indifference to Romania's plight. He wanted to send eight additional divisions to support an attack against Bulgaria.

Lloyd George was ignorant of the technical aspects of sending large numbers of troops to Salonika: for instance, how they would arrive in time on the Bulgarian front to be of any help to Romania and how they could be fed. But he was at home with the political implications. If Romania went the way of Serbia, he warned, British prestige "would have absolutely disappeared." He demanded that an inter-Allied conference meet immediately "to advise some measures which would enable our honour to be saved."[65] One result of Lloyd George's pressure was that the War Committee instructed Robertson to consult Joffre.

As Lloyd George's primary target, Robertson was livid. He told Repington on October 10 that he had drafted a letter of resignation, noting that "as L. G. constantly opposed his military opinions at the War Committee, he, R., saw no use in remaining where he was."[66] Derby, however, persuaded Wully not to take such a drastic step, at least not yet.[67] On reflection, Robertson decided not to resign without a fight. Powerful allies, such as the king and key elements in the press, might yet give him the upper hand over Lloyd George.

On October 11, he wrote Lloyd George a letter complaining that his position was being undermined: Lloyd George volunteered unwelcome strategic advice, and the expertise of a foreign general was sought. If the

War Committee ("whether on the advice of General Joffre or not") supported Lloyd George's demands for extensive Balkan operations over his advice, he would refuse to be responsible for their implementation.[68]

The consequences of Robertson's resignation to Lloyd George's political fortunes were immediately made clear. Lord Northcliffe stormed into Lloyd George's quarters at the War Office. Finding him unavailable, he blustered to the Welshman's private secretary: "You can tell him that I hear he has been interfering with Strategy, and that if he goes on I will break him." On the same day, Lloyd George received a note from Gwynne, who recently had launched a blistering attack against him over his interview with Foch in September. Gwynne made it clear that Lloyd George would destroy his image as the man who could win the war if he had a falling out with the army.[69]

Lloyd George clearly faced a dilemma. He believed that if Asquith continued to bow to the advice of the generals, Britain would lose the war. Yet Lloyd George knew that the national press would turn against him if he had a public break with the army. With memories of the Kut and Gallipoli disasters still fresh, the press overwhelmingly supported the professional over the amateur strategist. As a leading article in the influential *Morning Post* noted: "If the Army is again to suffer from the interference of civilian politicians [read Lloyd George] it can only be said that there will be more ignominious failures, more gratuitous bloodshed, and more criminal waste."[70] Although Lloyd George talked recklessly of resigning and taking to the people his strategic ideas, which represented a return to limiting Britain's liability to the land war in Europe, he didn't relish taking on the soldiers in public debate. He consequently gave his "word of honour" to Asquith that he had complete confidence in Haig's and Robertson's leadership. "If either of them were to go he knew no one who could fill their places," he asserted.[71]

In his response to Robertson's October 11 letter, Lloyd George, however, raised issues that put Robertson on the defensive. First, he wanted to know how journalists learned of the War Committee's secret discussions. "Of course you could not have authorised such a breach of confidence & discipline," he acidly noted. And it was not the first time that someone in the War Office had worked with the press against him. "In each of these cases I could not have defended myself against these press assaults without divulging information which in the interests of the army should remain secret." Lloyd George also dealt with the unresolved issue of where the authority of the CIGS ended and the civilian head of the War Office began. Robertson was the government's sole strategic adviser, but that surely didn't prevent the secretary of state for war from expressing views on the war. "You must not ask me to play the part of a mere dummy. I am not in the least suited for the part," he wrote.[72]

This latter point remained a sensitive one for civil-military relations during the war. Robertson's view that the technical expert couldn't be ignored when military operations were being planned had wide support. The British Empire's commitment of the bulk of its military resources to the trench warfare in France and Flanders was almost certainly the most realistic and direct military means to achieve London's stated political ends: the liberation of Belgium and the destruction of German militarism. Robertson believed that politicians and soldiers would work in harmony by keeping "within their respective sphere."[73] But could the roles of the civil and military authorities be neatly delineated? That was the rub. The excesses and sacrifices of total war put immense pressure on British manpower, industry, and finances. With Britain's staying power in question, the civilians sought to balance Britain's declining resources with Robertson's direct road to victory through the German army.

Robertson's strategic views were known to the civilians when he became CIGS, and he argued that his advice should be followed or another strategic adviser chosen. To ask for input from other generals such as Joffre was not just demeaning to his position as CIGS, it could portend a return to the pre-Robertson days, when Britain's commitment to the Continental war wavered. The government would be torn apart and paralyzed by a debate over alternative strategies. As Robertson was fond of saying, "If I were not in my present position I daresay I could find half a dozen different ways of rapidly winning this war. Being in the position I am and knowing what I know I find it not so easy to produce a scheme certain of winning in a short time."[74]

Lloyd George scored a minor victory over Robertson. The Army Council, at his prodding, went on record as opposing "unauthorized communications from official sources to the Press."[75] Not that the Army Council's position in any way interrupted the War Office's active channel of communication with Repington and other journalists.

Unable to mobilize support against Robertson (Asquith rather enjoyed the War Office row because it put the Welshman on the defensive for once), Lloyd George tried in the future to avoid a direct confrontation. "I never believed in costly frontal attacks either in war or politics," he later wrote, "if there were a way around."[76]

Lloyd George might be a lone voice in the War Committee for Balkan military operations, but he could count on support from Britain's allies. At an inter-Allied conference at Boulogne on October 20, Asquith supported Robertson's position that the Eastern Army without massive reinforcements wasn't capable of achieving significant gains. Moreover, before Allied reinforcements could arrive, the "season for operations" would "have passed."[77] Faced with the united opposition of their allies, however, the British were forced to send a second British division to Salonika, making total British reinforcements about thirty-nine thousand rifles (which included a division from the western front). "Had they refused to send the division they would have been left in the position of being the one Ally who refused to give assistance,"[78] Robertson informed Haig.

With critical political and military conferences scheduled for mid-November, Robertson feared that the planned reinforcements had brought the Eastern Army "a step nearer to embarking on extensive operations in the Balkans" where he believed "decisive results" were impossible."[79] General Sarrail, the commander in chief of the Eastern Army, wanted to capture Monastir, the principal town in Macedonia after Salonika. With no rail lines beyond Monastir and poor road communications, Robertson was convinced the results of such an attack would be limited. To cut the vital Nish-Sofia-Constantinople railway, the Allied force would have to make a distant advance across rugged country. Another obstacle to making Macedonia a major theater was that the Eastern Army was entirely dependent upon sea transport for their supplies.

When asked for his opinion, the commander of British forces in Macedonia, Milne, was in basic agreement with Robertson's opposition to transforming Macedonia into a major theater. But he saw possibilities that Robertson didn't. For the first time, a British officer suggested that Bulgaria's defeat was a distinct possibility, and that it might occur without a distant advance. If the Bulgarians were pressed hard, Milne suggested, they might break because they "did not appreciate a long and trying campaign." Milne also expressed concern about the location of his forces that were involved in a subsidiary operation to assist the Franco-Serbian advance on Monastir. He told Robertson that his troops in the waterlogged and malaria-infested Struma Valley must either retreat or advance. Milne did not exaggerate; by the end of the war, 160,381 British cases of malaria had been recorded in Macedonia. Robertson, however, was unmoved. "What I am concerned about is your statement that your Army will slowly waste away from disease next summer unless you get on the other side of the mountains," he responded. After promising all possible help, he suggested that Milne "keep up" his "pecker."[80]

Joffre was critical to Robertson's efforts to prevent Southeastern Europe from becoming a primary theater. His lobbying of the French commander in chief (I "most earnestly hope that you can assure me that you will be able to agree with my view that we must continue to make our main effort on the Western Front"[81]) eventually bore fruit when the Allied generals met at Chantilly on November 15. Joffre reversed himself, and according to Haig, "was more strong in argument against such a course [large reinforcements to Salonika] than even the British are!"[82] The resulting compromise between the generals was that, although a winter offensive by the Eastern Army was sanctioned, the extent of this offensive was to be determined by the Eastern Army's resources. On November 16, the Allied political leadership ratified the conclusions of the military conference. When Lloyd George spoke in favor of sending more divisions to Salonika, he was (in Haig's view) "crushed" by Joffre's dissent and Robertson's pessimistic assessment of supplying a force sufficient to defeat the Bulgarians.[83]

Romania's subsequent collapse rendered Allied plans to knock Bulgaria out of the war academic and contributed to the mounting gloom in London. Worn thin by Verdun and the Somme, France could no longer be counted upon to sustain the western front. The Russian offensive, which showed so much promise in its initial phase, had been checked and thrown back when German reinforcements arrived. Suffering enormous casualties, the Tsarist army seemed on its last legs.

Although Robertson had not promised an end to the war in 1916, many members of Asquith's government, concerned about precarious finances, a deteriorating shipping situation, and massive casualties, hoped for better. The 140-day Battle of the Somme ended on November 18. The German front hadn't been ruptured. No position of strategical importance had been captured: Bapaume, an important British objective for the first day, remained in German hands. The BEF's casualties almost matched its average ration strength during the previous year. The war's toll in 1916 had been especially tragic for the Prime Minister. In the space of a few days, he lost his oldest son, Raymond, and two nephews. Another son, Arthur, was invalided from the western front.

To the dismay of the civilians, Robertson reported in late October that the German army was "fighting with undiminished vigour" and had actually grown in size. On June 1, the Germans had 169$^{1}/_{2}$ divisions in the field; they now had 197, an increase of 27$^{1}/_{2}$ divisions. These additional divisions enabled the German high command to strengthen its position on the eastern front, with German divisions there increasing from 47$^{1}/_{2}$ on

June 1 to 70 on October 24.[84] When pressed for his views on the earliest the war might end, Robertson shocked some of the ministers with his response: the summer of 1918.[85] This turned out to be a remarkably accurate forecast, but the ministers can be forgiven for wondering if Britain's sacrifices on the Somme had been commensurate with the results.

Haig's and Robertson's defense was that it was necessary to "wear out" the German army as a preliminary to its defeat. They continued to emphasize an awkward truth to those who hoped to limit British involvement: Coalition warfare made it impossible for Britain to avoid heavy fighting in France. Lloyd George's alternative strategy of focusing on the Balkans went untested. But would Lloyd George's so-called "eastern" strategy have been more fruitful than Haig's hammering on the Somme? Although Sarrail took Monastir on November 19, his losses were extremely heavy. The Serbians were practically destroyed as a fighting force, losing some 27,000 men; the French suffered an additional 13,786 casualties.[86] The ratio between the size of the Allied force and its casualties offered no encouragement to those who believed that there was an inexpensive route to victory in Southeastern Europe.

Moreover, if the necessary resources had been committed to overrun Bulgaria and destroy Berlin's rail link to Turkey, Hindenburg surely would have focused on this front to retrieve the situation. With Romania's defeat and Russia's slide toward revolution in March 1917, London might have found itself waging a largely British campaign in rugged Balkan terrain, with lines of communication favoring the enemy. Germany's interior lines, railway communications, and effective U-boat campaign during 1917 gave it the logistical advantage over British sea power. With the defense of Paris obviously holding a higher priority than the fate of Sofia, there were clear limits on how many troops France would divert to the Balkans. Thus Britain would have carried the burden of sustaining the war in the Balkans, and the fighting there might well have approached the levels of the western front.

On the other hand, Robertson's plan of holding German troops on the western front and forcing Berlin to react to the British offensive had mixed results. British pressure forced Germany to suspend its Verdun offensive in July although the fighting remained heavy in this sector. But the continuation of Haig's offensive into November had not prevented Germany from transferring troops east to deliver devastating blows to the Russian army, reinforce Bulgaria, and defeat Romania. The tactical case for continuing the BEF's offensive into November was certainly weak. Improving German defensive tactics made it impossible for the artillery to clear the way for an infantry advance in rain and mud.[87] The weather, as one might expect for October and November, was in fact frequently awful, with the battlefield being reduced to a quagmire. Robertson must be given some of the responsibility for the prolongation of the offensive in almost impossible tactical conditions because he argued that the most realistic support that Britain could offer beleaguered Romania was for Haig to keep pressing the Germans.

The BEF after July 1 went through a very costly, one might say inevitable, process of adjusting to trench warfare and the modern technology of warfare. Every army had the same experience, including the U.S. Army, which suffered disproportionate losses in 1918 with its emphasis on open warfare and the rifleman.

As the BEF improved tactically, its offensive led to the progressive deterioration of the German Army. The official history argues that Somme was the "turning point" of the war.[88] After the battle concluded, Haig reported to Robertson that "95 German divisions have suffered defeat on the SOMME front—many of them twice over and a few three times. The enemy's losses have undoubtedly been very heavy—far heavier than those of the allies. . . . it is safe to conclude that an appreciable proportion of the German soldiers are now practically beaten men, ready to surrender if they could find opportunity, thoroughly tired of the war, and hopeless of eventual success."[89]

Any argument based on a comparison of Allied and German losses may be seen by some as both repugnant and immoral. Images come to mind of tens of thousands of young men being slaughtered in futile offensives planned by callous and intellectually bankrupt generals. But just as in World War II, if Germany was to be defeated, her reserves had to be depleted by hard fighting. That circumstances led to the Red Army doing most of the fighting and dying for the Allied cause in World War II doesn't change this. The Red Army destroyed or crippled 506$^{1}/_{2}$ German divisions; by some accounts the Soviets were responsible for 10,000,000 of the 13,600,000 German dead, wounded, and captured.[90]

If the point is accepted that Britain could not emerge victorious in World War I without casualties beyond anything in past experience, another question should be addressed. Did the evolution of BEF tactics and doctrine in 1916 translate into a manpower policy in line with Robertson's views? Casualty figures in most wars are open to debate and interpretation, and the Great War is no different. In 1922, the War Office published its *Statistics of the Military Effort of the British Empire during the Great War*. British casualties, excluding the sick, were put at 498,054 for the entire British front during the period of the Somme Offensive, July 1 to November 30, 1916. For the year, the BEF's casualties were given as 600,617 as against Germany's 297,351, a lopsided advantage of two to one for Berlin.[91] The official history later attempted to revise German casualties substantially upward by claiming that the Germans did not include their lightly wounded. But this seems a dubious assertion. The German ratio between killed and wounded was 1 to 2.35 whereas the British was 1 to 2.27, ratios that suggest that the Germans included their lightly wounded in their casualties.[92]

What has not come to light in this comparison of casualties is the estimate provided by the general staff on November 9, nine days before the battle ended. In its weekly "Summary of the Military Situation in the Various Theatres of War for the Seven Days Ending 9 November, with Comments by the General Staff," it inadvertently provided the civilians with a damning indictment of the BEF's performance by comparing British and French casualties. For German battalions engaged against the Anglo-French forces on the Somme front, the General Staff rather crudely assumed a 50 percent casualty rate. If an enemy battalion stayed in the line for three months or returned to action after being withdrawn to refit, it was counted twice. Using this method of calculation, German casualties on the Franco-British Somme front were put at 671,000 (which roughly matched GHQ's estimate of 680,000, about 180,000 greater than the figure given in the German official history).[93] British casualties were given as slightly greater than German, 350,000 to 327,000.[94]

What is startling is that on the French Somme front, the General Staff put French casualties at 180,000 as opposed to 344,000 for the Germans.[95] German casualties were surely inflated by the methodology employed, but it seems obvious that "the experience of Verdun had introduced realistic infantry and artillery tactics to the French."[96] Both Allied armies had been on the offensive, but the French, with a much greater concentration of heavy artillery, more-experienced gunners, and limited objectives, apparently made attrition work in their favor. The British didn't. This was partly due to the inexperience of British gunners, faulty shells, and the much greater weight of French artillery. The general staff took pains to explain why the accuracy and timing of French gunners were superior to the British. French artillery had expanded two and one-half times since the beginning of the war; whereas British artillery had increased tenfold.[97] But the BEF's leadership was also to blame. Haig's laissez-faire approach to his commanders, his exaggerated estimate of the effect of his offensive on German morale, and his emphasis on a breakthrough made him a flawed instrument to carry out Robertson's version of attrition, which depended on the BEF at the operational level having the better manpower policy.

As the "authoritative channel" for military advice, Robertson argued that his responsibility was to shift, examine, and present, "if necessary with reasoned conclusions," all "advice regarding military operations emanating from sources outside the War Office."[98] Yet, fearing a reorientation of British strategy, he hadn't shared his critical evaluations of Haig's break through mentality. A commander in chief more in line with French tactics on the Somme might have strengthened the resolve of the civilians for Britain to play a leading role in the destruction of the German army.

On November 3, the War Committee met without Robertson. This, according to Hankey, gave Lloyd George the opportunity to "air his views freely unhampered by the presence of that old dragon Robertson."[99] "We are not getting on with the war," the Welshman told a receptive audience. "We are now at the end of the third campaign of the war. Yet the enemy had recovered the initiative; he had in his occupation more territory than ever before; and he still had some four millions of reserves. At no point had the Allies achieved a definite, clear success." Lloyd George's criticism of the military's conduct of the war wasn't new. Asquith's general support of him was. The prime minister didn't accept the full force of Lloyd George's argument, but he accepted a conclusion that read: "The offensive on the Somme, if continued next year, was not likely to lead to decisive results, and that the losses might make too heavy a drain on our resources having regard to the results to be anticipated. It was therefore generally agreed that we should examine whether a decision might not be reached in another theatre."[100]

Asquith also welcomed two proposals by Lloyd George that meant trouble for Robertson: the dispatch of Robertson to Russia to attend a military conference, and an inter-Allied political conference to plot strategy that would upstage a scheduled meeting of Allied generals at Chantilly. The War Committee decisions were neither printed nor circulated. On November 7, after Robertson left the cabinet room, the ministers returned to a discussion of the proposed conferences in Russia and France.[101]

That afternoon an "intensely indignant" Robertson confronted Hankey. Having been told of the plan to send him to Russia to consult with General M. V. Alekseev, the Russian chief of staff, he accused Lloyd George of trying "to get him away & play hanky-panky behind his back."[102] What especially nettled Robertson was his apparent low standing with the political leadership. Hankey told him that all of the members of the War Committee, with the possible exception of McKenna, wanted him to meet with Alekseev.

When Hankey tried to reassure him that he was not being given the "Lord K dodge," Robertson wanted to know why the ministers developed their plans in secrecy.[103] "They are not so fond of me as at first—as I knew would be the case—for I am daily blocking some mad scheme or cheese-paring because they will not face the situation,"[104] he reported to Haig.

Prior to the inter-Allied political and military conferences in France, Robertson wrote Asquith a straight letter, insisting that he had "no questions of strategy to discuss with him [Alekseev], and I have no assistance to offer him, more than he already knows about."[105] Matters came to a head when Britain's allies accepted the idea of a Russian military conference. On November 21, after agonizing discussions over manpower, Asquith met with the ministers without any military advisers. Asquith clearly wanted Robertson to attend the Russian conference, but the War Committee was in general agreement that they couldn't order him to go.[106]

Although Robertson remained in London, his influence was waning. The limited results of the Somme offensive undermined his standing with the ministers, and it seemed certain that the general staff's stance was going to be reexamined. But a political crisis momentarily eclipsed any debate over Britain's future war policy. Lloyd George's triumph over Asquith at the beginning of December, however, meant that when strategic discussions resumed, they would be conducted in an atmosphere of Byzantine intrigue. Devious and crafty, Lloyd George had no equal among his colleagues in the art of intrigue.

NOTES

1. J. E. Edmonds, *Military Operations: France and Belgium, 1916* (London, 1932), vol. 1, 491.

2. G. C. Wynne, *If Germany Attacks: The Battle in Depth in the West* (London, 1940), 115–16.

3. Ibid., 117; and Middlebrook, *First Day on the Somme*, 267.

4. *Statistics of the Military Effort of the British Empire during the Great War 1914–1920* (London, 1922), 360, included only those who were killed in action (109,402); the number is put at 107,411 killed and 36,879 died of wounds by T. J. Mitchell and G. M. Smith in their *History of the Great War. Based on Official Documents. Medical Services: Casualties and Medical Statistics of the Great War* (London, 1931), 148.

5. H. C. Rees, "Notes as to the Battle West of Serre on the morning of 1st July 1916," enclosed in Sir A. G. Hunter-Weston to Robertson, July 2, 1916, Woodward, MCWR, 63–64.

6. Blake, *Papers of Haig*, 153.

7. J. H. Johnson, *Stalemate! The Great Trench Warfare Battles of 1915–1917* (London, 1995), 68.

8. Middlebrook, *First Day on the Somme*, 269.

9. Hunter-Weston to Robertson, July 2, 1916, Woodward, MCWR, 62–63.

10. Wynne, *If Germany Attacks*, 111.

11. John Keegan, *Face of Battle: A Study of Agincourt, Waterloo and the Somme* (New York, 1977), 234–36.

12. Hunter-Weston to Robertson, July 2, 1916, Woodward, MCWR, 62–63.

13. J. E. Edmonds and R. Maxwell-Hyslop, *Military Operations: France and Belgium. 1918* (London, 1947), vol. 5, 605.

14. Woodward, MCWR, 64–66.

15. Tim Travers, "A Particular Style of Command: Haig and GHQ, 1916–18," *Journal of Strategic Studies* 10 (September 1987): 368–69, and *Killing Ground*, 111, 189.

16. Bidwell and Graham, *Fire-Power*, 71–72.

17. Robertson to Maurice [following for His Majesty and War Committee], July 2, 1916, Woodward, MCWR, 61. Robertson also ignored the failure of British artillery in his weekly summaries for the War Committee. See WO 106/320.

18. Travers, "The Somme," 73.

19. Robertson to Maurice, July 2, 1916, Woodward, MCWR, 61.

20. Maurice to Lynden-Bell, June 29, 1916, Lynden-Bell MSS, vol. 1.

21. Robertson to Haig, July 5, 1916, Woodward, MCWR, 66–67.

22. De Groot, *Haig*, 254.

23. Wilfrid Miles, *Military Operations: France and Belgium, 1916* (London, 1938), vol. 2, 560.

24. Haig to Robertson, July 8, 1916, WO 158/21.

25. These figures are taken from *Statistics of the Military Effort of the British Empire*, 258, and are some fifty-six thousand more than the numbers that the general staff gave to the War Cabinet, perhaps because the higher number pertained to the entire British front.

26. Diary entry of July 31, 1916, Clive MSS, CAB 45/201.

27. Robertson to Haig, August 3, 1916, Woodward, MCWR, 77–78.

28. Robertson to Haig, August 5, 1916, ibid., 78.

29. Kiggell to Robertson, July 14, 1916, ibid., 71–72.

30. Robertson to Rawlinson, July 26, 1916, ibid., 72–73.

31. Robertson to Haig, July 29, 1916, Haig MSS No. 107. For GHQ's angry reaction to Robertson's letter, see diary entry of August 2, 1916, Clive MSS, CAB 45/201.

32. Kiggell to Rawlinson and Gough, August 2, 1916, Haig MSS No. 107.

33. Memorandum by Churchill, August 1, 1916, CAB 37/153/3.

34. See Robertson's letters to Haig and Archibald Murray, August 1, 1916, Woodward, MCWR, 73–77; and War Committee, August 1, CAB 42/17/1.

35. General Staff, "Summary of Military Situation in Various Theaters," August 3, 1916, WO 106/320.

36. War Committee, August 5, 1916, CAB 42/17/3.

37. Travers, Killing Ground, 19.

38. Robertson to Haig, August 7 and 8, 1916, Woodward, MCWR, 79–80.

39. Brett, Journals and Letters of Esher, vol. 4, 46.

40. Diary entry of September 26, 1916, Clive MSS, CAB 45/201. See also Travers, Killing Ground, 115–17; and De Groot, Haig, 291–95.

41. Robertson to Kiggell, September 29, 1916, Woodward, MCWR, 88.

42. Statistics of the Military Effort of the British Empire, 258.

43. Diary entry of June 6, 1916, Hankey MSS 1/1.

44. Trevor Wilson, ed., The Political Diaries of C. P. Scott, 1911–1928 (London, 1970), 217.

45. Memorandum by Stamfordham, June 15, 1916, RA Geo. V K. 951/14.

46. McEwen, "'Brass Hats' and British Press," 52.

47. See David R. Woodward, Lloyd George and the Generals (Newark, 1983), 98–102.

48. Robertson to Kiggell, June 26, 1916, Kiggell MSS IV/2.

49. "Proceedings of a Conference Held at 10 Downing Street," June 9, 1916, CAB 28/1/I.C.-8.

50. For Joffre's unhappiness with Robertson, see diary entries of June 29–30, 1916, Clive MSS, CAB 45/201.

51. "Note by the Chief of the Imperial General Staff on M. Cambon's Memorandum, dated July 1, 1916," July 5, 1916, WO 106/310.

52. War Committee, July 6, 1916, CAB 42/16/1.

53. War Committee, July 18, 1916, CAB 42/16/8.

54. Robertson, "The Position of Bulgaria," August 4, 1916, WO 106/310. This memorandum was probably written by Macdonogh, who later argued that a separate peace with Bulgaria might have ended the war in 1916 "with 1/3rd of our present debt, no Bolshevist revolution in Russia, & no American ascendancy." Macdonogh to Kirke, August 20, 1924, Kirke MSS WMK 13.

55. Robertson, "Possible Action of the Central Powers during the Autumn and Winter of 1916," September 9, 1916, WO 106/310; Repington, First World War, vol. 1, 323–24.

56. War Committee, September 1 and 18, 1916, CAB 42/19/1 and 20/3.

57. War Committee, September 12, 1916, CAB 42/19/6.

58. Prior and Wilson, Command on the Western Front, 243.

59. Ibid., 244.

60. Statistics of the Military Effort of the British Empire, 259.

61. Grigg, Lloyd George, 381.

62. Lloyd George to Asquith, September 26, 1916, Lloyd George MSS E/2/23/5.

63. Robertson to Haig, November 8, 1916, Woodward, MCWR, 104.

64. See Robertson to W. H.-H. Waters (head of British Military Mission at Russian military headquarters), September 28, 1916, Woodward, MCWR, 86–87; and War Committee, October 3, 1916, CAB 42/21/1.

65. War Committee, October 9, 1916, CAB 42/21/3.

66. Repington, *First World War*, vol. 1, 358–59.

67. Note by Stamfordham, October 11, 1916, RA Geo. V Q. 1200/3.

68. Robertson to Lloyd George, October 11, 1916, Woodward, MCWR, 90–91.

69. Gwynne to Lloyd George, October 11, 1916, Lloyd George MSS E/2/14/1.

70. *Morning Post*, September 28, 1916.

71. Memorandum by Stamfordham, October 12, 1916, RA Geo. V Q. 1200/6.

72. Lloyd George to Robertson, October 11, 1916, Woodward, MCWR, 93–96.

73. Robertson to Repington, October 31, 1916, ibid., 100–101.

74. Ibid.

75. See Army Council (190), October 13, 1916, WO 163/21.

76. Lloyd George, *War Memoirs*, vol. 2, 1371.

77. Conference of Allied Ministers at Boulogne, October 20, 1916, CAB 28/1/I.C.-11.

78. Robertson to Haig, October 25, 1916, Woodward, MCWR, 98.

79. Robertson, "General Review of the Situation in All Theatres of War, Together with a Comparison of the Military Resources of the Entente and of the Central Powers," October 26, 1916, WO 106/310.

80. Robertson to Milne, November 7, 1916, Woodward, MCWR, 102–4; Cyril Falls, *Military Operations: Macedonia*: vol 1, *From the Outbreak of War to the Spring of 1917* (London, 1933), 203–6; and Milne to Robertson, October 30, 1916, WO 106/1345.

81. Robertson to Joffe, October 27, 1916, Haig MSS No. 109.

82. Diary entry of November 15, 1916, Haig MSS No. 109. Haig's view is confirmed by a letter Maurice wrote Lynden-Bell on November 21, 1916, Lynden-Bell MSS, vol. II.

83. Diary entry of November 16, 1916, Haig MSS No. 109; Chantilly Conference, November 15–16, CAB 28/1/I.C.-12 (e); and "Note by the Secretary of the War Committee on the Result of the Paris Conferences, November 15 & 16, 1916," CAB 28/1/I.C.-12 (d).

84. Robertson, "General Review of the Situation in All Theatres of War, Together with a Comparison of the Military Resources of the Entente and of the Central Powers," October 26, 1916, WO 106/310.

85. Robertson to Lloyd George, November 3, 1916, WO 158/21.

86. *Military Operations: Macedonia*, vol. 1, 240.

87. On this point, see Prior and Wilson, *Command on the Western Front*, 255.

88. *Military Operations: France and Belgium, 1918*, vol. 5, 581.

89. Haig to Robertson, November 21, 1916, WO 158/22.

90. John Erickson, *The Road to Berlin: Continuing the History of Stalin's War with Germany* (Boulder, 1983), ix.

91. *Statistics of the Military Effort of the British Empire*, 324, 360.

92. Ibid., 358–62; Basil Liddell Hart, "The Basic Truths of Passchendaele," *Journal of the Royal United Service Institution* 104 (November 1959):437; and M. J. Williams, "Thirty Per Cent: A Study in Casualty Statistics," *Journal of the Royal United Service Institution* 109 (February 1964):51–55.

93. Holger H. Herwig, "The Dynamics of Necessity: German Military Policy during the First World War," in *Military Effectiveness*, vol. 1: *The First World War*, ed. by Allan R. Millett and Williamson Murray (Boston, 1988), 95.

94. WO 106/320.

95. Ibid.

96. See Travers, "The Somme," 70. The French, of course, had earlier been reckless in their employment of infantry. One study with a controversial scoring system gives the British a slight superiority in combat effectiveness over the French, putting German superiority over the French as 1.53 to 1 as opposed to 1.49 to 1 over the British. See Trevor N. Dupuy, *A Genius for War: The German Army and General Staff, 1807–1945* (Englewood Cliffs, N.J., 1977), 177–78.

97. "Summary of the Military Situation in the Various Theatres of War for the Seven Days Ending 21st December, with Comments by the General Staff," WO 106/320.

98. Robertson to Lloyd George, June 24, 1916, Robertson MSS I/19/2.

99. Diary entry of November 3, 1916, Hankey MSS 1/1.

100. War Committee, November 3, 1916, CAB 42/23/4.

101. War Committee, November 7, 1916, CAB 42/23/9.

102. Diary entry of November 7, 1916, Hankey MSS 1/1. It has been argued by Bentley Brinkerhoff Gilbert that Lloyd George had no ulterior motive in proposing that Robertson be sent to Russia. See his *David Lloyd George a Political Life: Organizer of Victory, 1912–1916* (Columbus, 1992), 360–65.

103. Hankey to Robertson, November 9 & 10, 1916, Woodward, MCWR, 106–9.

104. Robertson to Haig, November 10, Ibid., 111–12.

105. Robertson to Asquith, November 13 (but probably misdated), 1916, ibid., 113–14.

106. War Committee, November 21, 1916, CAB 42/25/2. See also Lord Beaverbrook, *Politicians and the War 1914–1916* (London, 1960), 319.

Chapter 5

The "Firework Strategy"

Robertson welcomed the outcome of the political crisis in December. Although inclined to defer to the general staff, Asquith lacked drive and decisiveness. When Asquith once fell ill, Kitchener sarcastically commented: "I thought he had exhausted all possible sources of delay; I never thought of the diarrhoea."[1] Conscription was only the most notable example of his reluctance to take a firm stand. Robertson found him "most intelligent and sympathetic," but he could never be "sure of a final and favourable decision."[2] The War Committee ballooned from five to eleven, with Asquith devoting much of his time to making peace between warring factions.

Robertson began to fear that the Asquith coalition wasn't capable of seeing the war through to victory. Its "wait and see" approach was in sharp contrast to Germany's stepped-up war mobilization. Pressed by the emerging Hindenburg-Ludendorff military dictatorship, the German government increased war production and passed the law of auxiliary patriotic service, which compelled all male Germans from the age of seventeen to sixty to work in the war economy.[3] Britain was obviously no Germany, but Robertson wanted the government run along military lines. He wrote Curzon that "we really need to *get on*. Don't forget my 3 war principles— courage, action, determination. We fall short of all. The War Committee is too big, and wastes much time in doing work that ought to be done inter-departmentally. The War Committee should give *orders*. Department chiefs should stay in their offices and obey orders. London should have the same organisation as there is in the Field."[4]

Although Asquith rejected American mediation, Robertson saw trouble ahead as the strain on the nation's manpower and economic resources increased. He told his confidante Repington on November 22 that the government "might succumb to any opportunity of an early peace."[5] The precarious political consensus on concentrating British resources against the main body of the German army had broken down, and Robertson feared a return to Kitchener's policy of limited liability and the confused and divisive strategic debate of 1915. The ministers now talked of victory not being possible unless the BEF's operations were "supplemented by greatly increased efforts elsewhere, and more especially in the east."[6] Of more immediate concern, Lord Lansdowne had just penned a memorandum that attacked the general staff's attritional policy. "In the matter of man-power we are nearing the end of our tether," the respected Unionist statesman noted. "We are slowly but surely killing off the best of the male population of these islands." Lansdowne suggested peace negotiations as an alternative to the chimera of a breakthrough on the western front.[7]

When Asquith asked for comments, Robertson angrily and abusively condemned Lansdowne. "There are amongst us," he thundered, "as in all communities, a certain number of cranks, cowards, and philosophers, some of whom are afraid of their own skins being hurt, whilst others are capable of proving to those sufficiently weakminded to listen to them that we stand to gain more by losing the war than by winning it. . . . We need pay no attention to those miserable members of society."[8]

Robertson's bellicose reaction was manifestly unfair to Lansdowne who raised a profound question: Was the price of defeating the German army too great to justify a continuation of the war? Britain, however, seemed to have little choice but to fight on. Berlin sought world power, and its minimum terms included Persian territory, military and political control of Belgium (with a German fort at Antwerp!), part or all of the Belgian Congo, and predominant German influence in Poland and the east coast of the Baltic.[9]

Robertson was determined to supply Haig with the soldiers to wear down the German army. To get some nine hundred thousand new recruits, he wanted a "*levée en masse act*," which included industrial conscription and raised the age for civil and military service to fify-five. The Army Council supported him, declaring, "not only should the present armies be maintained at full strength, but every effort should be made to augment them."[10]

Lloyd George's extremism on a war to the finish made him Robertson's ally. "Stick to it," Robertson told him during the height of the political crisis in early December that brought Asquith down.[11] Robertson also gave the Welshman advice on forming a war government. "The War Council could be you and two others, who need not necessarily be either 1st Lord or Secretary of State for War, provided you were satisfied with myself & the 1st Sea Lord as *advisers*." Put the foreign secretary on the new war directorate, he continued, and "get your *Cabinet* to efface itself and leave the *War Council* to run the war."[12]

Robertson's encouragement of Lloyd George led some to believe that he exploited his press contacts on the Welshman's behalf. Clive commented in his diary on December 4: "Government crisis on. To my mind W. R. is at the back of the whole thing; he has got Lord Northcliffe's support, and the two of them are working Lloyd George."[13] There is, however, no evidence to implicate Robertson in a conspiracy against Asquith. Nonetheless, he had to assure Buckingham Palace that he had "seen no one, & have had no communication with any one, for at least a week, except Northcliffe when I said 'good morning' to him Friday in the Secretary of State's room."[14]

When Lloyd George succeeded Asquith on December 7, 1916, a symbolic message was sent to the rest of the world: Britain would fight to the bitter end. The new government's commitment to victory was immediately put to the test, when on December 12, Berlin made a surprising and deceptive announcement that it was prepared to negotiate an end to the war. President Wilson then asked the belligerents to state their war objectives.

Robertson emphasized that any peace that left Germany preponderant in Europe was analogous to defeat. "The 'army' is everything in Germany," he wrote Lord Milner, "& it is very necessary we should *beat* it."[15] He warned the government that Berlin intended to establish a central European empire that would be the "strongest State in the history of the World, and tend to subjugate all other Western Kingdoms to that empire."[16]

Lloyd George rebuffed Wilson's efforts at mediation and stated terms that only a defeated Germany could accept. His ginger sentiments, however, didn't mean that the War Office got the recruits it requested. Growing concern about the nation's staying power did not by itself explain the new government's manpower policy. Fearing a repetition of the Somme, Lloyd George used recruiting as a means to control Haig. As he emotionally told Repington, he was "not prepared to accept the position of a butcher's boy driving cattle to the slaughter, and that he would not do it."[17]

Lloyd George's strategy resembled Kitchener's policy of hoarding British infantry and delaying an all-out British offensive against the formidable German defenses in the west until Britain's allies had exhausted Germany's reserves. On one occasion he defended an offensive on the Italian front by arguing that the wearing down of the enemy "would be taking place at the expense of the Italians and not of our men. . . . It would be very advisable for the Allies at last to make use of the great Italian superiority in men."[18] He also supported munitions and guns for Russia to enable the Tsarist army to wear down the enemy and welcomed the opportunity to give the French the primary responsibility for conducting the main offensive in the west.

Political factors shaped his advocacy of expanded British operations on the periphery at the expense of the western theater. Victories, even if not related directly to Germany's defeat, were necessary to maintain public support for the war. Military operations were also linked to gaining a British peace. Conquered Turkish territory, for example, might be used as bargaining chips at any peace conference.

The Haig-Robertson combination rather than Asquith had been central to the Welshman's bid for greater influence during the initial phase of the political crisis in December.[19] Lloyd George deemed Haig and Robertson incapable of seeing the war whole and devising a "plan" for victory other than tackling the German army. If he had failed to push Asquith aside, he planned to appeal to the country, using Romania as a club with which to beat Asquith and especially Robertson. His military secretary at the War Office, Colonel Arthur Lee, prepared a memorandum that blamed the "strong and insistent advice" of the general staff for the "tragic and inexcusable" Allied failures in the Balkans.[20]

Lloyd George expected things to be different now that he was prime minister. In his purple prose, "Was there any other chance left except once more to sprinkle the western portal of the temple of Moloch with blood? . . . I decided to explore every possibility before surrendering to a renewal of the horrors of the West."[21] When queried on Britain's future military prospects, Robertson's response reinforced Lloyd George's view that he lacked vision. "There is only one way of winning a war," Wully bluntly asserted, "and that is by defeating the chief enemy, and if this principle is kept in view by the War Council a very much smaller expenditure of brainpower will be required to carry on the war."[22] Robertson added an exclamation mark to this letter by giving a lecture on the danger of "side shows" at the first meeting of the new five-man directorate, the War Cabinet, which had replaced the larger War Committee.[23]

Prime Minister David Lloyd George at the front

Seeking strategic advice more in line with his views, Lloyd George turned to Hankey.[24] As the prime minister's confidante and secretary of almost everything that mattered, Hankey made himself an indispensable instrument of Lloyd George's war leadership. In contrast to Robertson's short and one-dimensional response on December 8, Hankey's lengthy memorandum was wide-ranging, covering naval and economic issues as well as future military strategy. Hankey endorsed a British offensive to capture either Jerusalem or Damascus and favored the dispatch of artillery from the western armies to assist an Italian offensive on the Carso. Guns and munitions would also be made available to the Russians if they could put them to good use. A jarring note for the Welshman was Hankey's argument that even if the Italian and Turkish plans succeeded, a British offensive in the west was "absolutely unavoidable."[25]

An obstacle to implementing Hankey's ideas over Robertson's was that Lloyd George was a prime minister without a party. To enlist the support of the Unionists, he had told their leaders that he would not remove Haig. He also selected the soldiers' ally Lord Derby as secretary of state for war.[26] If he openly violated the terms of Robertson's appointment as CIGS, Wully would resign, probably taking Derby with him. The pro-military press would react angrily, giving his Unionist and Liberal enemies a chance to destroy his government.

But Lloyd George was not without resources. Unionists such as Lord Curzon and Lord Milner, who had seats in the War Cabinet, had a dual focus. The Continental war was important, but so were the Turkish theaters where the security of the British Empire was at stake. Many Unionists also feared that the disintegration of Lloyd George's government would seriously undermine the nation's commitment to fight the war to a finish. As Bonar Law, the third Unionist on the War Cabinet put it, "he regarded Lloyd George as dictator and meant to give him his chance."[27] With victory doubtful in 1917, the imperial-minded War Cabinet saw merit in an approach that husbanded the nation's resources while protecting and advancing imperial interests.

Lloyd George was thus initially able to ignore Robertson, utilizing Hankey's December 8 appreciation as a blueprint for the War Cabinet's discussions on future military policy; that this was so is indicated by the filing of this memorandum in the Cabinet Papers instead of with Hankey's personal papers. The ministers began talking of taking divisions and big guns from Haig's forces and employing them in Palestine and Italy.

Robertson looked to Haig for support, sending him a list of practical objections to the dispersion of the BEF's resources. Using Wully's arguments, Haig did the talking at a December 20th meeting with Lloyd George and the CIGS. But to no avail.[28] Lloyd George and the ministers seemed determined to pursue their own war plans, perhaps even supporting the French in the Balkans.

Disturbed by renewed pressure from the French and Russians to reinforce the Eastern Army, Wully wrote Haig on December 24: "I do not exactly know what is in the mind of the Prime Minister or the other Members of the War Cabinet. . . . There is a very dangerous tendency becoming apparent for the War Cabinet to direct military operations."[29] The ministers had met the previous day, with Robertson being told not to attend.

The winds of change were also blowing in Paris. Several days after Lloyd George formed his new government, Premier Aristide Briand made portentous changes in his military leadership. General Hubert Lyautey, who had been Resident General of Morocco, became minister of war, and Joffre was kicked upstairs with the ceremonial title of Marshal of France. General Robert Georges Nivelle, the son of a French army officer and an English mother, replaced him as commander in chief.

New leadership in France and Britain brought into question the Allied plan of resuming the offensive in the west, perhaps as early as February. When an Anglo-French Conference at London on December 26–28 revealed deep divisions over issues ranging from reinforcing the Eastern Army in the Balkans, extending the British-manned front in France, and Haig's and Nivelle's offensive plans, Lloyd George saw an opportunity to revise Allied strategy. He suggested that Britain, France, and Italy meet immediately in Rome to decide the "general question of the whole campaign of 1917. . . with the object of finding the best method of common action all through."[30] On December 30 the War Cabinet gave him the authority to "conclude any arrangement" in Rome.[31]

With Hankey's assistance, Lloyd George set to work on a broad strategic review of the war. In a hit at the Chantilly agreement to resume simultaneous offensives in 1917, Lloyd George argued that the Allies had no common approach "except for each General to continue 'punching' on his own front."[32] It must be noted parenthetically that when Lloyd George spoke of seeing the war whole, he was discreetly quiet about an offensive to capture Jerusalem, a campaign that furthered British imperial interests but had no strategical connection to the liberation of Belgium and northern France.

If Lloyd George got his way, the centerpiece of Allied strategy in 1917 would be a powerful offensive to defeat Austria-Hungary. Because of the mountainous nature of the Italian theater, the most inviting area for an offensive was on the extreme Italian right flank, a sixty-mile strip of territory where the Isonzo River flowed from the Julian Alps to the Adriatic. Although flanked and enfiladed by Austrian positions on the higher ground, an advance along this corridor would threaten Trieste. Beyond this city of Italian national aspirations lay the Ljubljana Gap leading into the plain of the Danube River. Hankey and Lloyd George were especially attracted to the Carso, a rugged limestone plateau by the sea, some twenty miles in length and from four to six miles wide. Extensively fortified, it has been called "a howling wilderness of stones sharp as knives."[33] Since entering the war, the Italians had launched nine unsuccessful offensives on the Isonzo, three coming during the autumn offensive, September 14 to November 4, 1916.

Lloyd George sought to enlist the support of General Luigi Cadorna, the Italian chief of the general staff, through Sir Charles Delmé-Radcliffe, the chief of the British military mission at Italian GHQ. Cadorna, a Piedmontese nobleman and a gunner by training, was known for his dogged determination and iron discipline. "The superior is always right," he was fond of saying, "especially when he is wrong."[34] The Italians had long been handicapped by a shortage of heavy guns, and Lloyd George was prepared to supplement their artillery with guns from the west if they resumed their drive toward Trieste. In exchange for artillery, Lloyd George also hoped to persuade the Italians to send troops to Salonika. These Italian reinforcements, when combined with renewed pressure on the Isonza front, might assuage French concern over the Eastern Army in the Balkans.

Robertson responded to his deteriorating position by reminding the War Cabinet that the deployment of British forces was still based on accepting France and Flanders as the principal theater. If, as it appeared, the War Cabinet no longer agreed with this policy, "the sooner an alternative plan is adopted the better."[35] There was an implied threat to Wully's position. If the ministers reduced Britain's commitment in the west to fight in other theaters, it was likely that Robertson would resign.

Robertson viewed Lloyd George's musings in grand strategy as "firework strategy."[36] He had a point. After a talk with the prime minister, Lord Esher perfectly captured Lloyd George's frame of mind on the eve of the Rome Conference: "His active intelligence keeps casting about for solutions. Will he find one? Yes!—he has got one. He rushes at it. Then suddenly he has another idea. He switches off the great solution on to the greater. And so on."[37] Robertson believed that the prime minister's propensity "of jumping from one proposal to another, regardless of time, distance, and transport" was prompted largely by his desire "to avoid fighting Germans."[38]

Robertson didn't resign, because he knew that Lloyd George couldn't count on either French or Italian support. Robertson noted years later that his survival often depended upon the prime minister's inability to convince either the French or his ministerial colleagues that his approach to winning the war was better than the general staff's.[39] Robertson should have added another reason. The soldiers' support in the press made Lloyd George tremble before the prospect of a public fight.

When the British delegation reached Rome on January 5, the jockeying between Wully and Lloyd George intensified. When Hankey was sent to lobby Cadorna, he found him "not nearly as enthusiastic as he ought to have been; he said of course he could not have too many heavy guns, but he made a number of technical difficulties, and it was clear that he had been got at by Robertson."[40]

On the second day of the conference, with the generals excluded from the discussion unless needed for technical matters, Lloyd George circulated the paper that he and Hankey had prepared. When called before the ministers, Cadorna stressed the technical difficulties of transferring heavy guns to his front and returning them to France in May. "The old fellow does not want guns," a disgusted Lloyd George told Hankey under his breath. When Lloyd George offered Cadorna guns for a longer time, it was the turn of Albert Thomas, the French Minister of Munitions, to pour cold water on Lloyd George's scheme. "How," he asked, "could this be done without altering the whole equilibrium of the position on the Western front?"[41]

Franco-Italian opposition gave Robertson the upper hand. When the prime minister's plan for a combined offensive on the Italian front was referred to the generals, Robertson confidently reported to Buckingham Palace: "Cadorna is to prepare a plan for co-operation and then send it to the French and British military authorities to consider. . . . Not much will come of it!"[42] Robertson also played his resignation card after Briand made an impassioned speech in favor of reinforcing the Eastern Army. "I don't know what effect," he wrote Lloyd George, "Mr. Briand's oratory may have upon you in regard to the wretched Salonika business, but it seems only right and fair to you that I should tell you *now* that I could never bring myself to sign an order for the despatch of further British Divisions to Salonika."[43]

Lloyd George's later lament was, "When we came to the main purpose for which the Conference had been summoned—a real and not a sham coordination of strategy—the Conference reached no final decision and the military staffs were left in possession of the field."[44] The generals may have remained in control, but the British and French higher commands did not speak with a common voice. Joffre's demise contributed to a serious breakdown in the coordination of Anglo-French attacks in the spring. Despite serious, even violent differences over the Balkans, Robertson greatly regretted "Papa" Joffre's absence from the councils of war. Since his days as CGS at GHQ, Wully had enjoyed a good working relationship with the de facto generalissimo on the western front. Nivelle was an unknown commander with diminished authority. Unlike Joffre, who had spoken for all French armies, including those in Salonika, Nivelle had no exterior authority and commanded only French troops in northern and north-eastern France.

The new minister of war, Lyautey, demanded and got authority to issue orders to Nivelle and Sarrail. Hard of hearing and inclined to dominate conversation, he made an unfavorable impression on Robertson. On the train ride to Rome, Lyautey stood before a map and lectured Robertson on how the British should conduct their Palestinian campaign. Wully listened with only an occasional grunt. "Has he finished?" he asked Lloyd George when the avalanche of words subsided, and retreated to his bed. Although Robertson believed that Lyautey had "no grasp whatever of the war," he thought it essential that lines of communication be established between the British and French war offices. To Robertson's dismay, Lyautey kept his distance, preferring to work through political channels such as the French embassy in London.[45]

The disruption of the long-established relationship between Joffre and the British high command sowed the seeds of the controversial Nivelle affair. At the Chantilly Conference, the French, acknowledging that their military strength had peaked, agreed that the "British armies would take a larger, and the French armies a correspondingly smaller, share of the main offensive in the spring."[46] Haig accordingly turned his attention to an offensive that had appealed to GHQ since the first year of the war: an independent British operation to clear the Belgian coast of enemy naval bases and remove the German threat to the Low Countries. One of the last acts of Asquith's government had been to encourage Haig to conduct such an operation. On November 21, Asquith wrote Robertson that "the War Cabinet were absolutely unanimous on the very great desirability, if it is practicable, of some military action designed either to occupy Ostend and Zeebrugge, or at least to render those ports useless as bases for destroyers and submarines."[47] In subsequent negotiations with Joffre, Haig and Robertson gained support for making a northern operation the primary British military effort in 1917 following a wearing-out offensive by the British and French early in the year.[48]

Nivelle's ascendancy, however, threatened British plans to fight for the first time on a battlefield of their choosing. Nivelle's popularity with the politicians was due to his successful utilization of artillery and his promise to end the war in 1917. He was credited with the slogan, "The artillery conquers; the infantry occupies." Using rolling barrages, he had achieved notable success in two set-piece operations at Verdun, recapturing Fort Douaumont, and in a second offensive, penetrating the enemy's defenses from four to five miles. "The German army," he confidently predicted, "will run away; they only want to be off."[49]

Nivelle's local success combined with political considerations to give some French ministers renewed faith in the offensive. The tsar had strongly supported French territorial claims on Germany, but Russia's precipitous decline made France more dependent on the attitude of the Anglo-Saxon powers.[50] If Nivelle succeeded, the French might retain their dominant position in the Anglo-French alignment, play the leading role in driving the Germans from northern France, and secure a peace in the national interest.[51] Briand in particular seemed in awe of Nivelle. Nivelle, he told the Allied leaders at Rome, "had described exactly how he could conduct the operation, and had stated that he would send telegrams to him at such and such an hour from such and such points which he had captured. . . . And Nivelle carried it out absolutely as he had forecasted."[52]

Nivelle's grandiose scheme for a war-winning breakthrough had three phases.

(1) Attacks by both British and French forces on the Arras front and to the south, with the primary object of drawing in and exhausting the enemy's reserves. This phase was expected to occupy anything between a week and a fortnight.

(2) When it had produced the necessary effect, large French forces would deliver the main attack, as a surprise, on the Aisne front, the object being to break completely through the enemy's positions. A period of twenty-four to forty-eight hours was allowed.

(3) If at the end of this time the rupture made was considered by Nivelle to be sufficiently large, it would at once be exploited laterally and in depth by an overwhelming rush of armies, which would roll up the whole of the hostile forces and deal a paralysing blow at their communications. If, on the other hand, the rupture did not admit of being exploited, the battle would at once be broken off.[53]

Prior to the opening of the Allied offensives, Nivelle wanted the British to occupy some twenty miles of French front, which would strengthen

French offensive power while leaving Haig with fewer reserves for his big push.

Haig was delighted that the tactics of attrition might be replaced by an attempt to inflict a decisive defeat on the enemy.[54] What he didn't like was that Nivelle's plan relegated the BEF once again to a supporting role. Nonetheless, he was willing to cooperate during the first phase, for he had already promised Joffre that the British would participate in combined operations at the beginning of the year when preparations for his Flanders operations would be incomplete. But he feared that Nivelle's overly ambitious plan would make it difficult if not impossible for him to break off operations and concentrate on the Belgian ports.[55] He warned Nivelle on January 6, that if he were not "satisfied that this larger plan, as events develop, promises the degree of success necessary to clear the Belgian coast, then I not only cannot continue the battle but I will look to you to fulfil the undertaking you have given me verbally to relieve on the defensive front the troops I require for my northern offensive."[56] Nivelle responded by accusing Haig of having an obsession with the Belgian coast—"C'est une idée fixe"—and said that he was incapable of viewing "the front as a whole and in fact was always trying to draw all the blanket to himself."[57]

The politicians attempted to resolve the differences between the French and British commands at a conference in London on January 15–16. Fluent in English, Nivelle made a good impression. His two offensives at Verdun, though local, had by the standards of the British effort on the Somme been spectacular successes. "Nivelle has proved himself to be a Man at Verdun; & when you get a Man against one who has not proved himself, why, you back the Man!"[58] Lloyd George enthusiastically told his mistress Frances Stevenson.

Focusing on a broad front on the Aisne, from Reims to the Aisne-Oise Canal, Nivelle created the G.A.R., officially the Groupe des Armées de Réserve, but designed as the "Groupe des Armées de Rupture." With two armies in the line and two in reserve, a force of 1,200,000 men, the G.A.R. constituted a massive strike force. The gunner Nivelle planned to shell the entire depth of the multiple German defensive system. He anticipated waves of infantry sweeping across the whole German front in one great rush. Positions not immediately taken were to be bypassed and left to small supporting companies.

Nivelle's audacity no doubt was more appealing to Lloyd George than was Robertson's attritional strategy. His blitzkrieg thrust, which emphasized surprise, mass, and sophisticated artillery tactics, might just work. But just as importantly, the French assumed the primary burden of the offensive, and Nivelle "promised a smashing blow or nothing."[59] If he failed, Lloyd George might be able to revive his Italian plans as an alternative to continued stalemate on the western front. Cadorna in fact now talked of a decisive victory if the Italian Army were augmented by three hundred big guns or eight British divisions.[60]

To the high command's dismay, the government sided with the French on all key points. Haig, who wanted to delay his attack until May when the Italians and Russians might put pressure on Germany, was told to comply with Nivelle's timetable of attacking no later than April 1 and to occupy an additional part of the front to free French troops for the offensive. This decision was underscored through special instructions sent to Haig, which bluntly told him that he must live up to both the "letter" and "spirit" of his agreement with Nivelle and "on no account must the French have to wait for us owing to our arrangements not being complete." This unusual communication was almost certainly the result of French machinations against Haig. Lloyd George told Hankey that he had learned from confidential sources that "General Nivelle is very distressed about Sir Douglas Haig, whom he finds rigid & inelastic & unaccommodating."[61]

Robertson viewed support for Nivelle's bold scheme as a very high-risk decision. Wully no less than Nivelle placed his faith in artillery, but the French commander was more extreme than even Haig in his belief in the breakthrough. His assertion that he could rupture the enemy's front in twenty-four to forty-eight hours dangerously raised expectations. The French government would be plunged into despair if he failed. Robertson also predicted that the success or failure of the first two phases would not be as easy to determine as the civilians thought. The battle might continue, compromising Haig's northern operation. Another and more immediate danger was that Nivelle might rush the British into an ill-prepared offensive before the ground dried.[62]

GHQ reacted bitterly to being once again subordinated to the French. Kiggell thought Nivelle's proposal "purely selfish," "short-sighted," and reckless to boot. "We had only Nivelle's expressed belief," he noted, "to set against a good deal of previous evidence supported by our own experience of the German powers of defence & the French powers of attack."[63] When Haig responded to Nivelle's pressure by insisting that he could advance no faster his offensive preparations or the extension of his front because of the deterioration of French railways, Robertson began to suspect that he wasn't being well served by his staff. One way to sabotage the French plan was to exaggerate the material needs of the BEF, and Robertson wondered if Haig's subordinates were playing straight with estimates that called for twice as many railway cars and locomotives as the French for half as many troops.[64] Robertson gently chided Haig: "I do not for a moment wish to dispute our estimated requirements, because I know nothing about them, but I do wonder whether they represent the minimum, or whether they are surely the total of the detailed requirements sent in by the different Armies and different Departments of your Command. . . . subordinates have a way of putting forward outside figures."[65]

Robertson expected Haig to resolve his differences with Nivelle in a face-to-face meeting. When push came to shove, the British and French generals had "played the game" during the Joffre era. Rather than work matters out with the new and junior French commander in chief, however, Haig alarmed Robertson by sending a telegram requesting an immediate meeting between the ministers to resolve his transportation difficulties. "So long as Ministers take part in the discussion of plan of operation we shall always have trouble of the worst kind I am sure. . . . Whereas if you and Nivelle can come to some sort of a settlement the two Governments will have to agree," he wrote Haig on February 14.[66]

Robertson's vexation increased when Haig gave an interview to some French journalists. The *Daily Telegraph* published a "French Writer's Sketch" on February 15 that portrayed a confident British commander in chief predicting imminent victory: "Our cavalry is awaiting the opening of the gate, so that the enemy's defeat may be turned into a route. The enemy will not have the possibility of entrenching himself even far behind the lines. Shall we break the German front? Why without doubt we shall, completely, and at many places."

Haig's sentiments, if quoted accurately, were out of character. Whatever he might say in private, Haig very carefully avoided any hint of self-advertisement in public. On the other hand, he may not have wanted British arms to be left in the wake of Nivelle's optimism about what the French were about to achieve with their artillery. This interview created a sensation. Haig's bombast and apparent indiscretion about Allied plans concerned the king and provoked the War Cabinet. Curzon wanted to muzzle Haig, and Lloyd George was no less exercised.[67] A generally overlooked aspect of this episode was that Haig's interview made mention of a shortage of big guns. Lloyd George, a former minister of munitions and an advocate of supplying Russia and Italy with artillery, took this personally.

On February 15 the Welshman embarked on a conspiracy with the French to bind Haig hand and foot to Nivelle. The generals would be ambushed and the British public kept in ignorance. He had a long conversation with Major Bertier de Sauvigny, a French liaison officer attached to the War Office. His lines of communication were objectionable but not unusual for him. As minister of munitions and later as secretary of state for war, he had worked behind the scenes with French leaders to gain support for positions rejected by his own government. Lloyd George told the French major that the success of the next Allied offensive depended upon Nivelle's having total control. He was prepared to give Haig "secret instructions to this effect, and, if need be, to replace him if he will not give the support of all his forces when this may be required, with complete understanding and compliance."[68]

The Welshman's words were welcomed in Paris where the French had been discussing ways to harness the British to their depleted forces, either through an inter-Allied general staff in Paris or a formal agreement subordinating the BEF to Nivelle.[69] Robertson was aware of these sentiments and was uneasy about the new government's tendency to defer to the French. Over his opposition, for example, Milne had been subordinated to Sarrail at the recent Rome Conference. When Sarrail's movement of a British brigade outside the British area of operations prompted an appeal to London from Milne, the War Cabinet supported the French commander.[70]

On February 20 Robertson tried to head off a political conference by telling the War Cabinet that Nivelle and Haig were now in agreement about the timing of the British offensive. This was not good enough for Lloyd George, and the War Cabinet insisted on a meeting "so that a definite understanding might be reached and an agreement drawn up and signed by the Heads of the two Governments respectively, not only so far as the railways are concerned, but also in regard to the operations of 1917."[71]

The War Cabinet's conclusion quoted here doesn't support Robertson's later claim that he thought that the sole purpose of the Anglo-French meeting at Calais was to discuss the condition of French railways. The ministers made it clear that they desired a written understanding on the "operations in 1917." And Robertson in fact informed Haig that the coordination of French and British operations was going to be definitively decided.[72]

Conversely, Lloyd George clearly played a duplicitous game with Robertson and kept from him the drastic nature of the changes he contemplated. Prior to departing for Calais, the prime minister held a War Cabinet meeting without inviting either Robertson or Derby. Those present in addition to Lloyd George and the omnipresent Hankey were Curzon, Bonar Law, and Arthur Balfour, who had replaced Grey as foreign secretary. The influential Milner was away at the inter-Allied conference in Russia, and

Arthur Henderson, the token Labour representative in the War Cabinet, was absent.

No minutes were circulated initially. On the way to Calais, however, Lloyd George instructed Hankey to prepare a formal conclusion, which in due course would be circulated, but not until *after* the conference was over. Hankey's subsequent bare-bones record found in the Cabinet Papers is noteworthy for what was not included.[73] Curzon, however, later gave the king's emissary, Lord Stamfordham, the gist of the War Cabinet's discussion. Referring to "private information," Lloyd George told those present of "serious differences" between the British and French commands. A choice had to be made between Haig and Nivelle. According to Curzon's version, the War Cabinet was decisively influenced in Nivelle's favor by compelling military and political considerations. "Independent opinion shows that without question the French Generals and Staffs are immeasurably superior to British Generals and Staffs, not from the point of view of fighting but from that of generalship, and of the knowledge of the science and art of war." From a political perspective, Britain had to give wholehearted support to what would probably be the last great effort by the depleted French armies. If the French were given any reason to attribute failure to a lack of cooperation by the BEF, it might "break up the alliance."[74]

On the way to Calais, the veil of secrecy was lifted slightly for Robertson. According to the account that Hankey later gave to Lord Stamfordham, "the prime minister in the train on Monday morning gave Gen. Robertson in the presence of Gen. Maurice and myself, what struck me at the time as a very fair and full statement of the case, making it quite clear that he had full powers from the War Cabinet to take any decision he considered necessary. . . . He made it clear that he had a free hand to decide specifically between Generals Haig & Nivelle."

Having the power to resolve differences between the two commands, however, was very different from amalgamating the British forces with the French army under Nivelle's command. And Hankey had to admit to Lord Stamfordham that that question "had not specifically arisen in the conversation."[75] Nor did Hankey reveal to the king's representative the explosive contents of Nivelle's original proposal which represented supreme command with a vengeance.

A truly astonishing document awaited the British delegation at Calais. Encouraged by Lloyd George's lack of confidence in Haig, the French had crafted a proposal that was certain to enflame British national sentiment. Haig became a commander in chief in name only, and his troops, including their arms and food, were turned over to the French. Orders concerning the conduct of battle, logistics, and reserves originated with Nivelle. As a sop to British pride, Nivelle's orders to Haig were transmitted by a newly created British chief of staff residing at French headquarters. Any direct link between Haig and London was disallowed, with the British chief of staff at French GHQ serving as the channel for communications. Only personnel and discipline, which legally could not be put under French control, remained in the hands of Haig and the War Office. If this recipe for unity of command were accepted, the British army, in the indignant language of Spears, would cease to "exist as an entity. Its Commander-in-Chief had become a cipher, and its units were to be dispersed at the will of the French Command, like the Senegalese regiments, like the Moroccans, like the Foreign Legion, until its massed thousands had become mere khaki pawns scattered amongst the sky-blue pawns on the immense front controlled by the French from the North Sea to Switzerland."[76]

The prime minister's underhanded and bludgeoning methods unnecessarily raised the stakes in his relationship with the army. Lloyd George could make a case for unity of command, but at what price? His actions were akin to waving a match in a gas-filled room. The Welshman was a risk taker, both in his personal affairs and in politics. But this time he went too far in his conspiracy with Nivelle, linking his personal credibility and perhaps the survival of his government to an arrogant, overconfident, and untested foreign general.

NOTES

1. Turner, *British Politics and the Great War*, 71.
2. Brett, *Journals and Letters of Esher*, vol. 4, 55.
3. This measure, however, did not go as far as Ludendorff proposed: all labor, including women and children, under the army's control.
4. Robertson to Curzon, November 28, 1916, Woodward, MCWR, 114.
5. Repington, *First World War*, vol. 1, 392.
6. Hankey to Robertson, November 9, 1916, Woodward, MCWR, 107.
7. Memorandum by Lansdowne, November 13, 1916, CAB 37/159/32.
8. Memorandum by Robertson, November 24, 1916, CAB 37/160/15.
9. A.J.P. Taylor, *English History 1914–1945* (New York, 1965), 65, n 3.
10. Repington, *First World War*, vol. 1, 405–6; Adams and Poirier, *Conscription Controversy*, 185; and Turner, *British Politics and the Great War*, 112–51.
11. A.J.P. Taylor, ed., *Lloyd George: A Diary by Frances Stevenson* (New York, 1971), 132.
12. Robertson to Lloyd George, December 6, 1916, Woodward, MCWR, 128.

13. Diary entry of December 4, 1916, Clive MSS, CAB 45/201.

14. Robertson to Stamfordham, December 4, 1916, Woodward, MCWR, 120.

15. Robertson to Lord Milner, December 18, 1916, ibid., 130.

16. Robertson, "German Peace Proposals," December 14, 1916, CAB 37/161/25. Robertson ignored the future German naval threat in this note. Admiral von Holtzendorff, the chief of naval staff, sought a peace that would enable Germany to overtake Britain on the high seas. See David French, *The Strategy of the Lloyd George Coalition 1916–1918* (Oxford, 1995), 33.

17. Repington, *First World War*, vol. 1, 455.

18. War Policy Committee (10), June 21, 1917, CAB 27/6.

19. Woodward, *Lloyd George and the Generals*, 116–30.

20. Lee, "Our Salonika-Balkan Policy," with appendix giving the general staff's opinions on Balkan military policy, December 2, 1916, Lloyd George MSS E/5/1/3.

21. Lloyd George, *War Memoirs*, vol. 1, 818.

22. Robertson to Lloyd George, December 8, 1916, Robertson MSS I/19/9; and Lloyd George, *War Memoirs*, vol. 1, 619.

23. War Cabinet (1), December 9, 1916, CAB 23/1.

24. Prior to the war, Hankey had been a proponent of maritime or "blue water" strategy. Stephen Roskill, *Hankey: Man of Secrets*, vol. 1: *1877–1918* (London, 1970), 79, 149–53.

25. Memorandum by Hankey, December 8, 1916, CAB 42/19/2.

26. "Memorandum of Conversation between Mr. Lloyd George and Certain Unionist Ex-Ministers," December 7, 1916, Curzon MSS Eur. F. 112/130.

27. Hankey, *Supreme Command*, vol. 2, 618.

28. Robertson to Haig, December 12, 1916, WO 158/22; Blake, *Papers of Haig*, 185–86.

29. Robertson to Haig, December 24, 1916, Woodward, MCWR, 131–32.

30. Anglo-French Conference, December 28, 1916, CAB 28/2/I.C.-13 (d); War Cabinet (21), December 28, 1917, CAB 23/1.

31. War Cabinet (23), December 30, 1918, CAB 23/1.

32. Woodward, *Lloyd George and the Generals*, 138–39.

33. James E. Edmonds and H. R. Davies, *Military Operations: Italy 1915–1919* (London, 1949), 11.

34. C.R.M.F. Cruttwell, *A History of the Great War 1914–1918* (Oxford, 1934), 447.

35. Robertson, "Note on Our Future Military Policy," January 2, 1917, WO 106/311.

36. Repington, *First World War*, vol. 1, 590.

37. Brett, *Journals and Letters of Esher*, vol. 4, 81.

38. Robertson, "Observations on the First Seven Chapters of the 1918 Volume," December 1, 1932, CAB 45/193.

39. Ibid.

40. Diary entry of January 5, 1917, Hankey MSS 1/2. The Italian king was the titular commander in chief, but Cadorna as chief of general staff fulfilled that role.

41. "Secretary's Notes of Allied Conferences Held at the Consulta, Rome," on January 5, 6, and 7, 1917, CAB 28/2/I.C.-15 (b); Lloyd George, *War Memoirs*, vol. 1, 854.

42. Robertson to Wigram, January 12, 1917, Woodward, *MCWR*, 140.

43. Robertson to Lloyd George, January 6, 1917, Woodward, *MCWR*, 136.

44. Lloyd George, *War Memoirs*, vol. 1, 858–59.

45. Ibid., 469; Robertson to Wigram, January 12, and Robertson to Esher, February 21, 1917, Woodward, *MCWR*, 141, 153.

46. Robertson, *Soldiers and Statesmen*, vol. 2, 192.

47. War Committee, November 20, 1916, CAB 42/24/13; and "Draft of Letter from Prime Minister to C.I.G.S.," November 21, 1916, CAB 42/25/4.

48. For Anglo-French discussions on this issue, see Philpott, "British Military Strategy on the Western Front," 343–90.

49. James E. Edmonds, *Military Operations: France and Belgium, 1917* (London, 1948), vol. 2, 11.

50. David Stevenson, *French War Aims against Germany 1914–1919* (Oxford, 1982), 61–62.

51. See Douglas Porch, "The French Army in the First World War," in *Military Effectiveness*, vol 1: *The First World War*, ed. by Allan R. Millett and Williamson Murray (Boston, 1988), 190–228.

52. "Secretary's Notes of Allied Conference Held at the Consulta, Rome," January 6, 1917, CAB 28/I.C.-15 (b).

53. Robertson, *Soldiers and Statesmen*, vol. 2, 196–97. See also Spears, *Prelude to Victory*, 542–45.

54. *Military Operations: France and Belgium, 1917*, vol. 2, 13.

55. Haig's comments on Nivelle's proposed operation, January 11, 1917, Robertson MSS I/23/2/4.

56. Haig to Nivelle, January 6, 1917, Haig MSS No. 110.

57. Spears, *Prelude to Victory*, 65–67.

58. Taylor, *Diary by Stevenson*, 139.

59. Hankey, *Supreme Command*, vol. 2, 629.

60. Rennell Rodd to Lloyd George, January 12 and 15, 1917, Lloyd George MSS F/56/1/17 & 19; see also Robertson's opposition to reinforcing Cadorna, "Note on a Proposal for Combined Operations on the Italian Front," January 29, 1917, WO 158/22.

61. War Cabinet (36), January 17, 1917, CAB 23/1; and diary entry of January 17, 1917, Hankey MSS 1/1.

62. Memorandum by Robertson, January 24, 1917, WO 158/22.

63. "Conference at Chantilly Nov 1916" ; and "Notes. Chantilly Conference Nov. 1916 and subsequent developments," Kiggell MSS VI/2–3.

64. Lloyd George, *War Memoirs*, vol. 1, 892. It must be noted that Sir Eric Geddes, Lloyd George's choice as inspector-general for transportation in all war theaters, backed GHQ on the "unsatisfactory state of the railways in France." See War Cabinet (59), February 9, 1917, CAB 23/1.

65. Robertson to Haig, January 28, 1917, Woodward, MCWR, 154.

66. Woodward, MCWR, 151–52.

67. See Stamfordham to Derby, February 15, 1917, 920 Derby MSS (17); Derby to Lloyd George, February 19, 1917, Lloyd George MSS F/14/4/20; and Northcliffe to Charteris, February 21, 1917, Northcliffe MSS, vol. VII.

68. Spears, *Prelude to Victory*, 546.

69. Repington, *First World War*, vol. 1, 449; Robertson to Esher, February 21, 1917, Woodward, MCWR, 153; and diary entries of January 13 and February 13, 1917, Esher MSS 2/17–18.

70. Woodward, *Lloyd George and the Generals*, 144.

71. War Cabinet (75), February 20, 1917, CAB 23/1.

72. Robertson, *Soldiers and Statesmen*, vol. 2, 205; Robertson to Haig, February 24, 1917, Haig MSS No. 110.

73. Hankey to Stamfordham, March 4, 1917, RA Geo. V Q. 1079/17; and War Cabinet (79), February 24, 1917, CAB 23/1.

74. "Memorandum on a conversation between Lord Curzon and Lord Stam-fordham on Sunday 4 March 1917," RA Geo. V Q. 1079/6.

75. Hankey to Stamfordham, March 4, 1917, RA Geo. V Q. 1079/17.

76. Spears, *Prelude to Victory*, 143.

Chapter 6

The Nivelle Affair

Lloyd George's ambush of Robertson and Haig at Calais, scheduled for the first day of the conference, got off to a rocky start. Following a brief session, the transportation experts were dismissed, and Lloyd George, Robertson, Haig, Briand, Lyautey, and Nivelle gathered around a table in a small room in the railway station hotel. Nivelle, who was expected to provide a pretext for subordinating the BEF to his command, got his cue when Lloyd George asked him to express his views without "delicacy or reserve." Briand provided a further prod by noting that "if the two Generals are in agreement, the Governments had no more to do than to express their agreement." As Robertson and Haig looked on, Nivelle turned red with embarrassment. He praised Haig for his cooperation, said the two men were "veritable brothers in arms," and emphasized that "in every emergency the British commander-in-chief had always acted almost as though his army were part of the French army." Haig concurred and said that he had always "made every effort to 'play the game.'"

The closest Nivelle came to playing his role was his suggestion that "certain rules" should "guide the relations of the Generals themselves" and "be binding on their successors if either of them disappeared." The meeting concluded with Lloyd George asking Nivelle to put on paper his "rules" and Briand proclaiming that he "had confidence in both the Commanders-in-Chief, either in one or the other, but that he did not feel confidence in a system of duality."[1]

Several hours later the cat was out of the bag. Robertson, who was feeling ill, declined to dine with the other generals. Around 9 P.M., after finishing dinner, he was given a translation of Nivelle's proposal. When Lloyd George had become prime minister, Robertson had urged him to be "firm and ruthless" with Britain's allies, for Britain was "contributing far more to the war than any Power" and exercising "less general control."[2] Yet the prime minister now seemed set on reducing the largest British force ever sent abroad to a mere contingent within the French army. Wully's "face went the colour of mahogany, his eyes became perfectly round, his eyebrows slanted outwards like a forest of bayonets held at the charge—in fact he showed every sign of having a fit." He shouted, "Get 'Aig."[3]

Soon Haig and Robertson were at Lloyd George's door. Their anger was further fanned when they learned that Nivelle wanted Sir Henry Wilson, who was suspected of being a Francophile, as the British chief of staff at French GHQ. Objections poured forth from Robertson. Would Australians, Canadians, and New Zealanders serve Nivelle? How could a Frenchman, taking his orders from the French government, be responsible for the BEF's security? Lloyd George, in anxious anticipation of a confrontation with his generals, had worked himself into "an extra-ordinary frame of mind." He told an incredulous Haig and Robertson that he was acting on the War Cabinet's authority and showed them the door. His only concession was to agree that Nivelle's demands were excessive and required modification. "You must have worked out a scheme and be in agreement with the French by 8 o'clock to-morrow morning," he blustered.[4]

Robertson wanted to know the extent of this conspiracy against the high command. After a sleepless night, he asked to see Nivelle. When the French general arrived, he was unable to look Robertson in the face and tell him the truth. "Comment? You did not know?" With tears in his eyes, Nivelle also denied that the proposal had originated with him.[5] Hankey, Robertson's next visitor, found the CIGS in a terrible state. Taken in by Nivelle's emotional explanation, Wully's anger was directed at the politicians. He "ramped up and down the room, talking about the horrible idea of putting 'the wonderful army' under a Frenchman, swearing he would never serve under one, nor his son either, and that no-one could order him to."[6]

Retreating to Lloyd George's room, Hankey discovered that the prime minister was having second thoughts about his brinkmanship. Nivelle's formula went beyond anything contemplated by the War Cabinet when it gave him the authority to adopt "such measures as might appear best calculated, as the result of the discussion at the Conference, to ensure unity of command both in the preparatory stages of and during the operations."[7] When Hankey warned him that the "outrageous French document" would force Robertson and Haig to resign, he readily accepted Hankey's help in effecting a compromise.[8]

With his command at stake, Haig retreated into a dignified and injured silence, leaving Robertson and Maurice to defend the army. Believing that Lloyd George had exceeded his instructions from the War Cabinet, Robertson refused to produce an alternative proposal. The impasse was broken when Hankey produced a paper limiting Nivelle's control to the forthcoming operations. As the tense negotiations moved from room to room, Robertson and Maurice gained additional alterations. The concept of a British general staff and a quartermaster general at French headquarters was dropped. Prior to the commencement of operations, Haig could appeal to the War Cabinet through Robertson if he believed that Nivelle's orders compromised the safety of his army. When fighting began, Haig retained tactical control of his troops. The strategical direction of the campaign, however, remained firmly in Nivelle's hands. "Yes," Robertson admitted, when Lloyd George wanted to know if the revised document required Haig to take orders from Nivelle the same way as any French commander.[9] Robertson later regretted that he had persuaded Haig to become a party to this modified but still flawed system of unified command.[10] But he was under immense pressure. His prime minister told him that he must sign, or the conference would break up, and the British delegation would return to London.

When Lloyd George later described the negotiations at Calais to the War Cabinet, he suggested that the French had initially asked for too much, but that a reasonable compromise had been reached. The War Cabinet then confirmed the Calais agreement and not very convincingly instructed Derby to inform Haig that he had their "full confidence."[11]

It was difficult for Robertson to hold his tongue. Lloyd George downplayed both his role in the French proposal and the BEF's altered relationship to the French army. Kitchener's original instructions to Sir John French had stressed that he would "in no case come under the orders of any Allied General."[12] This had been modified by Kitchener when Haig became commander in chief. Although his command remained "independent," Haig was instructed that the "closest co-operation of French and British as a united Army must be the governing policy." In practical terms, this meant that Haig was expected to coordinate his operations with the French without subverting the British military role.[13] Under the Calais agreement, however, Haig could now be ordered around after joint operations began as if he were just another French general.

Lloyd George "is an awful liar," Robertson wrote Haig. "His story at the War Cabinet gave quite the wrong impression this morning. He accused the French of putting forward a monstrous proposal, & yet you and I know that he was at the bottom of it. . . . I cannot believe that a man such as he can for long remain head of any Government. Surely *some* honesty & truth are required."[14]

Although limited to the forthcoming Anglo-French offensive, Robertson feared that the flawed Calais arrangement might serve as the model for unity of command. Nivelle, or his successor, would consequently control the British army without any responsibility to the British government. Later Allied supreme commanders, Ferdinand Foch and Dwight D. Eisenhower, were responsible equally to the Allied governments.

In opposing the Calais agreement, Robertson was helped by the German withdrawal to the so-called Hindenburg Line, some seventy miles in length. This German retirement largely eliminated the large salient of almost one hundred miles between Arras and Soissons. Instead of attacking a vulnerable bulge, Nivelle would be throwing his forces against this deep, extensively fortified, and carefully sited defensive line.

The German high command had previously added some 300 battalions to their forces. By shortening their line by twenty-five miles, the Germans now released perhaps an additional fifteen to twenty divisions (or 135 to 180 battalions) for its strategic reserve. Robertson thought it possible that these reserves might be massed in the west for "an attack on a large scale towards the end of March." Robertson made no prediction where the Germans might attack, but Haig did.

On March 2, after discussions with Charteris and Kiggell, Haig sent both Nivelle and his government an alarmist paper suggesting that the Germans might attack his left flank and "threaten to cut me off within a few days from the three ports in northern France on which I rely for a considerable proportion of my requirements." Haig emphasized that his forces were endangered by the recent political intervention at the London and Calais conferences. "My centre of gravity has been shifted southwards by the extension of my line recently ordered and now completed. The railways on which I should be so dependent on [in] an emergency are not under my control and it has become evident that I can place no reliance on them." Political intervention had also deprived him of his reserves and limited his ability to position his troops for the offensive.[15]

The French were unimpressed by Haig's fears that he might be attacked. According to Spears, they believed that the BEF's leadership kept a "willing horse, a German attack on Ypres," to be trotted out when they didn't want to cooperate.[16] There was perhaps an element of truth to this. Once, when Robertson dispatched Macdonogh to the front in 1917 to explore GHQ's intelligence reports of an approaching German attack in the north, the DMI was told by Haig's subordinates that they had "invented the signs of a German attack in the north in order to prevent the Commander-in-Chief from cooperating with the French where they had asked for his aid."[17]

With Nivelle relying on the lash of the political whip to bring Haig into line, the relationship between the two commands went from bad to worse. Scarcely was the ink dry on the Calais agreement than Nivelle wrote Haig a peremptory note making it clear that he viewed Haig as his subordinate. "Briefly, it is a type of letter which no gentleman could have drafted, and it also is one which no C. in C. of this great British Army should receive without protest," an angry Haig noted in his diary.[18] More serious than Nivelle's brusqueness was his desire to revive the Calais agreement. He proposed a British general staff at his headquarters through which he would issue orders to Haig and that would report over Haig's head to Robertson.[19]

After writing Haig that his attack must "not be reduced by a single man or gun,"[20] Nivelle sent an explosive communication to London via Major Bertier de Sauvigny. Claiming that Anglo-French military cooperation was presently impossible, Nivelle suggested two alternatives. His favored recommendation was breathtaking in what it would have meant, the obliteration of the BEF's commander in chief and its unity: "The British Expeditionary Forces might be divided into two Army Groups, of which the Northern Army Group, consisting in the First and Second Armies, would have a defensive role, whereas the Southern Army Group consisted in the Third, Fourth and Fifth Armies, would take part in the combined Franco-British offensive, these two Army Groups being actioned by a British General acting in conformity with my plans and keeping in close touch with the War Committee."[21] If Lloyd George couldn't accept this radical recommendation, Nivelle wanted Haig replaced by Sir Hubert Gough, the commander of the Fifth Army.

Anxious over the unraveling of his all-or-nothing offensive, Nivelle crossed the line into never-never land. His understanding of both British national sentiment and Lloyd George's motives had no connection to reality. Astonishingly, he thought that Lloyd George's ulterior motive was to become the Allied commander in chief.[22] No less fantastic were his expectations of the self-effacement of senior British officers. His designated successor to Haig, General Gough, spoke for the soldiers when he wrote Wigram: "To put the British Army completely under the control of France is to take up the attitude of Servia & Rumania as regard to Russia, or Austria

as regard to Germany. . . . At the end of the war, what will be the position of England with its Army controlled & commanded by a French Chief, and possibly broken up & impotent?—What say or power will our Government have in the conditions of peace?"[23]

French politicians were hardly less extreme in their riposte to Haig's suggestion that his offensive preparations were affected by the enemy's threat to his left flank. Believing that Lloyd George was in its pocket, the French government on March 7 sent an insulting telegram to London that indicted Haig's leadership and demanded that he conform to instructions from Nivelle.[24] The full implication of the Calais agreement was now apparent. The French government through Nivelle wanted control of the British army, including its reserves.

This telegram arrived at a most fortuitous moment for Robertson. He had taken to his bed on Saturday, March 3.[25] Nivelle was no Joffre. Rousing himself, he wrote Haig, "I trusted Nivelle to play the game. It all depends upon him and I hardly dare trust him."[26] Three days later he noted, "no doubt he hopes to get hold of our Armies entirely, and it will be difficult to stop him now that he has once got in the thin end of the wedge but we must do our best."[27]

Initially Bonar Law and Curzon, who shared Lloyd George's view of the superiority of Nivelle's generalship and had been a party to the Calais conspiracy to the extent that they had kept Robertson in the dark, were unmoved. But Robertson would not be silenced. "It was all very unpleasant to listen to," Spears writes. "This old soldier would then, barrel-like, roll out and stopping at the door turn to declare that all one could do was to pray no emergency would arise which would put to the test the wisdom of handing our armed forces over to Monsieur Briand and his political friends. Which would receive a square deal at their hands, the French or the British armies? The door would bang and he was gone."[28]

Milner's return from the inter-Allied conference in Russia was especially welcomed by Robertson, who immediately sent him a copy of the minutes of the second session of the Calais conference.[29] Solid and industrious, Milner was a key member of Lloyd George's government, often serving as ballast for the Welshman's dynamic but at times erratic leadership.

Taking advantage of Haig's request to retain control of his reserves until German intentions became clearer, Robertson reopened the discussion of the Calais agreement, emphasizing that Haig no longer controlled the movement of his troops. "The whole of the Cabinet therefore know what the situation is," Robertson informed Stamfordham on March 6. "I mentioned that I could not understand how Nivelle should be responsible to the Government for the British Army and no one gave me any reply to this remark except Mr Bonar Law who said that he knew they had taken a great risk but they had decided to take it."[30]

But were the civilians really prepared to endanger the BEF with Nivelle's offensive in doubt and Haig warning of a German threat to the Channel ports? The arrival on March 7 of the intemperate telegram from the French government put Robertson in a commanding position. The Welshman's mandate to govern rested on his determination to defeat Germany, not handing the British army over to an unstable French government and a French commander in chief, who has been characterized in a recent study as "one of the most disastrous generals of his century."[31]

On the morning of March 8 Lloyd George paced up and down the Cabinet room, vigorously defending his actions against a devastating critique that he had asked Hankey to prepare. Hankey saw no successor to Haig worth putting the government in serious political danger. Moreover, Hankey bluntly asserted, "Haig is right and Nivelle is wrong." Germany's retirement from their vulnerable salient to the Hindenburg Line made a reexamination of Allied plans imperative. If Nivelle prevailed, the Allies would "expend a vast amount of effort, huge stores of ammunition, and involve much wear and tear to guns in bombarding and assaulting an empty shell."[32]

Following an animated debate with Hankey, Lloyd George attended an 11:30 A.M. meeting of the War Cabinet. With Robertson reporting "indications of preparations in Eastern Belgium for the reception of large numbers of enemy troops," the War Cabinet demanded another Anglo-French meeting.[33] With Lloyd George on the defensive, Robertson went on the attack the following day. He circulated a memorandum that emphasized that his signature on the Calais agreement should not be taken as approval of an underlying principle that might serve as "the thin end of the wedge which the French have for long desired to obtain for bringing the British Armies in France under definite French control."[34] He supplemented this memorandum with a personal statement, apparently so embarrassing to Lloyd George that he refused to include it in the minutes.[35]

As a rebuke to the prime minister, the ministers insisted that he take "any favourable opportunity" to make it clear to the French that Haig had their "full confidence."[36] The king then weighed in. In an unusually confrontational meeting, George V told Lloyd George that "if he were an Officer serving in the British Army and realized that he was under the command of a foreign General he would most strongly resent it & so would the whole Army. If this fact too were known in the Country it would be equally condemned."[37]

Although Robertson had not wanted another inter-Allied conference, he must have been satisfied with the results of the subsequent Anglo-French conference in London, March 12–13. Seeking to calm the rising storm, Lloyd George did a complete about-face to the bemusement of the French delegation. "Field-Marshal Sir Douglas Haig possessed the full confidence of the War Cabinet," Lloyd George exclaimed, "and was regarded with admiration in England." Lloyd George also dismissed any thought of an amalgam of Anglo-French forces, emphasizing that Haig's troops couldn't be "mixed up with the French Army."[38] As Lloyd George rebuked the French civilians, Robertson and Lyautey refereed a meeting between the warring commanders in chief at the War Office. The result was an amicable discussion that resolved the most-contentious issues to the advantage of the British.[39]

Robertson rescued the British army from the worst aspects of Lloyd George's plot with Briand and Nivelle without precipitating a constitutional crisis that might have undermined the war effort. But the French retained strategic control of the BEF. "As regards regaining control of our Armies," Robertson told Haig, "I do not think that we shall make any progress until after the next battle."[40]

Nivelle's political support evaporated when the French delegation returned to Paris. Lyautey resigned on March 15 when he was shouted down in a raucous session of the French Chamber. Briand's fall came four days later. Both Alexandre Ribot, the new premier, and Paul Painlevé, General Lyautey's successor, were hostile to Nivelle's offensive; and Robertson correctly characterized him as a commander "with a rope round his neck."[41]

France's uncertain political situation further clouded the War Office's vision of Allied prospects. Robertson still hoped to wear down the German army with a prudent attritional strategy. In crude form, the numbers greatly favored the Entente: Macdonogh estimated (March 30) that the Central Powers had 8,000,000 men in the field and another 2,750,000 in depots and garrisons at home. The Allies could count on 13,000,000 in the various theaters with an additional 3,700,000 in home depots and garrisons.[42] With the United States being torpedoed into the war by unrestricted German U-boat warfare, the numerical advantage of the anti-German coalition might be overwhelming; 24,000,000 Americans subsequently registered for the draft.

When subjected to a critical analysis, these numbers were not so encouraging. Robertson expected no significant personnel help from the United

States. American credit might save Britain from bankruptcy, but it was by no means certain that President Wilson would send troops to Europe. Even if he did, the U.S. Army seemed incapable of influencing the outcome of the Continental war. Assuming that ships and weapons could be procured, the British general staff estimated that it would take at least a year to field a U.S. Army of 250,000 men. Small wonder that Robertson discounted U.S. involvement: "What we want to do is to beat the German Armies, until we do that we shall not win the war. America will not help us much in that respect."[43]

With Britain's allies feeling the strain, a general staff memorandum was drafted (almost certainly by Macdonogh) that outlined how Allied fortunes had declined since Robertson had submitted his memorandum on war aims in August 1916. On the high seas, German undersea assault diminished Britain's ability to sustain the war in the periphery and supply her European allies. On land, Romania had been crushed, the Italians feared an Austro-German attack in the Trentino, and the French were worn thin, their railways deteriorating and their troop strength declining. Unlike some ministers, Robertson didn't believe that Nicholas II's overthrow on March 15 would regenerate the Russian war effort. He expected a passive Russian front and further internal disruption. As he told Repington, "the nation behind the Army is no good for anything 'except music and dancing and tommy-rot love stories.'"[44]

Viewing the war as increasingly a conflict between Berlin and London, this general staff memorandum suggested a mix of diplomatic and military moves to maintain Britain's world position. If any of Britain's allies should make a separate peace, British war aims should be adjusted accordingly. Russia's withdrawal, for example, might make it possible to negotiate peace with Turkey. The loss of one or more of her European allies might also require a retreat from Britain's commitment to the western front. "If the main trunk be found too great to fell," it was noted, "it may be necessary to proceed merely to lopping off the branches." Although using the imagery of Lloyd George, there was a critical difference between this appreciation and Lloyd George's position: The abandonment of the western front as Britain's "primary" theater necessitated a retreat from Lloyd George's "knock-out blow."[45]

Germany's unexpected ability to increase its field armies during the winter was especially worrisome. New recruiting and industrial policies freed an additional 1,700,000 men for military service. The influx of new recruits, when combined with the reduction of divisions from twelve to nine battalions, allowed Hindenburg to add eighty-nine divisions over the previous summer. Although these divisions would be weaker in infantry, the Germans by the beginning of summer would have a net increase of 1,250,000 men with a corresponding increase in guns. This impressive strategical reserve made Germany's decisive defeat in the near future unlikely.[46]

Faced with these discouraging numbers, Robertson revived his argument of a year earlier that diplomacy wasn't assisting the military effort. The ambitious war aims of Russia, Italy, and Romania, which were now out of line with their military contributions, robbed Britain of political flexibility. The burden of winning the Turkish Straits for Russia and Austrian territory for Italy was being shifted to Britain, but could Britain "sustain this burden sufficiently long to ensure such a victory?" Robertson wanted greater freedom of action in negotiations to detach Bulgaria, Austria, or Turkey.[47] In truth, Robertson pushed upon the Foreign Office the unlikely prospect that Russia and Italy, having hitherto sustained the land war with their treasure and blood in a maximum effort, would now sacrifice their war objectives to a British peace.

As Robertson pondered the shifting strategic landscape, the BEF attacked on the Arras front on April 9. British infantry advanced in short bounds covered by a deadly bombardment, ten divisions attacking at Arras and four at Vimy Ridge. The rain of steel that preceded the infantry represented the greatest improvement for the BEF since the beginning of the Battle of the Somme. The French retained the advantage in both quantity and effectiveness of their artillery, but the British were making marked progress. The BEF had had 3,911 field guns and 761 howitzers and heavy guns in mid-1916. By March 1917 this number had grown to 4,095 field guns and 1,468 howitzers and heavy guns; and Robertson hoped to have an additional 448 big guns in France by the end of June. Shells were also of a higher quality.[48] Careful preparation and weight of shell, along with unreformed German defensive tactics on this front, led to an encouraging start. Vimy Ridge was captured by the Canadian Corps, and the Third Army advanced to a depth of some three and one-half miles. German resistance soon stiffened, however, and the break-in could not be converted to a breakthrough. Haig, however, was obligated to fight on to fulfill his commitment to Nivelle to tie down German reserves.

After postponing his attack three times, Nivelle struck on the Aisne on the 16th. Lax security gave the Germans advance warning. An elastic defensive system, with forward positions being lightly defended, reduced German casualties due to artillery. Germans in forward positions often avoided being pulverized by positioning themselves on the reverse side of the Chemin des Dames, where they could not be seen by French artillery observers. Machine gunners were protected by concrete bunkers or pill-boxes. Heavy French casualties during the first week, some 117,000 with 32,000 dead, belied Neville's last words to his troops: "*L'heure venue! Confiance! Courage! Vive la France!*"

Even before the results of the French offensive on the Aisne were in, Robertson had a memorandum before the British government, stressing that Nivelle would be removed if his offensive didn't live up to expectations. He wanted the War Cabinet to revoke at the first opportunity the Calais agreement, warning the ministers about the dangers of subordinating the British army to "a Government which is neither stable nor far-sighted and which not unnaturally has an eye to French rather than to British interests. Our object is not primarily the direct defence of French soil, but to win the war and secure British interests."[49]

The fluid military and political situation forced the general staff to consider means of getting a decent peace if Britain's Continental allies faltered. Robertson, despite his apprehension about France's war leadership, believed that a good peace depended upon the outcome of the war in the west, but he wasn't blind to the possibilities of what might be called the "imperial front," the Turkish theaters where the British had greater strategic independence and special security concerns.

NOTES

1. Anglo-French Conference at Calais, second session, February 26, 1917, CAB 28/I.C.-17(a).

2. Robertson to Lloyd George, December 8, 1916, Robertson MSS I/19/9.

3. Spears, *Prelude to Victory*, 143.

4. Ibid., 146; Blake, *Papers of Haig*, 200–201; and diary entry of February 26, 1917, Hankey MSS 1/1.

5. Robertson, *Soldiers and Statesmen*, vol. 2, 208; Spears, *Prelude to Victory*, 147–48.

6. Roskill, *Hankey*, vol. 1, 363.

7. War Cabinet (79), February 24, 1917, CAB 23/1.

8. Roskill, *Hankey*, 363.

9. "Agreement signed at Anglo-French Conference held at Calais, February 26 and 27, 1917," Appendix III, War Cabinet (82), February 28, 1917, CAB 23/1; Robertson, *Soldiers and Statesmen*, vol. 2, 209–14.

10. Robertson to Haig, March 3, 1917, Woodward, MCWR, 156.

11. War Cabinet (82), February 28, 1917, CAB 23/1.

12. Richard Holmes, *The Little Field-Marshall Sir John French* (London, 1981), 201.

13. John Terraine, *Ordeal of Victory* (Philadelphia and New York, 1963), 181.

14. Robertson to Haig, February 28, 1917, Woodward, MCWR, 155.

15. Haig, "Review of present situation on the Western Front, with special reference to the German withdrawal on the ANCRE," March 2, 1917, WO 158/22.

16. Spears, *Prelude to Victory*, 131.

17. Macdonogh, however, put the time of his visit during the summer of 1917. Macdonogh to Spears, February 1, 1933, Spears MSS 2/3/70.

18. Blake, *Papers of Haig*, 203.

19. Haig to Robertson, March 11, 1917, Appendix III, War Cabinet (94), March 12, 1917, CAB 23/2.

20. Nivelle to Haig, March 6, 1917, Spears MSS 2/3/70.

21. Unsigned note, March 7, 1917 [given to Hankey on March 8 who passed it on to Lloyd George], Lloyd George MSS F/162/1; and diary entry of March 10, 1917, Hankey MSS 1/1.

22. Spears, *Prelude to Victory*, 181.

23. Gough to Wigram, March 3, 1917, RA Geo. V Q. 832/296.

24. Eric Drummond to Lloyd George, March 7, 1917 [with enclosed note in French communicated by French Embassy], Lloyd George MSS F/3/2/14.

25. Diary entry of March 11, 1917, Haig MSS No. 111.

26. Robertson to Haig, March 3, 1917, Woodward, MCWR, 156–57.

27. Robertson to Haig, March 6, 1917, Woodward, MCWR, 158.

28. Spears, *Prelude to Victory*, 184.

29. Robertson to Haig, March 6, and to Milner, March 7, 1917, Woodward, MCWR, 157–58, 160.

30. Robertson to Stamfordham, March 6, 1917, Woodward, MCWR, 159. Hankey makes no mention of Robertson's statement in his brief record for March 6.

31. Anthony Clayton, "Robert Nivelle and the French Spring Offensive of 1917," in *Fallen Stars: Eleven Studies of Twentieth-Century Military Disasters*, ed. by Brian Bond (London, 1991), 52.

32. Memorandum by Hankey, March 7, 1917, Hankey MSS, CAB 63/19; and entry of March 10, 1917, Hankey MSS 1/1.

33. War Cabinet (91), March 8, 1917, CAB 23/2.

34. "Note by the Chief of the Imperial General Staff Regarding the Calais Agreement of February 27, 1917," March 2, 1917, Appendix II, War Cabinet (92), March 9, 1917, CAB 23/2.

35. See the exchange of letters between Robertson and Hankey, March 17, 21, and 30, 1917, Spears MSS 2/1/20–22.

36. War Cabinet (92), March 9, 1917, CAB 23/2; and diary entry of March 10, 1917, Hankey MSS 1/1.

37. "Memorandum," March 12, 1917, RA Geo. V Q. 1079/35. Wild rumors circulated that Lloyd George sought the breakup of the British army because its

"loyal adherence" to the monarchy served as "his chief obstacle" to the creation of a republic. Diary entry of March 12, 1917, Rawlinson MSS 1/7.

38. Anglo-French Conference, March 12–13, 1917, CAB 28/2/I.C.-18.

39. Robertson, *Soldiers and Statesmen*, vol. 2, 222–25; and Spears, *Prelude to Victory*, 192–95.

40. Robertson to Haig, March 8, 1917, Woodward, MCWR, 161.

41. Robertson to Haig, April 14, 1917, Woodward, MCWR, 170–73.

42. General Staff, "Man-Power," March 30, 1917, Macdonogh MSS, WO 106/1512.

43. Robertson to Murray, February 13, 1917, Woodward, MCWR, 149.

44. Repington, *First World War*, vol. 1, 514.

45. Robertson chose not to circulate this memorandum to the civilians. General Staff, "Addendum to General Staff Memorandum of 31st August, 1916," March 28, 1917, Macdonogh MSS, WO 106/1512.

46. General Staff, "A General Review of the Situation in All Theatres of War," March 20, 1917, WO 106/311.

47. Robertson, "Addendum to Note by the Chief of the Imperial General Staff, dated 12th February 1916," Cabinet Paper G.T. 326 of March 29, 1917, CAB 24/9.

48. General Staff, "A General Review of the Situation in All Theatres of War," March 20, 1917, WO 106/311. See also Trevor Wilson, *The Myriad Faces of War: Britain and the Great War, 1914–1918* (Oxford, 1986), 449–55.

49. Cabinet Paper G.T. 477 of April 17, 1917, CAB 24/10.

Chapter 7

The Imperial Front

Britain was involved in three campaigns against Turkey when Robertson became CIGS in December 1915: Egypt, Mesopotamia, and Gallipoli. Gallipoli, which was winding down, required the new CIGS's immediate attention. The attempt to force the Dardanelles in 1915 and put Constantinople under the guns of British battleships had been sold primarily on its alleged political merits, the mobilization of the Balkan states against Austria and Germany, but many of the assumptions behind and the execution of this sea and land operation had been an absurdity.

Robertson had been a harsh critic of British involvement in the Dardanelles, more because it denied ammunition and men to the BEF, than because of its poor planning and execution. "Here we can beat the German," he wrote Buckingham Palace as troops were being assembled for a landing on Gallipoli. "No more d___d silly eccentric Dardanelles fiascos, pretty well doomed to failure & in no circumstances likely to help in decisive result. Fancy our fighting on a front from Calais to Constantinople!"[1]

Political considerations, however, made the complete abandonment of this failed campaign a difficult decision. British prestige in the east was at stake. Hankey argued that Britain's position in the east "resembles a line of children's bricks standing on end: all that is required is the momentum to upset the first brick, which causes the next one to upset its neighbour."[2] Hankey's domino theory is a good illustration of British anxiety about British possessions in the east. In October Serbia was overwhelmed, and Bulgaria cast its lot with Berlin. The Germans now had direct lines of communication to the Turkish Empire. Germany's ability to send troops and big guns to the Turkish theaters was not the only threat. German agents, claiming that the Kaiser had embraced the Moslem religion, sought to incite a Holy War against the British Empire, provoking fears in London that Persia, Afghanistan, and the northwest frontier of India were in peril.[3]

An increasingly untenable military situation in Gallipoli, with German 11" howitzers about to appear on the battlefield, pushed these political considerations into the background. Except at Cape Helles, the British troops had no place to retreat if their defensive positions were pulverized by German high-explosive shells.[4] On December 7, 1915, London decided to evacuate Suvla and Anzac. The fate of the last British position, Cape Helles, however, remained undecided, with the navy lobbying to retain the tip of the Gallipoli Peninsula as a base to assist British submarine warfare against the Turks.

Robertson's first act as CIGS was to gain the total abandonment of the Gallipoli Peninsula. But it was only the first of many conflicts that Robertson had with ministers over how best to fight a great war in France and simultaneously defend Britain's vast eastern lands. Balfour spoke for many civilians when he maintained that British prestige in the East had "a military value, and, irrespective of political interests or national pride, it may therefore be worth while sending soldiers away from the 'main theatre of war' in order to support it."[5]

Initially, Robertson got the best of this argument because of the disastrous results of putting political considerations over military and strategic factors. The successful evacuation of troops from Gallipoli took some of the sting out of the retreat in the Near East, but the British were not so fortunate in Mesopotamia when they put political objectives above military execution and strategy.

A small British and Indian force occupied Basra at the top of the Persian Gulf soon after Turkey entered the war. Its primary mission was to protect the Anglo-Persian oil pipeline, which was vital to the navy. A secondary objective was to impress Arab opinion in the area with a show of force. After the Union Jack was raised over Basra, the purpose of this expeditionary force evolved haphazardly from a limited, defensive stance to a distant advance to Baghdad.[6]

The capture of this ancient city offered no concrete military advantage in Britain's war with Germany. Hence political considerations dominated the discussions between London and Delhi. The Indian government was especially concerned that a Holy War against the British infidel might spread to India.[7] A strong British presence in Mesopotamia was thus considered vital. Efforts by the India Office and the Colonial Office to woo or influence Moslem opinion, however, were conducted with little consultation with the War Office. In the case of Mesopotamia there was also the problem of a divided command. With the bulk of the troops coming from India, the India Office conducted these operations, and the general staff in London was not directly involved in their planning and development.

As reinforcements arrived from India, the commander of the Mesopotamian forces, an aggressive cavalryman, General Sir John Nixon, encouraged by Delhi, extended his operations. Major General Charles V. F. Townshend, who commanded a reinforced division and a flotilla of ships, was ordered up the Tigris. Townshend had no definite strategic goal, but the temptation grew that he should advance to Baghdad.

Little consideration was made of the requirements of such a distant advance, some five hundred miles from Basra, especially how Townshend could defend Baghdad with woeful lines of communication and no reserves if the Turks sent reinforcements.[8] Nor were the terrible local conditions of this treeless, flat, inhospitable terrain fully appreciated. A more hostile theater of operations would be hard to find. Troops froze during the winter nights and were overcome by heat during the summer days, with temperatures reaching 120 degrees in the shade. Flies and mosquitos harassed them. Dust that covered them during the summer turned to mud when the banks of the Tigris overflowed during the rainy season.

By late September Townshend had taken Kut-el-Amara after heavy fighting and was only about one hundred miles from Baghdad. The ever optimistic Nixon encouraged both Delhi and London to believe that Townshend had adequate men and river transport to take the city. Political arguments in favor of advancing seemed overwhelming. Britain needed a concrete victory somewhere in the autumn of 1915. The Austrians occupied Belgrade on October 9, and five days later Bulgaria declared war on Serbia. With Allied casualties mounting in Gallipoli, a British retreat from the Dardanelles was daily becoming more likely.

Alarmed by German attempts to incite a Jehad in Persia and Afghanistan, the Foreign Office submitted a panicky paper in mid-October: "The advance to Baghdad may be regarded from the political or Foreign Office point of view as of the very greatest importance, not only on account of the situation in Asiatic Turkey. . . but more especially with regard to the present critical situation in Persia and even in Afghanistan."[9]

Townshend's close proximity to Baghdad largely determined his fate. General Sir Archibald Murray, then the CIGS, stressed that the Mesopotamian expeditionary force did not have either the lines of communication or the reinforcements to hold Baghdad against a determined Turkish counterattack. But the same was equally true if Townshend remained at Kut. Despite the risks, Townshend's force had gotten within striking distance of Baghdad. Why not advance the final one hundred miles, especially when Sir Edward Grey was speaking in apocalyptic terms about Persia's fate? "It was almost certain that Persia was going against us, and had been won over by the Germans," he told the Dardanelles Committee.[10]

Lord Kitchener's opinion might be expected to be decisive, but he no longer commanded the respect of the ministers. On October 21 he temporized even more than usual in the Dardanelles Committee. He argued that Townshend should advance on Baghdad because that is what "every Arab in the neighborhood" expected. On the other hand, he agreed with the general staff that the imperial forces in Mesopotamia were not strong enough to ensure that Baghdad could be held. Hence Townshend should take the city and then abandon it. His logic was: "If we moved back from our present position without going to Baghdad, it would be quite as bad as a retirement after a raid on that city."[11]

Given instructions to advance on Baghdad, Townshend met a sizable Turkish force at Ctesiphon, about twenty miles short of Baghdad. His subsequent attacks against the wired and dug-in Turkish defenders failed, and he lost approximately one-third of his force of some fourteen thousand men. With no arrangements for reserves, he had no choice but to retreat. A British soldier had the last word on this bungled campaign: "Of the officers, some calls it Tesiphon and some calls it Sestiphon, but we calls it Pistupon."

When Robertson arrived at the War Office, Townshend's force, which had fallen back to Kut, was surrounded by the Turks. Initially neither Townshend nor the authorities in Delhi and London thought his forces in grave danger. On his first day as CIGS, he submitted a paper asking the War Committee, which had replaced the Dardanelles Committee, to place the Mesopotamian force on the defensive and limit its reinforcements to troops drawn from India. Robertson got his passive policy in Mesopotamia, but not before February 29,[12] and not without opposition. Balfour and Lloyd George opposed the downgrading of the war against Turkey, which they refused to separate from the war with Germany. If the British were aggressive in Egypt and Mesopotamia, Lloyd George insisted, "the Turk must be there, and the German must come to his assistance."[13]

The general staff, of course, was not unmindful of the Turko-German threat in the East, but they sought alternative means to protect the British Empire. Macdonogh wanted to enlist Arab support. "A Turkish advance on Mesopotamia and Persia," he noted, "would be very difficult if opposed by the Arabs, and correspondingly easy if assisted by them."[14] Robertson wanted to detach Turkey. A compromise peace with Germany was unthinkable, not so with Turkey. He debated this point in an exchange of papers with Grey in February. The foreign secretary made an unanswerable point. Britain couldn't gain a satisfactory peace without assistance from Continental allies such as Russia. Having promised Petrograd both Constantinople and the Straits, Britain had its hands tied in negotiations with Turkey.[15] Robertson had to admit that Grey was right, but he lamented Britain's secret treaty with Russia. "It is a thousand pities we are at war with Turkey at all," he wrote a fellow general. "The part played by diplomacy during the present war is not as good as it could have been. . . . But for Constantinople Turkey would make peace to-morrow: of course Russia would not listen to such a suggestion."[16]

Wully also wanted to end the divided command of the Mesopotamia force, asking that its operations be placed under the general staff and that the commander in chief in India (who furnished most of the troops and supplies for the Mesopotamian theater) receive his instructions in the same fashion as the commanders in chief in other theaters.[17] The War Committee accepted Robertson's suggestion, and the new arrangement eventually made possible a dramatic improvement in communications and supplies, but not for many months, and not before the general staff assumed control of administration as well as operations from the India Office.

Meanwhile, as Townshend's position at Kut went from precarious to hopeless, an aggressive stance was required. Three desperate rescue attempts were launched by largely untrained and poorly equipped troops in January, March, and April, resulting in twenty-three thousand casualties, more than Townshend had suffered on his journey up the Tigris to Ctesiphon. On April, 1916 Townshend surrendered his exhausted and starving force of ten thousand men. Despite this defeat, the relief force, the Tigris Army of four understrength divisions, maintained its forward position within sight of the Crescent Flag flying over Kut. With Russian forces in Armenia and northern Persia being hard pressed, the War Office feared that a withdrawal from Kut might further undermine Britain's position in Persia and Afghanistan.[18]

Britain could survive defeat at Kut, but the loss of the jugular vein of the British Empire, the Suez Canal, might be catastrophic. A daring Turkish attack against this vital waterway in early 1915, although repulsed, had provoked exaggerated fears of Turkish strength; and an elaborate defensive system was constructed along the canal.

As the center for operations in the Mediterranean, Egypt housed some three hundred thousand men. Composed of partially trained reinforcements arriving from New Zealand and Australia, divisions evacuated from Gallipoli, and drafts sent out from England, this large body of troops was described by Robertson as a "chaotic jumble of units and personnel."[19] He wanted to transfer many of them to the battlefields of France; and he viewed as preposterous fears in London and Cairo that the Turks might invade Egypt with from two to three hundred thousand troops. How could the poor Turkish communications support such a large enemy force? "Think of the preparations," he noted, "we should have to make if we were marching some 700 miles, to be followed by 150 miles or so across the desert."[20] He slashed estimates of any invading Turkish force to one hundred thousand, and even this figure was too high.[21]

In January 1916, Sir Archibald Murray was dispatched to command British troops behind and on the canal, which soon came to be known as the Egyptian Expeditionary Force (EEF).[22] Murray took his removal as CIGS remarkably well and was prepared to subordinate his theater of operations totally to the demands of the western front. His instructions from Wully were straight forward: "To keep Egypt reasonably secure. To keep a reserve in Egypt for India as long as it seems likely to be required. To get everybody else to France."[23] By July 1916, Murray had shipped out some 240,000 troops, most going to Haig, including nine divisions, three independent infantry brigades, and nine batteries of heavy artillery.

With his forces reduced to four Territorial divisions and a sizable force of mounted troops, Murray wanted to extend his defense of the canal into the Sinai with the objective of establishing himself at El Arish, which blocked the only good road to Egypt. When Sir Arthur Lynden-Bell, his chief of general staff, advocated a strong defensive line on Egypt's eastern border, Murray had responded: "If you think I am going to stay here and do nothing, you are greatly mistaken."[24] Robertson supported Murray,[25] believing that a further advantage of extending the defense of Egypt was that it would reduce chances of unrest in Egypt in the event of a Turkish offensive.[26]

Robertson's desire to limit operations in Murray's theater, however, was threatened when Sherif Hussein, a prince who was keeper of the Holy Places in Mecca and Medina, led a revolt in June against Turkish rule of Arabia. Mecca fell and Medina was attacked. With their southern flank threatened, the Turks sent troops from Syria south to Medina, alarming imperial-minded ministers who feared that the Turks would crush this promising and welcome insurrection.[27]

When some ministers urged the dispatch of troops to Rabegh, a port on the Red Sea between Medina and Mecca, Robertson resisted, fearing that such a military venture might mushroom into a large enterprise. The ministers talked of sending some four thousand soldiers, but Robertson insisted that the government should prepare for maximum rather than minimum resistance. In his view, when support personnel were included, a Red Sea expeditionary force might involve sixteen thousand troops, a commitment that would force Murray to abandon his advance on El Arish.[28]

Robertson's technical views may have been a consequence of objective considerations. More likely, they were a reflection of his total opposition to intervention in Rabegh. Just as he made the strongest possible technical case for a campaign against the main body of the German army in France, he made the weakest case for a military venture he did not believe in. He would not be the first or last soldier to do so.

Robertson didn't mask his contempt for civilians who "lived from telegram to telegram and attached as much importance to a few scallywags in Arabia as I imagine they did to the German attack on Ypres two years ago."[29] His approach was to state his strategic principles and refuse to debate. When accused of not understanding the political ramifications, he responded: "In war there is no difference between political and military considerations. It is a commonplace that policy and strategy must be in harmony. Strategy is bad if it aims at results which are politically undesirable, and the converse is equally true. In a war of this magnitude neither policy nor strategy should be local in their aims."[30]

Murray loyally supported Robertson, writing that "both from military and from a Moslem point of view I am convinced you are right."[31] Events eventually proved that intervention at Rabegh was unnecessary to sustain the Arab revolt, But Wully's disdain for their views damaged his standing with the ministers, and for the first time they came very close to launching a military operation without his support.

Robertson had even greater difficulty dominating British policy in Mesopotamia. British prestige in that part of the world and the security of India constituted powerful arguments for a strong British presence. Robertson, who had almost been killed as a young officer defending the northwest frontier in the 1890s, recognized the connection between military operations in Mesopotamia and the security of India. "I do not think the Mesopotamian Campaign is a side show because as long as we keep up a good show there India and Persia will be more or less all right, whereas anything in the nature of a set back there might cause trouble in those countries," he wrote General Sir Charles Carmichael Monro, who had been chosen to replace Sir Beauchamp Duff as commander in chief in India.[32]

Keeping up a "good show," however, was not the same as conquering Baghdad. When the India Office pressed in late August for its capture, Robertson stressed the poor lines of communication, which he said were incapable of even feeding troops if they continued north. Robertson wanted to withdraw some ninety miles down river from Kut to Amara. Both technical and strategical arguments were employed. "We have not got," he noted in a paper for the War Committee, "and are not likely to have, available the number of troops required to seize and hold Baghdad; for a long time to come we cannot hope to maintain them there even if we had them; their position at Baghdad would be in a military sense unfavourable and would exert no decisive effect on the war."[33] The War Committee, however, was loath to accept a strategic withdrawal from Kut. Lord Curzon, the former Viceroy of India, and Austen Chamberlain, the Secretary of State for India, warned of a Holy War spreading to India; and the War Committee concluded, "The force saved in Mesopotamia would be much less than the force required in that event in India."[34]

On his way to India, Monro was scheduled to stop at Basra to review the situation with Robertson's choice as the new commander in chief in Mesopotamia, General Sir Stanley Frederick Maude. British policy in this theater remained on hold until Monro's recommendations were received.

Maude had dramatically improved his offensive capability. He commanded some 150,000 troops, with some 72,000 on the main front. His soldiers were now armed for modern warfare with airplanes, the latest grenades, and sufficient machine guns. The howitzers and medium guns he received enabled his artillery to destroy Turkish entrenchments. His lines of communications were improved, with Basra being transformed into a modern port, a railway and metal road under construction, and a significant increase in his river transportation.

A confident Maude convinced Monro that his forces should be aggressive. With the India Office, which supplied most of the men for the operation, supporting a resumption of the offensive, the War Committee sanctioned an aggressive policy for the Tigris Army. Robertson was unenthusiastic and made clear to Maude that he should limit his casualties and make no attempt to capture Baghdad. After Maude got to Baghdad, he would almost certainly have to push his front some sixty miles to the north to block the three approaches to the city. This would further extend his long lines of communication. In Robertson's mind, the capture of Baghdad was simply not worth the additional British commitment in this outside theater. Maude, however, went forward with an aggressive plan designed to destroy the Turkish force on the Tigris front. In the words of one commentator, "the historian who studies the orders and operations gains the impression that Maude's operations were contrived, consciously or unconsciously, to undermine the stability, not merely of the Turkish position, but of Robertson's instructions."[35]

Meanwhile Murray's deliberate advance across arid and barren land proceeded toward a point just south of the frontier of Palestine. The searing heat and vast expanse of sand presented tremendous logistical problems. A water pipeline (capacity of six hundred thousand gallons a day) and military railroad had to be constructed. A crude road, made of wirenetting held down by pegs driven into the sand, was prepared for infantry and cars. Thousands of camels with Egyptian drivers were also utilized to supply the British forces.

At the end of 1916, Murray had occupied El Arish without firing a shot and nearly completed his destruction of all organized Turkish resistance in the Sinai. Before him lay the Turkish defenses at Gaza and Beersheba, which defended the stony and rolling countryside of Palestine. Murray's limited military success coincided with Lloyd George's becoming prime minister. The Welshman hated Turks. On more than one occasion he had said that he would rather destroy Turkey than Germany; and he wanted to make the breakup of the Turkish Empire a central war objective.[36] Two days after taking office, he explored expanding Murray's operations into Palestine, telling Robertson that he wanted a victory to impress public opinion. When Robertson asked if the capture of Beersheba would do, the prime minister demurred. Beersheba would not catch the public's fancy, "but Jerusalem might!"[37] With major offensives planned on the western front in the spring and summer, Robertson opposed an advance into either Palestine or Syria. An additional consideration was that the French wanted Haig to extend his front; this meant additional divisions had to be found for the BEF.

Having gained the War Cabinet's support for a defensive policy, Robertson was not averse to a large-scale offensive by Murray in the autumn and winter. He shared the political leadership's concern about maintaining public support. A "second string to our bow" was required, he told Murray, and that "second string" was Egypt. A dramatic advance in Murray's theater offered only limited strategic rewards, but it might offset continued stalemate on the western front in the public's mind. "The autumn and winter are good seasons for you," he wrote, "and if we are still fighting then my desire is to give you a really big show and to let you do as much as you can and go as far as you can into Turkish territory."[38]

The general staff's offensive plans were made in great secrecy. With the exception of a "very secret" memorandum he submitted on February 22, Robertson sought to limit all discussion of war plans against the Turks to verbal communications between himself and the ministers.

A fascinating twenty-one-page document, "Note on Our Future Military Policy in the Event of the Failure of the Entente Powers to Obtain a Decision in the Main Theatres during the Coming Summer," was one product of the general staff's work. Though unsigned, it was clearly Macdonogh's work. If no military victory resulted from the combined Allied attacks in 1917, it was suggested that "peace agitation" by the United States and general war weariness might provoke irresistible demands for a compromise peace. In such circumstances, British security interests, which were more global and maritime than her allies', might be at risk. If Germany accepted a peace based on the evacuation of Northern France and Belgium, it would almost surely be a disaster for the security of Egypt, the Persian Gulf, and India, especially if the Turko-German alignment survived the war, with German influence predominant at Constantinople. German expansionism would be a constant threat to the Eastern empire, placing an "intolerable strain" on British efforts to defend Egypt and Mesopotamia.

If the war seemed likely to end in mutual exhaustion, Macdonough wanted to protect Britain's African and Asian possessions by establishing a defensive line in the Middle East. Aleppo, "the junction of the Syrian, Anatolian and Tigris railways, as well as of all the main roads connecting Syria and Mesopotamia with Asia Minor," was the key. Its capture would mean "the loss of the whole Turkish Empire with the exception of Anatolia and European Turkey."

An attack on Aleppo from Mesopotamia was considered and rejected. From Kut-el-Amara to Aleppo along the Euphrates was some 550 miles. The Tigris route was even longer, some 700 miles. Thus the best that might be realized from a Mesopotamian campaign was the capture of Baghdad, which might improve Britain's negotiating position, but it would "not involve the defeat of the main Turkish armies, nor would it have any effect in checking Germany's progress in Syria, Asia Minor and Arabia."

Aleppo was approximately 375 miles from Murray's present front, but the obstacles to reaching this vital communications hub were not pictured as being insurmountable. The EEF might require from nine to ten infantry divisions to go along with its existing large body of mounted troops. An advance from the Gaza-Beersheba line to the Beirut-Damascus line, a distance of some 200 miles, might be accomplished by this reinforced army within two months. Aleppo would then be within striking distance.

The Turks, faced with declining morale, terrible logistics, and mounting resistance from the Arabs, seemed to have most of the disadvantages. They seemed capable of massing at most some one hundred thousand troops in the Tarsus-Alexandretta-Aleppo area, less if Berlin sent reinforcements, because Germans required more supplies than the Turks. To collect one hundred thousand troops to defend Aleppo, the Turks would have to remove all of their soldiers from Europe. Even then, it would take them a minimum of ten weeks to transport them from Constantinople to Aleppo. "This number of one hundred thousand therefore represents a maximum which is unlikely to be reached, *while a force of this size could certainly not be supplied at any considerable distance south of Aleppo.*"

The optimism found in Macdonogh's paper when compared to later statements by the general staff and the future commander of the EEF, General Sir Edmund Allenby, about the potential Turkish threat to the EEF in southern Palestine is striking. But it must be emphasized that conditions were not the same in the autumn as they were when this paper was written in January 1917. The Russians were expected to maintain strong pressure on Turkey, and the author of this document also assumed that British sea power would be sufficient to establish bases along the Palestine and Syrian coasts to sustain the land campaign.[39]

Robertson initially agreed with Macdonogh's offensive philosophy. "The Turks in general are fed up," he wrote Monro. "If therefore we are still fighting next autumn and winter and could have a good thing based on Egypt we ought to get good value out of it, and moreover it is the only theatre where we can operate in winter time and so keep up public interest."[40] But when he advised the government in his "very secret" February 22 paper, he was restrained about the prospects of an autumn campaign. The Admiralty, when consulted, had been unable to promise the necessary tonnage required to establish bases along the coast and to transport and supply troops. Without naval support, the existing railroads probably couldn't sustain a rapid British advance.

Plans were currently underway to expand the EEF by autumn to six infantry divisions in addition to its two mounted divisions and Imperial Camel Corps of sixteen companies, with the possibility of additional troops, primarily Indian cavalry, being sent from France. But Robertson believed that the occupation of Palestine was probably the best that Murray's reinforced army could achieve after three months. Robertson made no estimate of the number of troops that would ultimately be required to make the Turks retire a considerable distance, perhaps even abandoning Syria. That figure depended upon numerous imponderables: sea transport; the navy's ability to open coastal bases to support an advance through Palestine; and the situation on the other Turkish fronts, especially Russian operations in Armenia and Kurdistan.[41]

The timetable for changing Murray's role from a defensive to an offensive position was moved forward by a string of setbacks for the Turks.[42] Given permission by Robertson to attack with limited objectives, Maude, whose force was vastly superior to the Turks in men and modern weaponry, had begun in December a series of assaults against the Turkish defenses that culminated with the virtual destruction of the Turkish 6th Army and the occupation of Kut on February 25. An excited Lloyd George asked Robertson, "Will Maude get to Baghdad?"[43] Robertson didn't need to be pressured. Given his strong preference earlier for a passive policy, a word of explanation is necessary. In March the Russians were active on their Turkish front. If they continued to press forward, as seemed likely, they might control the Tigris from Mosul to the sea and remove any threat to Maude's extended position at Baghdad.[44] Hence Robertson gave Maude the green light.

Baghdad's fall on March 11 opened up exciting possibilities. "I am hoping that Maude's occupation of Baghdad will enable the Russian columns to come out from the hills on the east and get firmly established on the Tigris as far as Mosul," Robertson wrote Murray. "When this is done, that part of the world will be pretty nearly finished so far as we are concerned, and the remainder will be for you to finish. I want you to have a good show and to pull off big things. . . . The Turk has never had such a shaking up as he is getting now, and the effect of it will be by no means local."[45]

Following his subsequent assault on Gaza on March 26, Murray sent London a very misleading report. "The operation was most successful, and owing to the fog and waterless nature of the country round Gaza just fell short of a complete disaster to the enemy."[46] Baghdad's fall and Murray's apparent success might herald the collapse of the Ottoman Empire. In the Hejaz the danger to Mecca had been removed, and the Turks had withdrawn from Medina. Arab resistance was on the rise in Syria with that country in the clutches of famine. Meanwhile, the Turks withdrew from Persia with the Russians pursuing them along a 250-mile front in wintry conditions.[47] An excited Milner wrote Lloyd George: "As things are, the Turk is crumbling . . . . Having got him on the run should we not keep him on the run?"[48] On March 30, Wully asked the War Cabinet for permission to instruct Murray "to develop his recent success to the fullest possible extent."[49]

Robertson had been misled by Murray's account of the First Battle of Gaza, later writing the compiler of the British official history, Sir James E. Edmonds, that "the early telegrams about the first battle of Gaza affected the action of the General Staff very much indeed."[50] Murray's initial assault actually didn't come close to inflicting a decisive defeat on the Turks. Lynden-Bell's view that the EEF had given "the Turks a jolly bad knock from which it will take them some time to recover" was rubbish.[51] A Turkish propaganda leaflet was much closer to the truth: "You beat us at communiques, but we beat you at Gaza."

Not surprisingly, Murray was unenthusiastic about resuming his assault and asked for reinforcements. Nonetheless, on April 17–19, his infantry attacked with limited artillery support, only 150 guns for a fifteen thousand-yard front. The EEF's few tanks either broke down or were put out of action by enemy artillery; and its poison gas shells failed. British losses were more than triple the enemy's.

Murray's defeat at the Second Battle of Gaza coincided with an abrupt downturn in Allied fortunes. General Nivelle's offensive failed. On the high seas, unrestricted U-boat warfare took a terrible toll, with an average of just over thirteen British ships being sunk each day in April; the daily average for 1916 had been three.[52] An alarmed Hankey believed that the success of the German submarine campaign "will probably ultimately compel us to withdraw our forces from Egypt."[53] Robertson was no less concerned, believing that Britain, with a shipping crisis in every theater, had lost the flexibility that command of the seas was expected to confer on British military efforts.[54] News from Russia was even worse. Serious unrest surfaced among Russian troops in the Caucasus and in Persia. All hope of a Russian advance to Mosul ended when General Alekseev informed Robertson that the Russians were incapable of any offensive action on their Turkish front.[55]

The prospect of a moribund eastern front had serious consequences for the western front.[56] But Russia's possible defection seemed no less ominous for Britain's imperial possessions. "It is in the East that the effect of Russia's collapse is being most acutely felt by us," Robertson warned the War Cabinet. Although still prepared to exploit "any favourable opportunity for striking the Turks,"[57] Robertson wanted a return to a passive policy on the imperial front.

NOTES

1. Robertson to Wigram, March 24, 1915, RA Geo. V Q. 2522/3/172.
2. Hankey, "The Future Military Policy at the Dardanelles," November 29, 1915, CAB 42/5/25.
3. David French, *British Strategy and War Aims 1914–1916* (London, 1986), 136–44.
4. See "Extracts from an account by Major General Sir Arthur Lynden-Bell," n.d., Lynden-Bell MSS 90/1/1.
5. Memorandum by Balfour, December 27, 1915, annexed to War Committee, January 13, 1916, CAB 42/7/5.
6. For the best account of the Mesopotamian campaign, see A. J. Barker, *The Neglected War: Mesopotamia 1914–1918* (London, 1967).
7. See Rothwell, *British War Aims and Peace Diplomacy*, 89.
8. Maurice later argued that these factors would have been taken into account if the General Staff in London had been in charge of the operation. Maurice to Kirke, December 19, 1920, CAB 45/91.
9. "Memorandum by the Foreign Office," October 7, 1915, Appendix VII, in Committee of Imperial Defence, "Report of an Inter-Departmental Committee on the Strategical Situation in Mesopotamia," October 16, 1915, CAB 42/4/12.
10. Dardanelles Committee, October 21, 1915, CAB 42/4/15.
11. Ibid.
12. War Committee, February 29, 1916, CAB 42/9/7.
13. War Committee, January 13, 1916, CAB 42/7/5.
14. Macdonogh to Sir A. Nicolson, January 6, 1916, CAB 42/11/9.
15. See Robertson's memorandum, February 12, 1916, and Grey's response, February 18, 1916, annexed to the War Committee, February 22, 1916, CAB 42/9/3.
16. Robertson to General Sir Beauchamp Duff, May 18, 1916, Robertson MSS I/32/27.
17. Robertson, "The Control of the Operations in Mesopotamia," January 31, 1916, CAB 42/7/16; War Committee, February 3, 1916, CAB 42/8/1.
18. Robertson, *Soldiers and Statesmen*, vol. 2, 69.
19. Ibid., 150.
20. Robertson to Callwell, October 26, 1915, Robertson MSS I/8/33.
21. Sir George MacMunn and Cyril Falls, *Military Operations: Egypt and Palestine* (London, 1928), vol. 1, 157; Cyril Falls, *Armageddon: 1918* (Philadelphia and New York, 1964), 5.
22. Sir John Grenfell Maxwell was the General Commanding Force in Egypt, but Robertson soon recalled him and gave Murray control of all the British forces in Egypt.
23. Robertson to Murray, March 15, 1916, Woodward, MCWR, 43.
24. "Extracts from an account by Major General Sir Arthur Lynden-Bell," n.d., Lynden-Bell MSS 90/1/1.

25. In an extensive commentary for Lloyd George on Murray's instructions, Hankey emphasized that Robertson acted on the War Cabinet's authority except when "he had obtained authority from you yourself." Hankey to Lloyd George, February 7, 1920, Lloyd George MSS F/24/2/8.

26. Robertson, *Soldiers and Statesmen*, vol. 2, 151.

27. See Rothwell, *British War Aims and Peace Diplomacy*, 87–95.

28. Robertson to Hankey, November 13, 1916, annexed to War Committee, November 20, 1916, CAB 42/24/13; Robertson, "Despatch of an Expeditionary Force to Rabegh," November 13, 1916, WO 106/310; and Robertson, *Soldiers and Statesmen*, vol. 2, 161.

29. Robertson to Lloyd George, December 8, 1916, Robertson MSS I/19/9.

30. Robertson, "Assistance to the Shereef," September 20, 1916, annexed to War Committee, September 25, 1916, CAB 42/20/8.

31. Murray's reference to "Moslem point of view" refers to his fear that there would be an adverse Moslem reaction to the introduction of Christian soldiers near the Holy Places. Murray to Robertson, December 12, 1916, Robertson MSS I/14/60/1.

32. Robertson to Monro, August 1, 1917, Robertson MSS I/32/65.

33. Robertson, "Situation in Mesopotamia," September 16, 1916, WO 106/310.

34. War Committee, September 18, 1916, CAB 42/20/3.

35. B. H. Liddell Hart, *The Real War 1914–1918* (Boston and Toronto, 1930), 269.

36. See Rothwell, *British War Aims and Peace Diplomacy*, 126–27.

37. Repington, *First World War*, vol. 1, 420.

38. Robertson to Murray, January 31, and to Monro, January 31, 1917, Robertson MSS I/32/53–54; and Robertson, "Note on a Proposal to Undertake a Campaign in Palestine during the Winter with the Object of Capturing Jerusalem," December 29, 1916, WO 106/310.

39. Author's italics. "Note on Our Future Military Policy in the Event of the Failure of the Entente Powers to Obtain a Decision in the Main Theatres during the Coming Summer," January 1917, Macdonogh MSS, WO 106/1511.

40. Robertson to Monro, January 31, 1917, Woodward, MCWR, 147.

41. Robertson, "Plan for a Campaign in Syria," February 22, 1917, WO 106/311.

42. My understanding of British operations in Palestine has been much enhanced by two deeply researched papers that have been shared with me. The authors did not always agree with my interpretation, but their work has been of great benefit to me. See John Hussey, "Defeating the Weak to Bring Down the Strong: The Palestine Argument, 1917–18," unpublished paper; and Matthew Dominic Hughes, "General Allenby and the Campaign of the Egyptian Expeditionary Force, June 1917–November 1919," Ph.D. thesis, King's College, University of London, 1995.

43. Robertson, *Soldiers and Statesmen*, vol. 2, 75.

44. Maurice to Lynden-Bell, March 7, 1917, Lynden-Bell MSS, vol. II.

45. Robertson to Murray, March 14, 1917, Robertson-Murray Correspondence 79/48/3.

46. Murray to Robertson, April 1, 1917, quoted in MacMunn and Falls, *Egypt and Palestine*, vol. 1, 319.

47. See "Summary of the Military Situation in the Various Theatres of War for the Seven Days Ending March 8, 1917, with Comments by the General Staff," WO 106/318.

48. Milner to Lloyd George, March 17, 1917, Lloyd George MSS F/38/2/3.

49. War Cabinet (109), March 30, 1917, CAB 23/2.

50. Robertson to Edmonds, February 4, 1926, CAB 45/80.

51. Lynden-Bell to Maurice, April 3, 1917, Lynden-Bell MSS, vol. II.

52. John Terraine, *The U-Boat Wars 1916–1945* (New York, 1989), 47.

53. Diary entry of April 30, 1917, Hankey MSS 1/3.

54. Robertson to Monro, April 19, 1917, Robertson MSS I/32/57.

55. "Summary of the Military Situation in the Various Theatres of War for the Seven Days Ending April 19, 1917, with Comments by the General Staff," WO 106/318.

56. See Keith Neilson, *Strategy and Supply: The Anglo-Russian Alliance, 1914–17* (London, 1984), 249–304.

57. Cabinet Paper G.T. 678 of May 9, 1917, CAB 24/12.

Chapter 8

"One Great Bog of Slime"

The Romanov dynasty's collapse in March 1917 greatly concerned Robertson. To obtain accurate intelligence, he asked British military authorities in Russia to "divest [their] minds of claptrap such as determination to win and fighting for freedom and so forth, remembering that without discipline and reasonable administrative efficiency, an army is merely a leaderless armed mob." Their answers confirmed his fears that the Russian army had "fallen to pieces" and would be unable to threaten the Central Powers in either Europe or Asia in 1917.[1]

Russia's decline required a rethinking of Allied strategy. If victory continued to be defined as a breakthrough leading to the German army's destruction, Robertson wasn't hopeful. "The decision may, in fact, be reached not by the breaking of the German lines or the retirement of the German armies, but by the exhaustion of the Central Powers, and nothing would be more fatal than to give the impression that we are staking everything on the result of one battle or on our ability to win a great strategical victory," he cautioned the War Cabinet. "It is certain that the war is entering on a phase which will impose a far severer strain on all the belligerents than they have yet had to bear, and victory will rest with that side which displays the greatest resolution and endurance."[2]

"Resolution and endurance," however, might not suffice if Britain took on the German army with little help from her European allies. Britain might be reduced to a second- or third-rate military power with no reserve to protect its eastern empire against the Turko-German threat. Hunkering down in their trenches and waiting for uncertain American assistance was equally dangerous. President Wilson in May promised to send troops to France, but his nation's lack of preparation and inadequate shipping suggested that it might be late 1918 or even 1919 before the Americans could play a significant role in the land war.[3] If the western front remained passive, the Germans might eliminate either Russia or Italy, or both. Robertson consequently advised his government to maintain pressure in the west. His choice of a British battlefield after Nivelle's grip on Haig was removed was Flanders.

The Flanders offensive, known officially as Third Ypres, but most remembered as Passchendaele after the village captured as the offensive concluded, has a special place of horror in the popular imagery of the war.[4] It may well be the most controversial land battle ever fought by the British, in large part because of the waterlogged and muddy battlefield. "What our men had suffered in earlier battles was surpassed by what they were now called upon to endure," writes Philip Gibbs, a British correspondent who covered the battle. "All the agonies of war which I have attempted to describe were piled up in those fields of Flanders. There was nothing missing in the list of war's abominations. A few days after the battle began the rains began, and hardly ceased for four months. Night after night the skies opened and let down steady torrents, which turned all that country into one great bog of slime."[5]

Robertson and his alter ego Maurice were well aware of the topographical drawbacks of fighting a major campaign to capture the Belgian ports. When Maurice had been Robertson's director of military operations at GHQ, he had prepared a topographical and strategical study of operations between Ypres and the coast. It stressed the clinging, heavy clay and the intricate system of drainage canals, dikes, and ditches that kept the at- or below-sea-level areas from flooding. Maurice was equally skeptical of distant objectives, arguing that the capture of the ports Ostend and Zeebrugge "would not materially improve the military situation of the Allies in the Western theatre" except in the unlikely event that it prompted a general withdrawal by the Germans. Extending the British left to the coast or as far as the Dutch frontier also gave the British a longer front to defend with only two single lines of railway to supply it. Served by better communications, the Germans might launch a counterthrust in a northwest direction. With their backs to the sea, the British would be at a "grave disadvantage."[6]

With Maurice concluding in 1915 that an offensive between Ypres and the coast "would be a very difficult enterprise so far as the nature of the country is concerned" and "might involve our being probably placed in a

British battery in action

rather dangerous position,"[7] how could Robertson possibly favor it in 1917? Robertson saw possibilities in the Ypres salient, not because he was excited about its strategical possibilities, but because he believed that the Germans must stand and fight, giving the British the advantage because of their growing artillery superiority. (By mid-July the Royal Regiment of Artillery had massed 2,868 guns in the Ypres salient, giving it an almost two to one advantage over the Germans.[8]) "I am hoping that I am right in thinking that our artillery is greatly superior to the German," Robertson wrote Haig. "If it is we can blast him out of the country and preserve our infantry as he is apparently intent on preserving his."[9] As Robertson explained to Hankey, Haig wanted "to attack the enemy in some spot where he is bound, either to fight, or to surrender some objective of strategical or political importance."[10]

Robertson's rejection of a passive role for the BEF didn't mean that he approved of Haig's squandering troop strength in a foolhardy attempt at a breakthrough. The most recent examination of Passchendaele suggests that the offensive "was undertaken on the premise that this war could prosper only as a result of mass offensives directed towards major geographical objectives,"[11] that is, the strategical breakthrough. But this was manifestly not Robertson's position.

On April 20, choosing his words carefully, Wully discussed tactics with Haig.

To my mind no war has ever differed so much from previous wars as does the present one, and it is futile, to put it mildly, hanging on to old theories when facts show them to be wrong. At one time audacity and determination to push on regardless of loss were the predominating factors, but that was before the days of machine guns and other modern armament. . . . Your recent splendid operations [at Arras] are a proof of this so far as I at this distance am able to judge, for its seems to me that your success was mainly due to the most detailed and careful preparation, to thorough knowledge of the ground by battalions and batteries and the higher units, and to well observed artillery fire. It seems to me that these factors will continue to the end of the war to be vitally essential, and if they are not so regarded success will be rather in the nature of a fluke, and will probably entail heavier losses than will justify the few hundred yards of trench or additional village gained. I cannot help thinking that Nivelle has attached too much importance to what is called 'breaking the enemy's front.' The best plan seems to me to go back to one of the old principles, that of defeating the enemy's army. In other words instead of aiming at breaking through the enemy's front aim at breaking down the enemy's army, and that means inflicting heavier losses upon him than one suffers oneself. If this old principle is kept in view and the object of breaking the enemy's army is achieved the front will look after itself, and the casualty bill will be less.[12]

In all of Robertson's surviving correspondence with Haig, this letter represents his most serious effort to address their differences over the prospects of a decisive defeat of the German army. His reluctance earlier to confront Haig during the Somme offensive was partly due to his belief that "no more foolish or cruel thing can be done than to crab a man's plans once they have been decided upon and approved. In fact no plan should ever be crabbed. It should either be accepted or rejected, and if accepted criticism should be practically silent."[13]

With Haig's Flanders operations still in the planning phase, however, there is no excuse for Robertson not having voiced his differences with Haig more forcefully. That he didn't is perhaps partly explained by Haig's recent promotion to field marshal, which altered the balance between the CIGS and the commander in chief of the BEF. Robertson had discouraged George V from giving Haig his baton while the Somme Battle was in progress.[14] But apparently the king could not be deterred once Lloyd George, known for his low regard for Haig, replaced Asquith.

Knowing that Wully's support was essential, Haig gave lip service to a cautious step-by-step advance, but the Haig of Ypres was no different from the Haig of Somme.[15] Subordinates such as Rawlinson and Sir Herbert Plumer—the commander of the Second Army who had fought in the Ypres salient since the spring of 1915—were dubious of GHQ's plan to break the enemy's front in a one-step-breakthrough and send British cavalry sweeping across western Belgium.[16] Shortly after receiving Robertson's lecture that emphasized breaking the enemy's army rather than his front, Haig replaced Rawlinson with the forty-seven-year-old cavalryman Gough, who has been called his "least qualified army commander."[17] Gough was known for his "cavalry spirit," and Haig instructed him to aim for a breakthrough.[18] Gough's immediate objectives consequently exceeded the range of all but his biggest guns.[19]

As Haig studied maps of Flanders, the disheartening effect of Nivelle's failed offensive on the French government became clearer. On April 30 Robertson got confirmation that Nivelle was finished. Although he retained his post for the moment, he received his orders from Phillipe Pétain, the new chief of the general staff, who was suspected of favoring a policy of "nibbling" and waiting on America.[20] "They [the French] have broken down and the only remedy is for us to take charge and at once," Wully bluntly informed his government.[21]

If Nivelle's demise led to a dramatic diminishing of France's military effort, Robertson was not prepared to recommend a Flanders offensive. Yet he opposed breaking off the present battle although British casualties at Arras were almost on the same level as the Somme.[22] "If the French stop now and once get away from the idea of heavy fighting and heavy losses," he reasoned, "it will be difficult, if not impossible to persuade them to undertake a big offensive again."[23]

On May 1 the War Cabinet met in a crisis atmosphere to determine Britain's position at a summit meeting with the French. The possibility that the BEF might be forced to take on the German army virtually single-handedly made the ministers sit uneasily in their chairs.

Robertson had a new and important ally, Jan Christiaan Smuts, who had come to London to sit in the Imperial War Cabinet, a new body designed to coordinate the British Empire's military and diplomatic effort. Having proven his mettle when he commanded Boer troops during the South African War, he had been directing the imperial military effort in German East Africa. With no previous involvement in the divisive strategic debates, the South African leader represented a fresh voice in London. Lloyd George, who admired his ability to relate military operations to the Empire's political objectives, dispatched him to the western front to survey the military situation. Robertson took a no less favorable view of Smuts, but for different reasons. When the War Cabinet invited Smuts to submit his strategical and military views, Robertson made no protest. As the constitutional military adviser to the government, Robertson might be expected to guard his prerogatives; he later reacted angrily, threatening resignation, when Lloyd George went over his head and asked Sir John French and Sir Henry Wilson to advise the War Cabinet. But this time he made no protest because he knew that Smuts saw "grave dangers" in the Calais agreement that gave the French strategical control of the western front.[24]

Smuts's advice for the War Cabinet couldn't have been more Robertsonian. Gambles in the outlying theaters were rejected and an attritional approach to exhausting the enemy endorsed. Smuts admitted that efforts to wear down the enemy were bound to be prolonged and costly, but he emphasized "that to relinquish the offensive in the third year of the War would be fatal, and would be the beginning of the end." The enemy would be encouraged and the Allies would fall into a state of "pessimism and despair." When Lloyd George departed for one of the most critical Anglo-French summit meetings of the war, his instructions from the War Cabinet were to "press the French to continue the offensive."[25]

Humbled by his championing of Nivelle, Lloyd George told Haig and Robertson on May 3 that he would support their plans. But whose plans? Robertson's or Haig's? Robertson's account of the meeting of the Anglo-French high commands on May 4 to the politicians suggested that his cautious policy "of destroying the enemy's divisions" had prevailed. "It is no longer a question of aiming at breaking through the enemy's front and aiming at distant objectives," Robertson asserted. "It is now a question of wearing down and exhausting the enemy's resistance, and if and when this is achieved, to exploit it to the fullest extent possible. . . . We are all of opinion that our object can be obtained by relentlessly attacking with limited objectives, while making the fullest use of our artillery. By this means we hope to gain our ends with the minimum loss possible."[26]

Lloyd George later asserted that Robertson's disclaimer about any attempt to break the enemy's front by implication ruled out the Flanders operation.[27] But Lloyd George was writing a lawyer's brief when he composed his memoirs. As he well knew, Robertson wanted a battlefield where artillery shells could be substituted for the flesh and bones of British soldiers. As Hankey had just explained to him, a distant advance in Flanders was not a requirement for success: "If the enemy retires he gives us what we want [the Belgian ports]. If he stands, he exposes himself to colossal losses from our heavy artillery. Either way we stand to gain." Hankey, in fact, favored an offensive with distant objectives. "Napoleon described Antwerp as a pistol pointed at the breast of England," he noted. "At the present time Zeebrugge is the barrel of the pistol and the submarines and destroyers based thereon are the bullets which daily strike their deadly blows at the heart of Britain's sea-power."[28]

Uncertainty about future French support rather than the menace of German undersea assault dominated Lloyd George's thoughts when he made an emotional speech during the Paris conference. "We must go on hitting and hitting with all our strength until the German ended, as he always did, by cracking." When Ribot cautioned against excessive losses, Lloyd George riposted: "We were ready to put the full strength of the British Army into the attack, but it was no good doing so unless the French did the same. . . . Tentative and feeble attacks were really more costly in the end." Lloyd George also supported the conference's conclusion that the time and place of future offensives should be left in the hands of the generals.[29]

The Welshman seemed especially interested in making his peace with Haig, whom he had treated brutally during the Nivelle conspiracy. Resorting to humor, he made Robertson his victim. Dining with Haig at GHQ, he performed a masterful imitation of Robertson's prickly demeanor when in the company of civilians. With every grunt and body movement, he evoked "fits of laughter" around the table. Charteris thought the prime minister's mimicry "as good, or better, than any music-hall turn."[30]

Robertson proclaimed the Paris Conference "about the best Conference we have had."[31] The Calais agreement was given a quick burial, and the strategical initiative on the western front passed to the British. But trouble lay ahead. The fluid political and military situation made it critical that British civil and military authorities work in harmony. That any decision was fraught with grave risk to Britain's ability to win a good peace, however, made any consensus difficult.

British anxiety would have been greater if the true state of the French army's morale after Nivelle's failed offensive had been known. In early May, soldiers of the 2nd Colonial Infantry Division appeared on parade without packs or rifles. "We're not marching," they chanted. Like a drop of oil on water the mutiny spread. Some troops sang the "Internationale," while others baaed, suggesting that they were sheep being led to the slaughter.

Unaware of the French army mutiny, the British remained more concerned about Russia's decline than France's. Lloyd George hoped to balance Russia's collapse through military-diplomatic operations to detach Germany's allies, especially Austria. Robertson, however, argued that Russia's decline made it less likely that either Turkey or Austria could be defeated. Given its limited resources, the British Empire couldn't conduct extensive military offensives on multiple fronts. With U.S. assistance in the distant future, it was crucial to concentrate British resources in the west so that a Russian defection would not be followed by France's collapse.[32]

Key imperialists, such as Smuts, Milner, and Curzon, accepted Robertson's view that the road to a sound peace lay through France rather than Jerusalem or Baghdad. Curzon stressed that the British needed the support of their Continental allies more than they needed Britain's help. His nightmare was that an unhumbled Berlin might offer terms that "would purchase the safety of our Allies by the acceptance of a grave peril to the future of the British Empire."[33]

Robertson's commitment to an active western front was not unqualified. On May 15, Pétain replaced Nivelle as commander in chief, with Ferdinand Foch taking Pétain's former position as chief of the general staff. When Esher wrote Robertson that the "jelly fish" in the French government were unlikely to live up to their commitments at the recent Paris conference, he passed this letter on to Lloyd George and informed Haig that the "Cabinet could never agree to our incurring heavy losses with comparatively small gains, which would obviously be the result unless French co-operate wholeheartedly."[34] Robertson recognized that it might not be easy for Haig to assess the truth of what Pétain told him. Nonetheless, if Haig had any doubts, Robertson wanted the War Cabinet immediately informed.[35]

Seeking to revive his pre-Nivelle working relationship with the French army, Robertson on May 23 wrote his French counterpart, General Foch: "I wish to learn your views in order that we may work in accord," he noted, "because our Governments are placed in a difficult position if and when their respective military advisers do not agree, and we therefore should first endeavour to come to an agreement before questions are laid before our Governments."[36] Robertson was especially interested in learning Foch's view of operations beyond the western front.

Robertson's meeting with Foch, which didn't take place until June 7, turned out to be a wide-ranging discussion of the new strategical geography. Foch opposed an all-out British offensive in Flanders, having just told Sir Henry Wilson that such an operation was "futile, fantastic & dangerous."[37] In more diplomatic language, he asked Robertson to put off attacks "on a grand scale" until the Allies had the clear superiority of force that America's entry into the war eventually promised. In the interim Foch favored detaching Germany's allies. In Austria's case, however, Foch expressed doubt that Vienna would agree to a compromise peace unless forced to. "Austria was very anxious to treat for peace," he said, "but would only treat when she was beaten. She was, in fact, asking to be beaten, in order to get out of the war with a good face." "This information raised the whole question of our military policy," Robertson responded. "Ought we now to concentrate against Austria."[38]

Foch's equivocal answer may have confirmed Robertson's earlier view that the French would ultimately accept only a limited role in the Italian theater. When Robertson had visited the Italian Army in late March, he hadn't been impressed with either the ability or morale of many of its army commanders—"white faces and white hands and other indications shew that these officers spend far more time in their comfortable headquarters than they spend at the front." He had concluded that success on the Italian front depended upon massive reinforcements in men and artillery, but he doubted if the French would imperil their own front by contributing the necessary troops and guns.[39]

Robertson and Foch appeared to be in general agreement in opposing "a great battle aiming at a distant objective." (Haig would have to advance thirteen miles before he could put Ostend under long-range fire from his artillery.) In response to Robertson's queries, Foch said that limited British operations would suffice to maintain French morale. Yet when Foch and Robertson parted, the Flanders operation was still alive. Until he had talked with Haig, Robertson emphasized that "he could not give any definite engagement as to the English programme."[40]

A new British offensive, designed to secure Haig's right flank on the Messines-Wytschaete ridge, began on the same day that Foch and Robertson conferred. British sappers had been tunnelling since August 1915 to plant mines under the German defenses. When the almost four hundred tons of explosives were ignited before dawn on June 7, Hankey in his home in Surrey and Lloyd George at Walton Heath were awakened. The massive artillery bombardment was almost as impressive and also could be heard in southern England. The stunned German defenders had no chance. By 9 A.M. the British had possession of the whole ridge. Messines was exactly the type of operation Robertson favored. Artillery had been concentrated and objectives limited; the planning had been meticulous and the advance methodical.

On June 9, Robertson and Haig had a lengthy discussion. Unable to extract the new recruits he requested from a government that was using manpower as a way to restrain Haig,[41] Robertson was acutely aware that a prolonged offensive with heavy British casualties might gravely weaken the BEF. "When Autumn came round," he said, "Britain would then be without an Army!"[42] He had just informed Haig that he would receive "only scraps" in future drafts. Haig's angry reaction must be quoted: "For the last two years most of the soldiers have realised that Great Britain must take the necessary steps to win the war by herself, because our French Allies had already shown that they lacked both the moral qualities & the means for gaining the victory. It is thus sad to see the British Govt. failing at the XIIth hour!"[43] Haig was convinced that the war was at its XIIth hour. Robertson wasn't, and he posed the question to Haig. Might not British support of an Italian attack against Austria be more prudent under the circumstances? Heartened by the brilliant victory at Messines, Haig was dismayed at what he took as Robertson's lack of faith in the BEF's ability to defeat the German army.[44]

At this critical juncture of the war, Haig and Robertson were in fundamental disagreement about three vital and related questions pertaining to the Flanders offensive: the possibility of a strategic breakthrough, Germany's staying power, and the necessity of substantial French assistance. After his meeting with Robertson, Haig's optimism shown brightly in a paper, "Present Situation and Future Plans," dated June 12, that he for-

warded to London. If the Germans were unable to transfer massive reinforcement from the eastern front, Haig said that he had a good chance of
clearing the Belgian coast during the summer. "The defeats on the German
troops entailed in doing so might quite possibly lead to their collapse."[45]

Haig had unwavering faith in Charteris, who fed the field marshal's
appetite for a war-winning battle with reports of declining German morale
in both the trenches and the home front. Within the War Office, however,
Charteris was regarded as a "dangerous fool because of his ridiculous
optimism."[46] When Haig argued in an appendix to his June 12 appreciation
that German troop strength was nearing the breaking point,[47] Robertson
refused to show the ministers Haig's numbers. "I cannot possibly agree with
some of the statements in the appendix," he telegraphed Haig.[48] Haig was
unmoved. His "conviction that he could defeat the German army in the
west grew in inverse proportion to the apparent decline in French morale"
is the conclusion of a recent examination of the origins of the Flanders
offensive.[49]

Robertson's refusal to discuss with the civilians his differences with Haig
on Germany's staying power is indefensible. An even more serious failing
was his suppression of crucial intelligence about the French army's morale,
information that he had always said was essential to any decision to go
forward with the offensive. On June 6, the War Cabinet received its first
official confirmation of unrest in the French army when the general staff
reported that "there was serious trouble practically amounting to mutiny,
in a number of French regiments."[50] At this point the general staff did not
have enough data to make any firm conclusions. Lieutenant-Colonel
Edward Spears, a British liaison officer with the French army, initially
forwarded somewhat ambiguous reports. On June 6, he described the
situation in France as "serious," but eight days later, he was more encouraging, writing Maurice that "the general situation in France is improving;
the morale of the Army is also better though not yet what it should be by
any means." The tone of Spears's reports changed dramatically after he
visited the front and saw firsthand the situation. After conferring with
French officers, he reported on June 19 that the mutiny, although under
control, "was more serious than I or any one else thought at the time."
Instead of a few regiments, at least five corps had been involved. His
ominous conclusion was that it wasn't possible to predict "when the troops
in which trouble has occurred will be fit to attack, or how long it will be
before the whole Army is right again."[51] Robertson didn't share this
alarming information with the civilians. Just as he had kept from the

civilians Haig's unrealistic estimates of the German army's staying power, he now suppressed Spears's report.[52]

When Robertson returned to London following his meeting with Haig, he found that the consensus of the previous month for continuing the offensive had broken down. On June 8, Lloyd George, conveniently forgetting the Nivelle affair, told the War Cabinet that the government's war policy had hitherto been guided "entirely by the views of their naval and military experts," whose assessments had often been wrong. To take a fresh look at the military situation, the War Cabinet created a Cabinet Committee on War Policy, composed of Lloyd George, Curzon, Milner, and Smuts.[53] The stage was now set for a critical and necessary debate on the pros and cons of a Flanders campaign, for which an almost irresistible momentum had developed. During the next six weeks, this committee held sixteen meetings before it submitted a report for the War Cabinet's approval.

Robertson shared the civilians' concern about Haig's ability to wage a prudent campaign, yet he didn't serve as an honest broker between the War Cabinet and Haig. His reaction to the creation of the Cabinet Committee on War Policy was to close ranks with Haig. "There is trouble in the land just now," he wrote Haig. "The War Cabinet, under the influence of L. G., have started, quite amongst themselves plus Smuts, to review the whole policy and strategy of the war, and to 'get at facts.'"[54]

The divide between the CIGS and prime minister prevented an open-minded discussion of either the merits of Haig's Flanders plan or alternatives such as Messines, a set-piece operation with limited objectives. The Welshman failed to inspire confidence with his flip-flopping from one plan to another, and the price (a diminishing of Britain's commitment to the western front and either Haig's resignation or dismissal) seemed too high for cooperating with him. Nonetheless, Robertson's suppression and doctoring of information was indefensible.

Lloyd George made clear his preference for switching off to Italy at the first meeting of the War Policy Committee. He read a private letter from the British ambassador in Rome who reported that Cadorna believed "that the Italian front provided the enemy's most vulnerable point on the Western Front." On the following day, with Robertson absent, the War Policy Committee heard a report from General Delmé-Radcliffe, who predicted that the Italians (if supported by Allied artillery) would be in Trieste by September if Russia's decline didn't lead to a considerable strengthening of the Austrian defenses.[55]

When Robertson was asked for his estimates on moving three hundred heavy guns and twelve divisions from the western front to Italy, he dug his heels in. "They will never go while I am C.I.G.S.," he wrote Haig on June 13. He also succinctly stated the position that he wanted Haig to take. "Argue that your plan is the best plan—as it is—that no other would even be safe let alone decisive, and then leave them to reject your advice and mine. They dare not do that. Further, on this occasion they will be up against the French."[56]

Attempting to enlist Foch's support in knocking out Lloyd George's Italian project, Robertson worked behind the scenes through Spears. "I impressed on General Foch the importance of keeping the gist of my conversation, based on Sir William Robertson's letter, secret, and I asked him expressly not even to hint at it to his Ministers, and he promised to do this," Spears informed Maurice.[57] Robertson had mixed results in his lobbying of Foch. The French chief of general staff opposed sending troops but retained an open mind on deploying Anglo-French heavy guns against Austria if the Italians "really mean to attack."[58]

Robertson also put pen to paper to debunk Lloyd George's Italian schemes. With battles on the western front becoming increasingly artillery duels, Robertson wanted every available shell and gun devoted to exhausting Germany's artillery. "I think we should follow the principle of the gambler who has the heaviest purse and force our adversary's hand and make him go on spending until he is a pauper."[59] Germany's advantage of interior lines was stressed. By rail Hindenburg could rapidly transfer troops and equipment to rescue Austria from any defeat on the Italian front. Robertson also exploited the ghost of Nivelle, warning of the dangers of entrusting British military fortunes once again to foreign hands, especially Cadorna, a general who had never shown "any marked ability," who commanded an army that was "miserably afraid of the Germans." Moreover, an advance to Trieste, which would have to overcome many natural obstacles, would not be sufficient to defeat Austria. Its capture might even encourage the Italians, who had come "into the war to fight Austria, not Germany," to make peace.[60]

Robertson made a good case against concentrating on the Italian front in 1917. But could he make an equally strong case for Haig's Flanders campaign? If Haig's forces adopted a standstill policy, it was possible that the European war might be lost. On the other hand, if Haig took on most of the German army, Britain might have little left to fight with in 1918.

An additional consideration for the War Policy Committee was Admiral John Jellicoe's dire warning that British security depended upon the conquest of the Belgian coast. Rather than submarines, the commander of the Grand Fleet now emphasized the possibility that German destroyers operating from Ostend and Zeebrugge might break Britain's Channel link to the Continent.[61] The future as well as the present concerned Jellicoe. If the war ended in stalemate, he suggested that Germany might "have at our front door a standing menace, and it would be quite certain that Germany would not be content with Belgium alone: Holland would follow, and we should have the whole North Coast of Europe from the Elbe to Ostend in German hands. Such a situation would be a menace to the existence of Great Britain."[62]

Jellicoe was well known for his pessimism, even suggesting that the shipping crisis would prevent Britain from continuing the war past 1917, and the political leadership didn't find his fearful warnings convincing. Nonetheless, Jellicoe's insistence that it was vital that the Belgian ports be captured in 1917 could not be ignored. "To get the enemy away from the Belgian coast was worth half a million men,"[63] Milner proclaimed at the seventh meeting of the War Policy Committee.

To reach the Belgian coast, however, meant a longer advance than British arms had yet achieved in the west. Balancing this ambitious and uniquely British strategical goal with the ability of the BEF to fight on into 1918 and beyond was difficult. Haig presented a formula to the ministers that attempted to combine Robertson's attritional strategy with his desire for a decisive victory. He said that he had no "intention of entering into a tremendous offensive involving heavy losses. His plan was aggressive without committing us too far." If there was not a "reasonable chance of success," he promised to halt his attack.[64]

But was it really possible to reconcile capturing the Belgian ports with Robertson's prudent attritional strategy? Robertson hoped that the superior weight of artillery would give the British the advantage against German troops nailed to their defensive position, and he emphasized that he didn't "advocate spending our last man and last round of ammunition in an attempt to reach that [Belgian] Coast if the opposition which we encounter shows that the attempt will entail disproportionate loss."[65] But how easy would it be to interpret "disproportionate loss" especially with a commander in chief inclined to believe that if he pushed in just one more attack the enemy would break?

Robertson's opposition to a strategic breakthrough offensive and his rejection of GHQ's views on the staying power of the German army clouded his relationship with Haig, who on the eve of Messines, wrote his wife that Robertson seemed "tactless, wishing to be here during the Battle! It is all for his own advertisement, and no doubt he tells the War Cabinet that we here in France cannot get on without him."[66] Shortly thereafter Haig became involved in an unsuccessful plan to have Robertson replace Sir Edward Carson as First Lord of the Admiralty. The Admiralty clearly needed shaking up, and Robertson was widely recognized for his firmness and organizational ability, but Haig's enthusiasm for removing his protector seems extraordinary. Perhaps the best explanation is that Haig believed that Wully had outlived his usefulness.[67] He could not have been more wrong, because his survival during the next months depended upon Robertson's remaining CIGS.

On July 18, the War Policy Committee finally sanctioned Haig's Flanders offensive. Two days later the War Cabinet ratified this decision. The ministers had discussed alternative operations from the Balkans to Alexandretta to the Italian front, but they kept coming back to Flanders. Although Robertson sought to minimize the seriousness of the French mutiny from them, the ministers unquestionably were aware that the BEF would be attacking with little expectation of strong French assistance. Rather than nullify a large-scale British offensive as Robertson had initially suggested should be the case, France's decline tipped the scales in favor of applying pressure on Germany in the west.[68] Haig might not achieve the success he expected, but it seemed necessary that he try, especially in light of what appeared to be the remarkable recovery of the Russian army. The so-called Kerensky Offensive (named after the then Russian minister of war), was having unexpected success against the Austrians in mid-July.[69]

The ministers did place a very important condition on Haig's offensive: "If it appears probable in the execution of these plans that the results are not commensurate with the effort made and the losses incurred, the whole question should be re-examined by the War Cabinet with a view to the cessation of this offensive and the adoption of an alternative plan."[70] Haig thought these conditions most unreasonable and was inclined to blame Robertson. Although he planned a breakthrough, he had avoided Nivelle's hype, describing his offensive in Robertson's language, a methodical step-by-step approach to maximize German casualties. Yet Robertson now seemed prepared to evaluate his success or failure on the ministers' terms. "I hope that your operations will be sufficiently successful to knock out the project for sending the artillery [to Italy]," Robertson wrote him on July 19. Two days later, Robertson sounded a bit more encouraging, but not by much. "Unless there were very great miscalculations on your part, and unless the first stage proved to be more or less a disastrous failure—which I certainly did not expect it would be—I did not think it would be possible to pronounce a verdict on the success of your operations for several weeks."[71] Several weeks before a decision was made on its offensive was cold comfort to GHQ.

When Robertson arrived in France on July 22, he was handed a memorandum, written by Kiggell but "concurred in & approved by C in C," which made it clear that GHQ had no intention of altering its plans. "We could see Italy and even Russia drop out, and still continue the war with France and America," Kiggell noted. "But if France drops out we not only cannot continue the war on land but our Armies in France will be in a very difficult position." As for assisting Cadorna, "the chance of anything positive being achieved in Italy is—to anyone acquainted with the A.B.C. of war—infinitesimal." Later, when Robertson dined with Haig, he was told to "be firmer and play the man; and, if need be, resign."[72] Robertson departed knowing that his standing with GHQ was at stake if he honored the War Policy Committee's conditions for continuing the offensive. "I can assure you that I never omit to impress upon the War Cabinet. . . the necessity of supporting wholeheartedly a plan which has once been approved," he wrote Haig.[73]

On July 24, Wully met with Cadorna and Foch prior to a meeting of an inter-Allied meeting in Paris. They agreed with him that only after the planned simultaneous offensives on all fronts were over could a joint effort on the Italian frontier be considered. When his Italian plans were also rebuffed by the Allied political leadership at a conference in the French Foreign Office, Lloyd George began emotionally talking of resigning and taking his case to the public.[74]

An especially alarming note had been sounded by Foch at Paris: Russia's defection might result in an overwhelming enemy superiority on the western front.[75] Just as Haig's forces were about to go "over the top," news from the Russian front suggested that this calamitous development might be sooner than later. On July 29 Robertson reported the results of an Austro-German counterattack: "The Russians broke, with the result that three Russian armies comprising some 60 to 70 divisions, well equipped with guns and ammunition, are now running away from some 18 Austrian and German divisions." In Robertson's view, there was "no good reason for the Russian retirement other than their refusal to fight." Robertson's advice was to moderate Allied war aims. If Russia and Romania dropped out of the war, "it would be folly to expect to realise existing aims, and therefore the sooner the hostile Powers concerned are made aware of any modifications which can be made the better."[76]

On July 31 the War Cabinet held a secret meeting to discuss the consequences of Russia's military collapse. The mood was grim though steadfast. Britain's war leaders agreed with Smuts that the issues at stake were "too vast" to accept "a peace which will in effect mean a defeat." But the cost of sustaining the Continental war with the eastern front moribund was great, almost certainly beyond Britain's capacity. Britain, it was noted in the War Cabinet, "might have to contemplate a situation in which the burden of the War was sustained entirely by the British Empire and the United States of America." Following the meeting, Lloyd George and some of his colleagues talked of getting President Wilson to come to Britain "and swear to support us."[77]

Amid all of the doubts and uncertainties in London, Haig began his infantry assault. The greatest battle in the history of the Royal Artillery had in effect been underway since Messines. According to Bidwell and Graham, eight gunners were in action for every ten infantrymen. Some three million shells were expended during the eighteen-day prelimary bombardment. The effect of the massive use of artillery, however, was not as great as Robertson and other artillery enthusiasts contemplated. British gunners, firing out of a salient, were themselves exposed to German artillerymen whose guns were concealed on the reverse slopes of the semicircle ridges overlooking the battlefield.[78] German experimentation with elastic defensive tactics also meant that the British bombardment frequently fell on "a position the Germans already regarded as a derelict extension of no-man's land."[79] The heavy rains that began on the evening of the first day of the assault further served to diminish the effectiveness of the artillery. Not in twenty years had it rained so much in Flanders in August. Shells buried in the deep mud, and poor visibility hampered counter-battery fire against the enemy artillery.

The big guns churned up the earth and destroyed the extensive drainage system. As the advancing British troops navigated this obstacle course, German machine gunners, secure in concrete pillboxes, inflicted heavy losses. Adding to the woes of the infantry, the heavy rain turned the battlefield into pools of water and mud. "In many places the men could only get forward by assisting each other out of the breast-high mud and water in the shell holes," Haig reported to Robertson on August 21. Rifles were "so clogged by mud as to be temporarily useless."[80]

Although stymied in his efforts at a breakthrough, Haig put the best possible face on matters. The first days' fighting, he told the War Cabinet, "confirm our ability to overcome the enemy's artillery even under the most unfavourable conditions, and to assemble our troops for assault and launch the assault even under the enemy's direct observation. They confirm further that the British Armies can be relied on to drive the enemy from any position by the combined efforts of the infantry, artillery and aeroplanes and to do so without undue loss." Claiming that German casualties probably exceeded British by 100 percent, Haig persisted in his offensive.[81] Gough launched attacks on August 10 (the battle of Gheluvelt plateau) and August 16 (the battle of Langemarck). Both achieved little, and the "thruster" Gough apparently advised Haig to call off the offensive.[82]

As usual, GHQ was stingy in its information for the War Office. "Not unnaturally the Cabinet ask me my opinion every morning as to how matters are going and it is rather difficult for me to say much as I have nothing to rely upon but the Communiqué and the slight additions you occasionally send to me,"[83] Robertson wrote Kiggell. As the offensive continued in appalling conditions with disappointing results, Robertson was faced with a quandary. His faith in artillery had been shaken. "A year ago we thought that victory lay in having a large amount of heavy artillery," he wrote Haig. But the employment of high-explosive shells to destroy the enemy's machineguns "entails the entire destruction of the surface of the ground and renders it almost impassable, especially in Flanders. We would therefore seem to be confronted with the problem that unless we use a great deal of artillery fire we cannot get on, and if we do use it the ground is destroyed."[84]

One word from Robertson would have given Lloyd George and his colleagues the confidence to terminate the Flanders attack. This word never came. Robertson remained under intense pressure from GHQ to "play the game." "You can rest assured," Derby wrote Philip Sassoon, Haig's private secretary, "that there are two people here, Robertson and myself, who will absolutely uphold him."[85] More importantly, Robertson feared that a suspension of the offensive would result in diminishing the British role on the western front, where he believed the war would be won or lost.

When Lloyd George pressed for diverting Allied artillery to assist Cadorna in his forthcoming offensive at an inter-Allied Conference in London on August 7–8, Robertson took the position that atrocious weather had extended Haig's time frame for taking Clercken ridge, his "first main objective." Supported by Foch, the CIGS argued that it was "quite impossible to send guns to Italy in time for work next month."[86] Lloyd George wouldn't allow the issue of loaning guns to Italy to die. In mid-August he attempted to enlist the support of the monarchy for his plan of "throwing our weight on to the side of Italy in order to smash Austria, take Trieste and then shake hands and make Peace with Austria." Seeking George V's support to halt the futile Flanders offensive, he impressed upon Stamford-ham that he and the king were the joint trustees of the nation. The generals, he emotionally charged, were "hammering not with steel and iron, but with human flesh and blood."[87]

The Eleventh Battle of the Isonzo, which began on August 18, gave him another opportunity to switch off to Italy. On August 26 the British ambassador in Rome reported that Cadorna's offensive might lead to "a complete smashing of the Austrian Army."[88] Lloyd George, who was on a much needed break at Sir George Riddell's home near Hurstpierpoint in Sussex, immediately wrote Robertson, asking him to consider sending reinforcements to the Italian front to turn "the Austrian retreat into a rout."[89]

Robertson initially told the War Cabinet that "no plan is of any good unless carried out with confidence and resolution," and that it was "false strategy to close down the offensive on the Western Front in order to give General Cadorna support which would only reach him too late to be effective."[90] Despite his firm stand, Robertson was in an uncomfortable position because of his earlier opposition to loaning Cadorna guns.

On the following day, Robertson drove to Sussex to confront Lloyd George. To lower Robertson's guard, his favorite dish, apple pudding, was served at lunch. In the end, Robertson agreed to a telegram to Cadorna promising reinforcements to the Italian front, but Robertson didn't give ground until an unrealistic condition was included: Cadorna had to prom-ise a decisive victory over Austria. Perhaps fearing Haig's reaction, Robert-son immediately tried to disassociate himself from this telegram, writing Maurice that he liked "the telegram sent to Italy less every day. It is bound to lead to trouble. Further Prime Minister & Milner will swear I agreed to it. I did not. I said if it represented their policy I saw no harm in it, but there was much to be said against the policy, which to my mind was impracticable."[91]

The Anglo-French political leadership in early September decided to send one hundred French guns to Cadorna, fifty of them from the French forces on Haig's left flank, a meager reinforcement when compared to the some three hundred guns desired by Lloyd George. This was the closest that Lloyd George came to overruling the soldiers and shutting down the Flanders offensive. In Hankey's words, "Ll. G. had been very truculent about the idea of overruling the soldiers, but when he came to the point, he funked it."[92] As it turned out, supporting Cadorna over the British high command might have been disastrous for his premiership. Just as Cadorna received his guns, he shocked the British with an announcement that he had no plans for another offensive. The stunned War Cabinet found the Italian general's decision "inexplicable."[93]

As hopes for an Allied success at the head of the Adriatic faded, attention focused once again on Flanders. Following the limited success of the Fifth Army in August, Haig admitted that his breakthrough attempt had failed, shifting the focus of his attack to Plumer, known for his set-piece operations. Plumer's assignment was the capture of the Gheluvelt plateau.

As Plumer readied his Second Army for a resumption of the offensive, anxiety grew in London. Bonar Law wrote Lloyd George on September 18 that he didn't know when the next attack was to take place, but "it may happen at any time. It is evident, therefore, that the time must soon come when we will have to decide whether or not this offensive is to be allowed to go on." Having just talked with Robertson, Bonar Law had gained the impression that Robertson had little hope "of anything coming of Haig's offensive."[94]

Bonar Law may well have gauged Robertson's state of mind correctly. Although Robertson continued to argue that the best means to keep the alliance together was military action in the western theater,[95] it now appeared certain that Russia was beyond salvation and that France and Italy were unwilling or unable to provide Britain much military assistance. Under the circumstances was it prudent to continue the offensive and run the risk of exhausting Britain's remaining troop strength?

Britain's staying power was much on the War Cabinet's mind in late September when it explored German peace feelers. One, originating from Spain, made no mention of peace terms. Another by way of France, which had mysterious and unofficial roots, seemed too favorable to British interests to be rejected outright. Belgium and Serbia were to be liberated, Alsace-Lorraine returned to France, Italy compensated with territory, and Britain granted colonial concessions. For its part, Berlin apparently expected to be compensated in Poland and along the Baltic coast (Courland and Lithuania). But such a peace left German expansionism unchecked, and Milner warned that "it would mean Germany coming out of the war more powerful than she entered it, and another war in 10 years' time."[96]

On September 26 Lloyd George and Robertson met with Haig in France to discuss the possibility that Germany might be willing to give the western powers generous terms on the condition that Russian territory be sacrificed. Robertson stated the Prime Minister's view of the military situation as follows: "Russia is practically finished for the purposes of the war—a view he held himself. The Italians are not fighting, and the French are not fighting. How, then, does the war look? We cannot singlehanded [sic] defeat the German army." Haig remained upbeat. Plumer's first attack, the battle of Menin Road, had been launched on September 20. His methodical approach reduced casualties and inflicted heavy losses on the counterattacking Germans.[97] Having gained his modest objective, an advance of only one kilometer, Plumer attacked again on September 26, the battle of Polygon Wood. Plumer's successes, limited though they were, put Haig in a confident mood. He told Robertson and the prime minister that the "Germans were now very worn out and had some very poor material in the fighting line."[98]

The German peace feelers came to nothing when Chancellor Georg Michaelis proclaimed: "We must continue to persevere until the German Empire on the continent and overseas establishes its position."[99] The prospect of continuing the war into 1918 or 1919 had serious consequences for British manpower. As he had done in the past, Robertson was inclined to blame diplomacy for the continued dispersion of the empire's limited and declining resources in the outer theaters. Believing that Bulgaria might make peace if the Allies promised to unite all Bulgarians under one flag, Robertson urged Lloyd George to press the Foreign Office. "We must detach some of the enemy countries if we possibly can," he wrote. "I have no right to address you on this subject. It is a Foreign Office matter. But I feel very strongly that we are not doing all we could do and ought to do."[100] Robertson also wanted an aggressive diplomatic offensive to detach Turkey if Russia fell out of the war.[101] Just as Russia's accelerating decline suggested that Allied war objectives be revised downward, it also encouraged the Bulgarians and Turks to believe that they were on the winning side. With the British determined to win a victor's peace, there seemed no alternative but to fight on.

While at GHQ discussing the German peace feelers, Robertson apparently questioned Haig in private about the advisability of continuing his offensive. When Haig suggested that he caucus with his army commanders, Robertson protested, "You know I could not go to your Army Commanders and discuss your plans in your absence."[102] Haig was thus present when Wully talked with the army commanders. Under his steely gaze, they kept whatever doubts they had to themselves. "Haig and his Army commanders being better judges of the enemy's condition than I could claim to be," Robertson later wrote, "I was not prepared to carry my doubts to the extent of opposing him, and of thereby obstructing the application of that little extra pressure upon the enemy which experience has so often shown may convert an inconclusive battle into a decisive victory."[103]

Returning to London, Robertson wrote Haig an equivocal letter: "Germany may be much nearer the end of her staying power than available evidence shows, but on the other hand France and Italy are not much to depend upon, and America will require a long time. Further, it is agreed that stagnation will destroy the Nation's determination. It is not an easy business to see through the problem when present resources of both sides and hostile gains are considered."[104] Haig possessed none of Robertson's doubts. His offensive continued.

After a promising start at Broodseinde on October 4, the BEF's assault was hampered by the return of wet weather. The mud and water surpassed the terrible conditions of August. High-explosive shells sank harmlessly into the deep mud, mortar base plates were submerged in it after every firing, small arms became clogged in short order, tanks were useless, and men and horses on occasion actually drowned in the pools of water. When Rawlinson talked to C. F. Macready, the Adjutant General to the forces in early October, he was told that the BEF could be kept "up to strength if we do not lose more than another 50,000 men before the offensive stops for the year."[105] Haig's persistence and Robertson's reluctance to buck him, however, cost the BEF an additional one hundred thousand casualties.[106]

Perhaps as serious as these losses was the decline in British morale because of the continued assaults under impossible conditions. When the offensive concluded in early November with the capture of Passchendaele ridge, the Belgian ports remained in German hands, as did some of the initial objectives of his first offensive on July 31. Among the troops, an alarming rise in drunkenness, desertions, and psychological disorders occurred. Auckland Geddes, the Minister for National Service, told the Cabinet Committee on Man Power that soldiers returning from the front were bitterly complaining of "the waste of life during the continued hammerings against the Ypres Ridge."[107] An even more significant witness was Haig, who characterized his forces as "much exhausted and much reduced in strength. Many divisions in the line urgently require relief, while the great majority of those for the first time being in reserve are neither sufficiently rested to relieve them nor really fit to be thrown into a fight to meet an emergency."[108]

Robertson's failure to advise a halt to the Flanders campaign undermined his position with War Cabinet members such as Smuts and Milner who earlier had accepted his position that Britain must maintain pressure on Germany during the summer. Disillusioned with the results of the Flanders offensive and concerned about the staying power of Britain's remaining European allies, they now rejected what Milner called "the policy of

Hammer, Hammer, Hammer on the Western Front,"[109] and increasingly looked to the eastern theaters. If Germany triumphed in Europe, Britain's position in Palestine and Mesopotamia would be vital to the security of the British Empire. Perhaps even more than his support of Haig, Robertson's attempts to limit Allenby's operations in Palestine and Syria cost him the support of Lloyd George's colleagues.

NOTES

1. Neilson, *Strategy and Supply*, 254; and Robertson to Monro, April 19, 1917, Woodward, MCWR, 177.

2. General Staff, "A General Review of the Situation in All Theatres of War," March 20, 1917, WO 106/311.

3. See Woodward, *Trial by Friendship*, 44–68.

4. For the origins of the Passchendaele offensive, see French, *Strategy of Lloyd George Coalition, 1916–1918*, 94–123; Woodward, *Lloyd George and the Generals*, 160–86; Andrew A. Wiest, *Passchendaele and the Royal Navy* (Westport, Conn., 1995); John Terraine, *The Road to Passchendaele: The Flanders Offensive of 1917: A Study in Inevitability* (London, 1977); and Hankey, *Supreme Command*, vol. 2, 670–84.

5. Philip Gibbs, *Now It Can Be Told* (New York, 1920), 472–73.

6. Maurice, "General Staff Note Regarding Operations between YPRES and the Coast," March 15, 1915, WO 158/17.

7. Ibid.

8. Martin Farndale, *History of the Royal Regiment of Artillery: Western Front 1914–18* (Dorchester, 1986), 199.

9. Robertson to Haig, April 14, 1917, Woodward, MCWR, 173.

10. Memorandum by Hankey, March 7, 1917, Hankey MSS, CAB 63/19.

11. Robin Prior and Trevor Wilson, *Passchendaele: The Untold Story* (New Haven, 1996), 35.

12. Robertson to Haig, April 20, 1917, Woodward, MCWR, 178–89.

13. Robertson to Haig, April 14, 1917, ibid., 171.

14. Robertson to Stamfordham, August 10, 1916, ibid., 81.

15. Graham and Bidwell, *Coalitions, Politicians and Generals*, 105–25.

16. *Military Operations: France and Belgium, 1917*, vol. 2, 18–19.

17. Prior and Wilson, *Passchendaele*, 53.

18. Travers, *Killing Ground*, 216.

19. Farndale, *Royal Regiment of Artillery: Western Front 1914–18*, 196.

20. See Esher to Lloyd George, April 24, 1917, Lloyd George MSS F/16/1/5.

21. Robertson, "Operations on West Front," April 30, 1917, WO 158/23.

22. The War Office reported that the BEF's casualties for the first six weeks of the Battle of Arras were 157,034. If the first day's horrendous casual-ties of the Somme were omitted, the BEF's casualties (206,357) for the first six

weeks of the Somme were roughly the same. General Staff. "Battles of the Somme and of Arras: Comparison of 42 Days—6 Weeks' Casualties," May 27, 1917, WO 106/311.

23. Robertson, "Operations on West Front," April 30, 1917, WO 158/23.

24. See Smuts to Robertson, Cabinet Paper G.T. 549 of April 13, 1917, CAB 24/11.

25. Cabinet Paper G.T. 597 of April 29, 1917, CAB 24/11; and War Cabinet (128 A), May 1, 1917, CAB 23/13.

26. Cabinet Paper G.T. 657 of May 5, 1917, CAB 24/12.

27. Lloyd George, *War Memoirs*, vol. 1, 927.

28. Memorandum by Hankey, April 18, 1917, Hankey MSS, CAB 63/20.

29. Anglo-French Conference, May 4–5, 1917, CAB 28/2/I.C.-21.

30. Charteris, *At G.H.Q.*, 223.

31. Robertson to Stamfordham, May 7, 1917, Woodward, MCWR, 183.

32. Cabinet Paper G.T. 678 of May 9, 1917, CAB 24/12.

33. Cabinet Paper G.T. 703 of May 12, 1917, CAB 24/13.

34. Robertson to Lloyd George (Esher to Robertson, May 11, enclosed), May 13, 1917, Lloyd George MSS F/44/3/12. Robertson to Haig, May 14, 1917, Haig MSS No. 113.

35. Robertson to Haig May 17, 1917, Woodward, MCWR, 186.

36. Robertson to Foch, May 23, 1917, ibid., 188.

37. Diary entry of June 2, Wilson MSS.

38. "Conference held at ABBEVILLE on the 7th June, 1917, between General Foch and General Sir William Robertson," Macdonogh MSS, WO 106/1513.

39. "Note by C.I.G.S. on his visit to Italian Headquarters 22nd to 24th March, 1917," WO 106/311.

40. "Conference held at ABBEVILLE on the 7th June, 1917, between General Foch and General Sir William Robertson," Macdonogh MSS, WO 106/1513.

41. Woodward, *Lloyd George and the Generals*, 174–75.

42. Blake, *Papers of Haig*, 236.

43. Robertson to Haig, May 26, 1917, Haig MSS No. 113; and Haig to Robertson, May 28, 1918, Robertson MSS I/23/28.

44. Blake, *Papers of Haig*, 236.

45. Terraine, *Road to Passchendaele*, 134.

46. Diary entry of June 8, 1917, Wilson MSS.

47. Terraine, *Road to Passchendaele*, 135.

48. Blake, *Papers of Haig*, 239.

49. French, *Strategy of Lloyd George Coalition*, 111.

50. War Cabinet (156), June 6, 1917, CAB 23/3.

51. Spears [originally spelled Spiers] to Maurice, June 6, 16, and 19, 1917, Spears MSS I/13/1.

52. See David French, "Who Knew What and When? The French Army Mutinies and the British Decision to Launch the Third Battle of Ypres," in *War*,

Strategy, and International Politics: Essays in Honour of Sir Michael Howard, eds. Lawrence Freedman, Paul Hayes, and Robert O'Neill (Oxford, 1992), 149.

53. War Cabinet (159 A), June 8, 1917, CAB 23/16.

54. Blake, *Papers of Haig*, 239.

55. War Policy Committee (1 and 2), June 11 and 12, 1917, CAB 27/6.

56. Blake, *Papers of Haig*, 239.

57. Spears to Maurice, June 16, 1917, Spears MSS I/13/1.

58. "Note by the C.I.G.S. on the Prime Minister's Memorandum regarding future military policy," June 23, 1917, WO 106/312.

59. Lloyd George, *War Memoirs*, vol. 2, 1462.

60. "Note by the C.I.G.S. on the Prime Minister's Memorandum regarding future military policy," June 23, 1917, WO 106/312.

61. Wiest, *Passchendaele and the Royal Navy*, 104.

62. "Note by the C.I.G.S. on the Prime Minister's Memorandum regarding future military policy," June 23, 1917, WO 106/312.

63. War Policy Committee (7), June 19, 1917, CAB 27/6.

64. War Policy Committee (9), June 20, 1917, CAB 27/6.

65. "Note by the C.I.G.S. on the Prime Minister's Memorandum regarding future military policy," June 23, 1917, WO 106/312.

66. Haig to his wife, May 30, 1917, Haig MSS No. 151.

67. Woodward, *Lloyd George and the Generals*, 181–82.

68. French, *Strategy of Lloyd George Coalition*, 117–22; and Woodward, *Trial by Friendship*, 76.

69. For an account of Russia's last offensive of the war, see Louise Erwin Heenan, *Russian Democracy's Fatal Blunder: The Summer Offensive of 1917* (New York, 1987).

70. War Cabinet (191 A), July 20, 1917, CAB 23/13.

71. Robertson to Haig, July 19 and 21, 1917, Robertson MSS I/23/39–40.

72. Kiggell, "Note," July 22, 1917, WO 158/22; and Blake, *Papers of Haig*, 246.

73. Robertson to Haig, July 28, 1917, WO 158/24.

74. Woodward, *Lloyd George and the Generals*, 191.

75. "Military Conference of 26th July," (attended by Cadorna, Pershing, Robertson, Foch, and Pétain), Cabinet Paper G.T. 1533 of July 26, 1917, CAB 24/21.

76. Robertson, "The Present Military Situation in Russia and its Effect on Our Future Plans," July 29, 1917, WO 106/312.

77. War Cabinet (200 A), July 31, 1917, CAB 23/13; Memorandum by Smuts, Cabinet Paper G.T. 1573 of July 31, 1917, CAB 24/21; and Roskill, *Hankey*, 418.

78. Bidwell and Graham, *Fire-Power*, 89–90; and Farndale, *Royal Regiment of Artillery: Western Front 1914–18*, 196.

79. Captain G. C. Wynne, "The Development of the German Defensive Battle in 1917, and Its Influence on British Defence Tactics, Part I," *The Army*

Quarterly 34 (April 1937): 23; Timothy T. Lupfer, *The Dynamic of Doctrine: The Changes in German Tactical Doctrine during the First World War* (Washington, D.C., 1981), 11–35; and Martin Samuels, *Command or Control? Command, Training and Tactics in British and German Armies, 1888–1918* (London, 1995), 194–97.

80. Cabinet Paper G.T. 1814 of August 21, 1917, CAB 24/24.

81. Cabinet Paper G.T. 1621 of August 4, 1917, CAB 24/22.

82. Wilson, *Myriad Faces of War*, 466.

83. Robertson to Kiggell, August 2, 1917, Woodward, MCWR, 211–12.

84. Robertson to Haig, September 15, 1917, ibid., 223.

85. Derby to Sassoon, July 30, 1917, 920 Derby MSS (17).

86. Robertson to Milner, August 7, 1917, Woodward, MCWR, 212; and Woodward, *Lloyd George and the Generals*, 193.

87. Note by Lord Stamfordham, August 14, 1917, RA Geo. V K. 1185/4.

88. *Military Operations: Italy, 1915–1919*, 35–36; and decipher of telegram from Rodd, August 26, 1917, Lloyd George MSS F/56/1/47.

89. Lloyd George to Robertson, August 26, Woodward, MCWR, 219–20.

90. War Cabinet (225 A), August 28, 1917, CAB 23/13.

91. Woodward, *Lloyd George and the Generals*, 197; and Robertson to Maurice, August 31, 1917, Woodward, MCWR, 221–22.

92. Anglo-French Conference held at 10 Downing Street, September 4, 1917, CAB 28/2/I.C.-26; and diary entry of September 4, 1917, Hankey MSS 1/3.

93. War Cabinet (237), September 21, 1917, CAB 23/4.

94. Bonar Law to Lloyd George, September 18, 1917, Lloyd George MSS F/30/2/25.

95. Robertson, "The Present Situation in Russia," September 24, 1917, WO 106/312.

96. Woodward, *Trial by Friendship*, 99–100.

97. Griffith, *Battle Tactics of Western Front*, 88.

98. Hankey's minutes of this meeting are in CAB 1/25/16. Two pages are in Hankey's handwriting, dated September 26, and there are typed minutes, dated September 29, 1917. The latter were apparently prepared after Hankey returned to London.

99. See Woodward, *Trial by Friendship*, 102–3.

100. Robertson to Lloyd George, September 29, 1917, WO 106/1515; and Rothwell, *British War Aims and Peace Diplomacy*, 140–41.

101. Robertson, "The Present Situation in Russia," September 24, 1917, WO 106/312.

102. Spears, *Prelude to Victory*, 342. October prior to the Italian setback at Caporetto is perhaps a more logical time for this discussion to have taken place, but I have not been able to place Robertson at GHQ during this period.

103. Robertson, *Soldiers and Statesmen*, vol. 2, 262.

104. Robertson to Haig, September 27, 1917, Woodward, MCWR, 229.

105. Diary entry of October 2, 1917, Rawlinson MSS 1/9.

106. Griffith, *Battle Tactics of Western Front*, 88–89.

107. Cabinet Committee on Man Power (2), December 11, 1917, CAB 27/14.

108. Haig, "Memorandum on the Question of an Extension of the British Front," December 15, 1917, M.P.C. 21, CAB 27/14.

109. Milner to Curzon, October 17, 1917, Curzon MSS Eur. F 112/113.

Chapter 9

Robertson and Allenby

With the downturn in Allied military fortunes during the spring and summer of 1917, long-range strategic considerations began to dominate British policy in the Turkish theaters. If the war went wrong on the Continent, Lord Curzon argued in a paper for the War Cabinet, it would be to Britain's advantage to take Jerusalem and drive the Turks out of Syria, "or at any rate advance to a strong defensive position in the northern part of Palestine."[1] Leo Amery, a member of the new War Cabinet Secretariat who played the role of a geopolitical guru for Lloyd George and the Milnerites, was even more alarmist about the Turko-German threat.

With a reorganised German-Turkish Army, as a vanguard of the Armies of Central Europe, in a position to strike effectively either at Baghdad or the Suez Canal, and with submarine bases in the Eastern Mediterranean and the Red Sea, our position both in Mesopotamia and in Egypt would be increasingly precarious. The collapse of Russia has, in fact, made Palestine, of the issues still left undecided by the war, one of the most vital for the whole future of the British Empire.[2]

Lloyd George wanted a commander "of the dashing type"[3] on a front where British operations had greater latitude from coalition politics. Smuts, who saw significant strategical consequences in the capture of Palestine for the British Empire, was his first choice to replace Murray.[4] But the South African leader, despite intense lobbying by the prime minister for more than a month, wouldn't accept the command unless promised sufficient resources for a decisive victory. With Russia in decline and sea transport in

General E.H.H. Allenby

question, Robertson could make no such commitment. Smuts had to agree and bluntly informed Lloyd George that "our present military situation on all Fronts does not really justify an offensive campaign for the capture of Jerusalem."[5]

On June 5, the War Cabinet, on Robertson's recommendation, chose a large and forceful cavalryman, General Sir Edmund Allenby, who had been one of Robertson's contemporaries at Staff College. The son of a country gentleman, he was known for his rough manner and explosive temper. Having not gotten on with Haig as a commander on the western front, he was delighted to be in control of his own theater. Before departing for Egypt, the prime minister told him that his objective was "Jerusalem before Christmas," and if he needed reinforcements and supplies, he only had to ask for them.[6] Robertson, however, made it clear that there were limits to the assistance he could expect. His official instructions sensibly made the point that Allenby must coordinate his operations with what was occurring in other theaters and that the "precarious nature" of sea communications limited his potential reinforcements.[7]

At this juncture Britain had no fixed policy in Palestine. Lloyd George obviously wanted a decisive victory, but the minutes of the meeting when Allenby was selected noted: "The policy to be adopted in that theatre of war would not be settled until General Allenby had assumed control."[8] Wully sought to restrain the prime minister's exuberance, arguing that unless Allenby's assessment of the situation differed from his, a decisive defeat of the Turks wasn't possible with the resources that Allenby would have at his disposal, even including reinforcements that were being sent to him from England and Salonika.[9]

After arriving in Egypt on June 27, Allenby toured the Palestine front. Estimating the enemy's "fighting force" in southern Palestine at 46,000 rifles and 2,800 sabres, he concluded that he might take Jerusalem if the Turks were not "materially increased," and estimated his troop requirements at seven infantry and three cavalry divisions. To advance beyond and perhaps to maintain a front from Jaffa to Jerusalem, however, he wanted a "considerable addition" to his strength.[10] If Robertson prevailed, Allenby would limit his objectives. "It is my present opinion that the purely military advantages to be gained [from occupying Jerusalem] would not justify the expenditure of force required and the risks incurred," he informed the War Cabinet in July, "though I do not say that this opinion may not be modified later."[11]

A new element of uncertainty had just been introduced to the Turkish theaters. Intelligence sources from Switzerland suggested that the Germans were about to send as many as 160,000 men to the Middle East, where they might concentrate against Maude, whose forces were not as strong as Allenby's and were vulnerable because of Russian military inactivity. Robertson viewed these reports of massive German reinforcements as fantasy.[12] When consulted, French intelligence agreed, informing the general staff that "the distance, the transport and supply difficulty and the number of troops available will—none of them—allow the Germans to part for so long a time with even a limited number of Divisions."[13] Nonetheless, the presence of some Germans with artillery might stiffen Turkish resolve; and Robertson believed that the "Turks and Germans combined may make things very unpleasant in Persia and possibly for Maude."[14] To protect the Mesopotamian front, Wully wanted Allenby to pressure the Turks to force them "to divert to the Palestine front troops and ammunition, which might otherwise be sent to Mesopotamia."[15] His dilemma was that any success by Allenby would encourage the civilians to become more deeply involved in Palestine.

On August 1 he sent one of his "secret and personal" notes to Allenby:

With reference to the general situation we need to be careful as to the extent to which our commitments are increased. With Russia practically out of the war we have got to consider the necessity for economising shipping and men and also for being strong on the West front. . . . I am therefore taking the line at present that it will be a good thing to give the Turk in front of you a sound beating, but that the extent to which we shall be justified in following him by an advance into Northern and Central Palestine is a matter which for the moment must be left open. The further we go north the more Turks we shall meet; and the greater will be the strain upon our resources. Of course if we can so knock the Turk about that he throws his hand in, nothing would be better. On the other hand it is nearly 400 miles from where you are to Aleppo and the Turks' home lies beyond Aleppo. Do not take these remarks too definitely. . . . I again ask you not to take too definitely what I have said about the advance into Palestine. As you know the Prime Minister is very much in favour of it and eventually the Government may decide to do it. The only point I wish to make is that in deciding to go forward we will have to bear in mind what the situation will be after we have gone forward and whether we can, having regard to all the circumstances of the war, maintain ourselves after going forward and to a useful purpose.[16]

On August 10 the War Cabinet instructed Allenby "to strike the Turk as hard as possible during the coming Autumn and Winter," but gave him no specific "geographical" objective. Rather, Allenby was told to defeat the Turks opposing him and "follow up your success as the situation allows."[17]

Robertson added in a personal note: "I think the Instructions will be clear to you. They simply amount to doing the best you can with what you have got; to giving the Turk as hard a knock as you can; and at the same time avoiding going too far forward and getting into a position from which you can neither advance nor go back and which might involve us in commitments which we could not properly meet having regard to other places and to our resources."[18]

In reference to Robertson's personal notes of August 1 and August 10, Allenby responded: "The War Cabinet's instructions are sufficient and clear; and, with your explanatory remarks, I feel that I understand exactly."[19] In sum Allenby knew that Robertson expected him to limit his operations.

Meanwhile, working at cross-purposes with the CIGS, Lloyd George tried to expand the British role by including an amphibious Anglo-French attack at Ayas Bay (Alexandretta).[20] Robertson, emphasizing the shipping crisis, argued against this ambitious and risky project. He, however, expressed confidence that Allenby could take Jerusalem without reinforcements, telling the War Policy Committee on September 24, 1917, that

he would be disappointed if, General Allenby did not defeat the Turks at Gaza, and then he would be only some 50 miles from Jerusalem. Water was the chief difficulty in connection with any advance, which must be in steps from one source of water-supply to another. He would be surprised if Allenby could not reach Jerusalem with his present force but he asked, what General Allenby was to do when he got there, and what would we get out of an advance through Syria, for which he would need far more men. Aleppo, the first really important point from Gaza, was some 400 miles distant.[21]

As Robertson applied the brakes to Allenby's operations, Lloyd George continued to push hard on the accelerator. On October 3, with Robertson absent, the Welshman lobbied the Committee on War Policy for a smashing defeat of the Turks, which he believed in conjunction with a diplomatic offensive would force them out of the war. Curzon demurred, insisting that Allenby couldn't possibly get to Aleppo this year, but Lloyd George, emphasizing poor Turkish morale and the deterioration of Turkish rail transport, wanted Allenby to exploit to the fullest any victory over the Turks. The ministers then officially recommended that two of Haig's divisions be sent to Egypt.[22]

Russia's collapse strongly suggested that the stalemate would not be broken in France in 1918. As Wully confessed to Haig, he still supported " 'defensive' in all theatres but the West. But the difficulty is to prove the wisdom of this now that Russia is out. I confess I stick to it more because I see nothing better, and because my instinct prompts me to stick to it, than to any convincing arguments by which I can support it."[23] On the other hand, prudence dictated that all available British soldiers be concentrated in France, where the war would be won or lost. If the Germans gained the strategical initiative—as Robertson feared—those soldiers would be needed for defense, especially because the British government had just agreed in principle that the BEF would take over more of the French line.

Angering the prime minister, Wully reversed himself on sending troops from France to Allenby.[24] Any troops sent, he now argued could not be "relied upon for fighting in France next Summer." Whatever local success was achieved by Allenby was not worth the risk of getting more deeply involved in this peripheral theater, especially because Robertson planned to draw on Allenby's forces in the spring to reinforce Haig.[25]

Pressed by the War Policy Committee, Robertson wired Allenby for his requirements to advance to the Jaffa-Jerusalem line, roughly fifty miles between the Jordan River and the sea, as compared to Allenby's existing front of some thirty miles between Gaza and Beersheba. He also took this opportunity to warn Allenby of the possibility that he might be attacked by the Turks reinforced by the Germans. "Beyond the arrival of one Turkish regiment," he noted, "we have no information of enemy concentration towards Mesopotamia east of Aleppo and therefore are still in doubt whether enemy's reported contemplated offensive will be in that theatre or in Palestine. You should also remember that two German divisions are reported to be preparing for the East and German facilities for increasing this force, should be borne in mind."[26]

Though instructing Allenby to take no chances in his estimates of the potential enemy threat, it must be noted that Robertson cautioned Maude not to exaggerate his needs. The ministers "cannot always put correct military interpretation upon them," he wrote the commander of British forces in Mesopotamia, "and are apt to become unduly anxious and therefore prone to expect me to take action giving complete security everywhere which is impossible."[27]

The Turkish Minister of War Enver Pasha's plan to retake Baghdad was a pipe dream. General Erich von Falkenhayn, the commander of a Turko-German force, known as Yilderim or "Thunderbolt," had neither the troops nor the lines of communication to support a distant and large-scale offensive against either Maude or Allenby. Allenby in fact believed that if Falkenhayn "comes my way he will have great difficulty in supplying his Army; and with his present strength has not a chance against me."[28] The general staff was equally aware of the deterioration of the Turkish army. Its troops were deserting freely, and when Enver Pasha visited Beirut in June, it was reported that soldiers were forbidden to be stationed along his route for fear that he would be assassinated.[29] And then there was the weakness of Turkish communications. Robertson had noted in February that "owing to lack of rolling stock troops are frequently detrained at Damascus, and are marched hence to Southern Palestine."[30] The tendency of some civilians, especially Lloyd George, to support peripheral operations, stretching British resources to the breaking point, however, overrode all other considerations in Wully's mind.

A private and personal note accompanied Robertson's official communication requesting Allenby's requirements to secure the Jaffa-Jerusalem line:

You will understand that my 42625 of today does not originate with me because apart from the strategy I do not believe that the policy if successfully executed would have the anticipated result. However you are concerned only with framing your reply and, in it you should take no chances because of the many uncertain factors. You should also remember that transport, supply, water, time and space are imperfectly realised here and therefore they may need emphasising. I find it impossible to convincingly prove the great difference between the needs and facilities of Turkish and British troops in these and similar matters.[31]

On October 9 Robertson submitted his estimates of Allenby's requirements to occupy the Jaffa-Jerusalem line. He had planned to await Allenby's assessment, but the unexpected arrival in London of the French premier, whom he suspected of being used by Lloyd George "to carry me off my feet," prompted him to put his views before the government immediately. Robertson's intent was clear. As he wrote Haig, "the Palestine thing will *not* come off."[32]

With the civilians hostile to his strategical views, Robertson resorted to technical arguments that would be more difficult to challenge. He told the civilians to expect a "large scale" battle to rupture the Turkish Gaza-Beersheba front, and then "at least two more such battles" before Jerusalem was captured. To relieve battle-exhausted forces, the EEF would require at least three fresh divisions. If Allenby acquired the Jaffa-Jerusalem line, he might face sixteen divisions (some 120,000 combatants) north of Jerusalem, more if the Turks abandoned their position in Mesopotamia. An additional two divisions were thus necessary to meet this potential threat, making a total reinforcement of five infantry divisions, all of which had to be taken from Haig's forces.[33]

If Robertson's assessment is thought unrealistic, Allenby's could be deemed fantastic. The EEF's commander suggested that he might have to take on virtually the entire Turkish Army, with troops from as far away as Romania and the Caucasus being sent to oppose him. If two German divisions were sent, he might face twenty divisions. To secure the Jaffa-Jerusalem line, he wanted an additional thirteen divisions, clearly an impossible request for the British government to meet, even if the BEF went on the defensive.[34]

Robertson had encouraged Allenby to exaggerate his needs, but his outlandish estimates gave the game away. Prior to his offensive, he had written Robertson that the "Turks are deserting freely, and their morale is reported to be poor." If his initial attack succeeded, he thought a rout possible.[35] Yet he now claimed that he needed massive reinforcements to capture and hold Jerusalem and southern Palestine.

On the eve of Jerusalem's fall, Allenby (reacting to Robertson's continued concern about expanding British commitments in a peripheral theater) argued that it would be easier to hold the Jaffa-Jerusalem line than the Gaza-Beersheba line. Significantly, he noted: "If I can get Jerusalem-Jaffa line I ought to be able to hold it with the force I now have if my establishments are maintained."[36]

Although unaware of his private letters, members of the War Cabinet suspected Robertson of using language in official correspondence designed to discourage Allenby from exploiting any success. Maurice's and Derby's attempts to defend Wully against this charge had little effect. The ministers believed that the general staff, in collusion with Allenby, presented the worst-case scenario for a campaign it didn't favor.[37] Every technical argument seemed to be raised against campaigns thought to have a weak strategical foundation. Conversely, technical difficulties were glossed over to support what was thought to be sound strategy. The contrast between Robertson's and Allenby's fearful estimates of Turkish capabilities and the general staff's support of Haig's offensive when the rains resumed in Flanders in October, returning the battlefield to a muddy quagmire once again, was striking. Despite the decline of Britain's allies and BEF's disappointing progress, the general staff wanted the clearing of the Belgian coast to remain the focus of Britain's military effort. Only in this way, it was argued, could Britain force Germany "to conform to British strategy and to divert her strategic reserve to the British front."[38] Facing a serious manpower crisis, the last thing that Lloyd George's government wanted was to attract most of the German army to Haig's front.

The military authorities were on the spot when Allenby encountered less resistance than either he or the general staff had encouraged the civilians to believe. Forty days after his attack on Beersheba, "Bull" Allenby reached Jerusalem. As the Holy City fell into British hands, Macdonogh told the civilians that Turkish rifle strength on all fronts from Romania to the Caucasus to Mesopotamia was just 110,000—with only 21,000 in Palestine![39] The two German divisions expected to arrive in the Middle East hadn't materialized, although three battalions of infantry eventually arrived.

Lloyd George was furious. "It is quite clear that the information which had been given to us about the number of Turkish troops available in that theatre was utterly wrong," he wrote Wully, "and that the more recent information supplied to me as to the complete breakdown of the Turkish transport is nearer the mark."[40] Robertson defended himself by telling the prime minister, that "if we had under-estimated the Turk and failed we should have deserved to be hung."[41] Success it seems was just as threatening to Robertson's position, and Lloyd George wanted his head. But Lord Derby refused to cooperate, threatening to resign if Robertson were removed.[42]

Nonetheless, the drumbeat of criticism continued. "When General Allenby," it was noted in the War Cabinet, "had been asked how many men would be required, in his opinion, to capture Jerusalem and hold it, he had replied that the Turks could bring against him 18 divisions in addition to 2 German divisions that were available. General Allenby had estimated that 20 British divisions would be required to take Jerusalem. What had finally happened was that only 20,000 Turkish rifles had opposed our 100,000 rifles."[43]

Attempting to explain the inflated estimates, Maurice said that intelligence in Syria couldn't be attained before it "was too stale to be of use."[44] Robertson also defended his and especially Allenby's professional advice to the civilians. The flanking movement by the cavalry at Beersheba, he explained, had exceeded expectations when the Turks failed to destroy their water supply. Even then the margin between success and failure had been razor thin. Some cavalrymen had lived for forty-eight hours on a single water-bottle. The rapid British advance also made it impossible for the Turks to bring up the anticipated reinforcements. In essence, Wully seemed to suggest that the military authorities had prepared their estimates on everything going wrong when almost everything had gone right.[45]

Irritable and excitable, the prime minister at times seemed on the verge of a nervous breakdown.[46] Having failed to switch off to Italy during the summer, he became obsessed with Palestine, even to the extent of wanting to abandon "all activity on the Western Front to concentrate our efforts against Turkey."[47] Infuriating Robertson almost to the point of resignation, he asked Field Marshal French and General Sir Henry Wilson to assess present and future British strategy. To Lloyd George's disappointment and Robertson's relief, they argued that although a campaign against Turkey was good strategy, it was too late to prepare for a winter campaign.[48]

Undeterred, Lloyd George used the rout of the Italians at Caporetto to create an inter-Allied war council on November 7 at Rapallo, Italy. The new Supreme War Council (SWC), with its inter-Allied military staff at Versailles, served to divide Robertson's control of British strategy. Wilson, thought to be more flexible than Robertson on the deployment of British forces, became Lloyd George's soldier on the inter-Allied staff.

Jerusalem's capture gave Lloyd George a fresh opportunity to redirect British strategy. The War Cabinet instructed the general staff to consider two policies: a) the conquest and defense of all of Palestine; or b) an advance to the vicinity of Aleppo to cut Turkish railway communications with Mesopotamia. When consulted, Allenby said that he could take Palestine with his present force. An additional advance of 250 miles to Aleppo (the Damascus-Beirut line) would require sixteen or eighteen divisions besides his mounted corps, an addition to his force of from eight to ten divisions.

Despite this demand for massive reinforcements, Robertson was unhappy with Allenby's assessment because it suggested that Palestine could be occupied and defended without additional divisions. In October, it should be remembered, Allenby had asked for an additional thirteen divisions just to conquer and hold southern Palestine, the Jaffa-Jerusalem line.

Raising many technical points against becoming more deeply involved in Palestine, Robertson on December 26 stressed the manpower drain: "The vital point to remember is that the conquest of Palestine requires men and material which can be provided only at the expense of the Western front." According to Robertson's estimates, Palestine's conquest might mean an additional fifty-seven thousand battle casualties with twenty thousand more troops put out of action due to sickness.[49]

Robertson's influence was now at its nadir. His support of the Flanders campaign lowered his standing; Palestine now destroyed what was left of his credibility. "I have seen General Robertson's [December 26] Memorandum—an amazing document even from him," Amery wrote Lloyd George. "The line of argument adopted in it would have disproved the possibility of success of almost any great campaign in history."[50]

Amery conspired with Lloyd George to deny Robertson any role in future military operations against Turkey. Military and strategical questions in the Turkish theater were referred to the Permanent Military Representatives (PMRs) of the inter-Allied staff at Versailles. Lloyd George also toyed with placing Smuts, who would bypass the CIGS and report directly to the War Cabinet, in charge of naval and military operations against Turkey. "With Wilson at Versailles & the East delegated to Smuts," Amery suggested, "I don't think the old gang can give too much trouble—if they do you can deal with them."[51]

Meanwhile, Wilson, Lloyd George's general on the inter-Allied staff at Versailles, discussed questions about military operations against Turkey with him and other members of the War Cabinet without going through Robertson.[52] "The Boches," he told Smuts, "could not get a decision agst. us, that we could not get one agst. him in the West & that thereupon we ought to try to knock out the Turk."[53] With German troops massing on the western front, there may have been too much imagination and brainstorming at Versailles about the Turkish theaters. Amery reported to Lloyd George that French officers were enthusiastically discussing a landing on the Syrian coast, assisted by "a Japanese Expedition to take the Dardanelles."[54]

Apparently convinced that the west was "safe & two or three divisions from Palestine would make no difference,"[55] Wilson persuaded the PMRs to support a major effort to defeat Turkey. The differences between Versailles and the British general staff on the feasibility of a Turkish campaign were great. Putting Turkish military strength at "250,000 at the utmost," the PMRs asserted that "the existing Allied forces in Palestine and Mesopotamia are already sufficiently superior to the enemy in numbers, equipment and moral to justify the hope that successful operations can be carried out with these forces provided they are maintained at full strength." The general staff, however, estimated Turkish ration strength at 425,000, which included 250,000 combatants, and emphasized that Allenby's infantry was 17,500 below strength.[56]

Believing that Wilson was maneuvering to drive him from the War Office and viewing the work of Versailles as "d___d rot," Robertson refused to give an inch. He emphasized that Versailles, especially the Italian and French staff officers, didn't "appreciate the difficulty if not impossibility of providing the means required" to execute their Turkish plans. "I have told the War Cabinet they cannot take Palestine," he wrote Haig, "& I shall stick to my guns and clear out if I am overruled."[57] But Robertson was now virtually irrelevant. The War Cabinet sent Smuts to Egypt to oversee plans for the "most vigorous prosecution of the war against Turkey."[58] The South African conferred with Allenby and Lieutenant General Sir William Raine Marshall, who had become the commander in chief of the Mesopotamian theater after Maude died of cholera.

Robertson made his last stand on Palestine when the Supreme War Council considered the recommendation (Joint Note No. 12) of the PMRs on February 1. Assisted by Wilson's horse trading at Versailles, Lloyd George gained qualified support for a military enterprise against the Turks. A skeptical and agitated Georges Clemenceau wanted to know how the British could contemplate such a peripheral campaign when northern France was occupied by Germany and Paris itself might be menaced in 1918. According to Robertson, the French premier "poured scorn on the plan, and drove in point after point, leaving L. G. smaller and smaller until he was almost shrivelled up."[59] When the fierce-tempered premier had finished with Lloyd George, he turned to Robertson for his opinion. Despite the embarrassment that he knew it would cause the prime minister, Wully didn't hesitate. It would "be dangerous and detrimental to our prospects of winning the war," he responded.[60] Lloyd George subsequently had to promise that not a single British soldier would be sent from the western front to Palestine.

Robertson immediately wrote Allenby that it would:

be folly for you to try to give advice as to what can be attempted in it [Palestine] without having some information with respect to the main theater the security of which is now authoritatively admitted to be vital to the Allied interests. . . . I see no insuperable difficulty in your going further forward for a considerable distance, but I fail to see any useful gain thereby. . . . I have not mentioned this in the official letter I am sending you because I do not wish you to think that I am trying to tie your hands, but I do wish to prevent you finding yourself in the cart later on.[61]

This letter was hand delivered by Colonel Walter Kirke, chosen by Robertson to accompany Smuts as his general staff adviser. The language was similar to earlier private messages that Allenby had received from the CIGS. As Kirke later admitted, "my instructions from the C.I.G.S. were to do everything possible to prevent him [Smuts] making any plan, which would keep troops in Palestine, and I had written instructions to Allenby to the same effect."[62]

When accused by the civilians in December of "cooking" his estimates, Robertson had written Allenby insisting that he had never "deliberately" overstated "the enemy's power of resistance in order to knock out" the Palestinian project; and he was sure that "no such idea" had ever entered

Allenby's mind.[63] But it surely had, and what Allenby did next strongly suggests that he believed that Robertson was trying to "tie his hands" and manipulate the appreciations that he sent to the general staff. No longer fearing Robertson's authority, he told Smuts of Robertson's instructions and worked with the South African to develop an ambitious offensive strategy. Marshall was given the role of standing on the defensive and supplying Allenby with reinforcements. With as many as three divisions from Mesopotamia, Allenby was expected to get to Haifa by June and Damascus by Autumn, the speed of his advance being determined by how rapidly the British could construct a military railroad. Turkish forces confronting the EEF were not considered formidable, and poor Turkish lines of communication limited the number of Turkish reinforcements that could be transported and supplied on the Syrian front.[64] Encouraged by Smuts's reports, the War Cabinet authorized Allenby to "advance to the maximum extent possible, consistent with the safety of the force under his orders."[65]

With few exceptions Robertson in 1916–1917 sought to impose a passive role on British arms in the Turkish theaters. But he didn't rule out an aggressive policy under the right circumstances. In February, when Maude had annihilated the Turkish 6th Army and the Russians seemed about to occupy Mosul, he supported a forward policy. But the rapid decline of the Russian army after the March Revolution and Murray's setback at Gaza made Robertson cautious once again. Robertson tried to control Maude's successor Marshall, handpicking the key members of his staff and making it clear that his future role in the war was strictly limited.[66] The British gained the political prize of Baghdad and upheld British prestige in the Moslem world, but some 50,000 Turks tied down a huge imperial force with a ration strength of over 400,000 at the beginning of 1918, including 117,471 British troops. Almost half of this force, however, were noncombatants, a vast and ever-increasing army of followers or labor, composed of Indians, Egyptians, Arabs, Kurds, Chinese, and other nationalities.

With a passive policy in Mesopotamia, Robertson had been prepared to give Allenby a "really big show" during the winter of 1917–1918, in part, to sustain public support for the war. But declining Entente military fortunes and the shipping crisis led him, in Maurice's words, to oppose a "goose chase which will interfere with the main theatre."[67]

Fearing more personnel-draining offensives, the civilians were increasingly unimpressed by Robertson's advice. Defending India from a Moslem holy war made Mesopotamia a critical theater in their eyes. Fearing a mutual stalemate, the civilians also linked the future security of the British Empire to achieving a strong position in Palestine and Syria. Wully's "cooking" of estimates for military operations against the Turks alienated former supporters. The British Empire will "never get on with the War so long as Sir William Robertson remained CIGS," Smuts told Lloyd George before he departed for Egypt.[68] When he returned, Robertson had been replaced by Wilson.

Palestine became the litmus test for those who wanted to give British strategy flexibility. Wilson initially passed this test, but his approach to a major military effort in Palestine eventually resembled Robertson's. With the British front in peril in 1918, Allenby had to send almost sixty thousand men to France to stem the German tide. Notwithstanding the Allied setbacks on the western front, the authorities in London, which now included the Dominion prime ministers, continued to emphasize the protection and expansion of the British Empire in the east as an insurance policy if total victory over Germany proved unobtainable. Wilson gave lip service to peripheral operations designed to give the British Empire a good peace, whether it were gained on the battlefield or at the peace table.[69] But when he presented his views in July 1918 on British military policy in 1918–1919, he maintained that an improved military situation for the anti-German coalition meant that Britain must continue to give primary emphasis to fighting the main body of the German Army. Any diversion of British troops to Palestine was opposed. "Wully redivivius" was Lloyd George's furious reaction.[70]

NOTES

1. Cabinet Paper G.T. 703 of May 12, 1917, CAB 24/13.
2. L. S. Amery, "The Russian Situation and Its Consequences," Cabinet Paper G.T. 831 of May 20, 1917, CAB 24/14.
3. War Cabinet (115 A), April 5, 1917, CAB 23/13.
4. See David R. Woodward, "The Imperial Strategist: Jan Christiaan Smuts and British Military Policy, 1917–1918," *Military History Journal* 5 (December 1981): 134–37.
5. Robertson to Smuts, May 26, 1917, Robertson MSS I/33/50; and Smuts to Lloyd George, May 31, 1917, Lloyd George MSS F/45/9/4.
6. Lloyd George, *War Memoirs*, vol. 2, 1089–90.
7. Robertson to Allenby, June 13, 1917, WO 106/718.
8. See War Cabinet (155), June 5, 1917, CAB 23/3.
9. Robertson, "Military Policy in the Various Theatres of War," June 12, 1917, WO 106/312.
10. Allenby to Robertson, July 12, 1917, Macdonogh MSS, WO 106/1513.
11. Robertson, "Palestine," July 19, 1917, Macdonogh MSS, WO 106/1513.

12. Robertson, "Military Situation in Mesopotamia," July 31, 1917, WO 106/312.

13. Spears to Cox, July 10, 1917, Spears MSS I/13/1.

14. Robertson to Haig, September 24, 1917, Woodward, MCWR, 225–26.

15. Robertson, "The Present Military Situation in Russia and Its Effect on Our Future Plans," July 29, 1917, WO 106/312.

16. Robertson to Allenby, August 1, 1917, Woodward, MCWR, 210–11.

17. War Cabinet (210 A), August 10, 1917, CAB 23/13; and Robertson to Allenby, August 10, 1917, WO 106/718.

18. Robertson to Allenby, August 10, 1917, Robertson MSS I/32/68.

19. Allenby to Robertson, August 26, 1917, Robertson MSS I/32/73/1.

20. This was a plan that Smuts had been advocating since July. See Smuts, "Suggested Programme for Paris Conference," July 8, 1917, W.P. 36, Curzon MSS Eur. F. 112/135.

21. Cabinet Committee on War Policy (17), September 24, 1917, CAB 27/6.

22. Cabinet Committee on War Policy (18), October 3, 1917, CAB 27/6.

23. Robertson to Haig, September 27, 1917, Woodward, MCWR, 229.

24. See Robertson to Haig, September 24, 1917, ibid., 226.

25. Hankey was sick, and minutes were not taken for the October 5 Cabinet Committee on War Policy. Diary entry of October 6, 1917, Hankey MSS 1/3; the position that Robertson took at this meeting was restated in his "Future Military Policy," October 9, 1917, WO 106/313.

26. Robertson to Allenby, October 5, 1917, WO 106/313.

27. Robertson to Maude, September 24, 1917, Woodward, MCWR, 227–28.

28. Repington, First World War, vol. 2, 116. Nor apparently did the general staff expect Falkenhayn to attack Allenby. See Robertson's comments in War Cabinet (238), September 24, 1917, CAB 23/4.

29. See "Summary of Intelligence," August 2 and September 5 and 6, 1917, WO 106/347. Macdonogh had also given the government figures indicating that Turkish reserves were exhausted. Lloyd George referred to these figures on October 3, 1917. Cabinet Committee on War Policy (18), October 3, 1917, CAB 27/6.

30. Robertson, "Plan for a Campaign in Syria," February 22, 1917, WO 106/311. See also Falls, Armageddon, 3, 14.

31. Robertson to Allenby, October 5, 1917, Woodward, MCWR, 232.

32. Both quotes are from Robertson to Haig, October 9, 1917, Woodward, MCWR, 234–35.

33. Robertson, "Occupation of Jaffa-Jerusalem Line," October 9, 1917, WO 106/313.

34. Allenby to Robertson, October 9, 1917, WO 106/313.

35. Cyril Falls, The Great War (New York, 1961), 326; and Allenby to Robertson, October 19, 1917, WO 106/718.

36. Author's italics. Allenby to Robertson, December 7, 1917, Woodward, MCWR, 262.

37. War Cabinet (274), November 15, 1917, CAB 23/4. See also Lord Milner's comments during Cabinet Committee on War Policy (21), October 11, 1918, CAB 27/6.

38. See Macdonogh, "Note by D.M.I.," November 17, 1917, WO 106/1516.

39. Cabinet Committee on Man-Power (1), December 10, 1917, Macdonogh MSS, CAB 27/14.

40. Lloyd George to Robertson, December 11, 1917, Lloyd George MSS F/44/3/38.

41. Robertson to Allenby, December 14, 1917, WO 106/718.

42. Derby to Lloyd George, December 11, 1917, Lloyd George MSS F/14/4/83.

43. War Cabinet (296), December 12, 1917, CAB 23/4.

44. Ibid.

45. Robertson to Hankey, December 14, 1917, WO 106/313.

46. See Woodward, *Lloyd George and the Generals*, 199.

47. Diary entry of September 16, 1917, Hankey MSS 1/3.

48. Memoranda by Wilson and French, October 20, 1917, W.P. 60 and 61, CAB 27/8.

49. See Robertson, "Future Operations in Palestine." The Allenby-Robertson correspondence during the last half of December can be found in the appendix to this memorandum. Cabinet Paper G.T. 3122 of December 26, 1917, CAB 24/37.

50. Amery to Lloyd George, December 30, 1917, Lloyd George MSS F/2/1/10.

51. Amery to Lloyd George, January 12, 1918, Lloyd George MSS F/2/1/11.

52. See, for example, Wilson to Lloyd George (Joint Note 12 enclosed), January 20, 1918, Lloyd George MSS F/47/7/9.

53. Diary entry of January 16, 1918, Wilson MSS.

54. Amery to Lloyd George, December 29, 1917, Lloyd George MSS F/2/1/9.

55. Diary entry of February 9, 1918, Maurice MSS 4/3.

56. "Joint Note to the Supreme War Council by Its Military Representatives. 1918 Campaign," January 25, 1918, and "Comments by the General Staff upon Joint Note No. 12 to the Supreme War Council by its Military Representatives," January 25, 1918, WO 106/314.

57. Robertson to War Office, January 25, 1918, WO 106/314; diary entry of January 28, 1918, Wilson MSS; and Robertson to Haig, January 24, 1918, Woodward, MCWR, 274.

58. War Cabinet (332), January 28, 1918, CAB 23/5.

59. Repington, *First World War*, vol. 2, 247; and Robertson to Derby, February 2, 1918, Woodward, MCWR, 280.

60. Supreme War Council, February 1, 1918, CAB 28/3/I.C.-41.

61. Robertson to Allenby, February 2, 1918; Woodward, MCWR, 281–82.

62. "General Kirke's typescript memoirs, with manuscript amendments and additions, probably written in the late 1940's." Kirke MSS WMK 13.

63. Robertson to Allenby, December 14, 1917, WO 106/718.

64. Robertson to Allenby, February 2, 1918, Woodward, *MCWR*, 281–82; diary entry of March 2, 1918, Hankey MSS 1/3; "Palestine and Mesopotamia. Future Military Policy" included in Smuts to Wilson, Cabinet Paper G.T. 3648 of February 15, 1918, CAB 24/42; and comments by Smuts in War Cabinet (358 A), March 4, 1918, CAB 23/13.

65. War Cabinet (360 A), March 6, 1918, CAB 23/13.

66. Barker, *Neglected War*, 435.

67. Maurice to Lynden-Bell, December 13, 1917, Lynden-Bell MSS, vol II.

68. See Stamfordham memorandum on Robertson's removal from office, February 16, 1918, RA Geo. V F. 1259/32.

69. Imperial War Cabinet (18), June 18, 1918, CAB 23/43.

70. Wilson, "British Military Policy 1918–1919," July 25, 1918, CAB 25/85; diary entry of July 30, 1918, Hankey MSS 1/5.

Chapter 10

The Strategical Nadir

British success in the imperial theater boosted morale on the home front and blunted the Turko-German threat, but it couldn't compensate for the widening cracks appearing in the anti-German coalition. Russia, with its army demoralized, was not revived by the overthrow of the Romanovs. The Bolsheviks, committed to "peace," seized power in November. Although it was by no means certain that Lenin's regime could survive, Robertson told the War Cabinet that his intelligence sources made it "quite clear that, whatever happened politically in Russia, the bulk of the Russian army refused to continue the war."[1] Russia's subsequent defection gave relief to the Central Powers, undermined the Allied blockade, and threatened Britain's Asian flank.

Italy's ability to fight on was also in doubt. Reinforced by the six divisions of the German strategic reserve (employed earlier on the Russian front), the Austrians in late October attacked the Italian Second Army's front near Caporetto. On the third day of the Austro-German assault, October 26, a rout was in progress. British observers reported nightmarish scenes of roads and mountain paths clogged with vehicles, soldiers, and civilians in full flight. In the background supplies burned and ammunition dumps exploded. "The real cause of the trouble was the determination of a portion of the troops to leave the field. . . . It was not a question of troops fighting moderately well, but of their fighting at all,"[2] General Radcliffe reported. Anglo-French reinforcements rushed across the Alps, but Robertson, having made a personal inspection of the Italian front, feared the worst. "Italy now appears to be in a position somewhat similar to that of Russia in 1915," he informed the War Cabinet. "She has suffered a great disaster, and the extent to which she will be able to recover from it is very doubtful."[3]

Recent news from France was fortunately more hopeful. Clemenceau became premier on November 16 following the fourth political shakeup of 1917. There was no defeatism in "the Tiger." When asked in Parliament about his war policy, Clemenceau simply stated: "I make war!" The French army also showed signs of recovering with an offensive on the Aisne. Although he believed that the French "can still fight well," Robertson feared that their depleted reserves might "render a sustained offensive in 1918 difficult if not impossible."[4]

With the strain of a prolonged and exhausting war being felt in every quarter, the War Cabinet anxiously pondered Britain's next move. The War Cabinet was scheduled to discuss war policy on November 26; Hankey woke at 6 A.M. on the 24th with a "brain wave," analyzing the changed strategical geography by candlelight. He accepted Robertson's dictum that the western front was the decisive theater, but "with no reasonable prospect" of a "decisive" Allied superiority in the west in 1918, he opposed British operations that would reduce Britain to "an exhausted nation" at any peace conference. On the other hand, he thought that few of the belligerents would last until 1919. "Russia has collapsed under the strain; Italy is near collapse; France's arms are held up until the hour of sunset by Britain and America; Austria and Turkey are exhausted. Germany, Great Britain, and the U.S.A. are still stalwart. The contest has become one of endurance, and on the whole the balance of advantage lies with us, provided we do not deliberately exhaust ourselves prematurely."[5]

Lloyd George had already made up his mind about Allied chances in 1918, betting Derby one hundred cigars that victory would not come until 1919. He told Hankey on November 23 that he was ready "to risk his whole political reputation, if necessary, in order to stop these bloody attacks of the Somme, Flanders type."[6] Robertson was well aware of the prime minister's mood for he had been told that "very serious trouble was brewing" for him "unless he could see his way to drop the idea that the only way to win the war was by hammering away at the same spot on the western front."[7] Although he hoped to maintain pressure on Germany, Robertson was as eager as Lloyd George to avoid another Somme or Passchendaele, and he favored adjusting the BEF's operations to the existing balance of forces. "The only practicable thing to do is to make ready to the full extent of our power by the early Spring," he advised the War Cabinet, "and then decide to what extent we should fight."[8]

Wully regretted that he had not followed his instincts and ordered Haig to halt his offensive. When some of the BEF's divisions (five in all) were diverted to the Italian front following the Caporetto disaster, Haig had no choice but to suspend his operations, the results of which he admitted to Robertson were extremely disappointing from a strategical perspective. His advance had fallen short of what he hoped "to secure before the winter cessation of active operations," he wrote. "Our present position about PASSCHENDAELE, and between that place and the YPRES-STADEN Railway may be difficult and costly to hold if seriously attacked."[9]

Unable to rupture the German line, Haig justified the continuation of his offensive by its "wearing out" effect. The War Office, however, was skeptical of GHQ's inflated estimates of German exhaustion. On October 8, for example, Haig asserted that out of the 147 German divisions on the western front "135 have been driven from their positions or withdrawn broken by their losses since the 1st April 1917—many of them twice and some three times." Robertson circulated to a disbelieving War Cabinet this appreciation, which included Haig's claim that the German army could be defeated in 1918 even if Russia made a separate peace.[10] But Wully cautioned Haig: "Numbers and morale are largely matters of guess work and opinion." German morale could "best be estimated, I suggest, by what takes place in battle, and, so far as I am in a position to judge, it would seem to be a denial of the well-known efficiency of our own troops to say that the enemy troops do not continue, as a whole, to fight well, although there may be and are exceptions to this."[11] Haig was unmoved and rejected the notion that he was being misled by Charteris. "My judgment is not formed on the information collected by him alone," he wrote Derby, "but on the views of commanders under me, who are in close daily touch with the troops and the situation on the battle fronts, and on my own experience of the German forces from the commencement of the war until now."[12]

That plenty of fight was left in the Germans was about to be dramatically demonstrated. In great secrecy, Haig had prepared a new thrust southwest of Cambrai by the Third Army. On November 20 surprise obtained by an unregistered (or no preliminary ranging fire) bombardment and the employment of some four hundred tanks enabled the British to penetrate the three main German defensive systems by nightfall. When his cavalry didn't follow up this stunning success, Haig was dismayed. "The object of the operations of the Infantry aided by Tanks is to break through the enemy's defences by surprise and so to permit the Cavalry Corps to pass through and operate in open country,"[13] he told his commanders on the eve of the attack. When an investigation revealed that the cavalry officers were in no mood for Light Brigade heroics, Haig minuted the document: "They must be blind," and added, "they [cavalry officers] fail to realise that the horse is our weapon, that we can do anything if we use it, and that the German is the feeblest of foes if pushed. . . . Risks must never be considered & the objective must be obtained no matter what the losses are."[14]

The 1916–18 version of the tank, because of its unreliability, limited life span, and snail-like battlefield speed, wasn't capable of converting a break-in into a breakthrough.[15] The cavalry represented a more mobile force, and Haig saw it as a means to maintain the momentum of his attack. But horse soldiers failed to demonstrate that they had an offensive role on the western front in 1917; it was Haig who seems "blind" on this point.[16]

Unable to sustain their offensive, British troops found themselves in a dangerous salient some six miles deep and seven miles wide. On November 30 the Germans counterattacked. The church "joy bells" that had earlier celebrated the BEF's advance were replaced by near panic in Parliament when Sir John French's military secretary reported that "the situation in France was worse than it had been at the end of 1914."[17] Although the British line stabilized, the Germans succeeded in capturing more territory than they had originally lost.

Given the precarious Allied military situation, a sharper edge began to characterize Robertson's relations with Haig. The field marshal believed that Robertson was violating correct principles of war by diverting divisions to rescue Italy. He emphasized the importance of capturing the Belgian coast and told Robertson "that nothing should be done to stop our offensive next Spring."[18] Robertson demurred and didn't resort to the familiar argument that Britain could best assist its Allies by applying pressure in the BEF's sector. As he later wrote Edmonds, "We could not disregard her [Italy's] shrieks for help, though we certainly cut down her requests a good deal. It would not have satisfied her, when the enemy was overrunning her country, to be told that we would help her by fighting in Flanders."[19]

Robertson believed that Haig was still the best commander available, but he had no confidence in the Scotsman's sycophantic staff. Lloyd George and the civilians were sharpening their knives, and the press was becoming restless. "There is the memory of a dead man or the knowledge of a missing or wounded man in every house. Outside the War Office I doubt whether the Higher Command has any supporters whatever," Lord Northcliffe wrote Philip Sassoon, Haig's private secretary.[20] On December 12, the *Times* demanded an inquiry into the Cambrai disaster and "the prompt removal of every blunderer." In addition to blunting public criticism, Robertson hoped to save Haig from himself by surrounding him with better men. The War Office's purge list included Charteris, Kiggell, Lieutenant-General R. C. Maxwell, the quartermaster-general, and Lieutenant-General G. H. Fowke, the adjutant-general.[21]

On December 15 Robertson crossed the Channel for a delicate meeting with Haig. In his pocket he carried a letter from Derby demanding staff changes. If Haig balked, Robertson planned to use this letter as a direct order from the secretary of state for war.[22] Whether Robertson resorted to a direct order is not known, but Haig generally gave way, with Fowke being the only survivor of the shake-up.

Robertson wanted Maxwell's head because he was "not up to the job & is not helping us with man power."[23] As manpower drove a wedge between the civilians and the army, so also did it divide the War Office and GHQ as the British assumed the brunt of the fighting on the western front. Haig was nettled by the failure of the government to replace his infantry losses, believing that the War Office as well as the civilians were to blame. Wully was equally disturbed by implications that he was retaining combat soldiers at home. His response was to cast a critical eye toward GHQ's deployment of its ration strength. On August 17, 1917, he suggested that Haig "immediately take steps to scrape up" infantry behind his front (some forty-one thousand were found from the administrative units) and emphasized that every possible man from the home service divisions was being sent across.[24]

With British casualties, including Dominion troops, surpassing eight hundred thousand on the western front in 1917, Britain's depleted manpower was uppermost on the minds of the civilians.[25] When another manpower committee, the fourth such committee, was created in December, Hankey succinctly described how the new committee's work differed from previous committees:

First: that the economic crisis, instead of being a danger to be guarded against, is actually present; and second: that the seriousness of the military man-power crisis is not merely that we shall not smash the enemy if the men are not forthcoming, but that the enemy may smash us. The problem that confronts the Committee, therefore, is to avert a military catastrophe without plunging us into an economic catastrophe equally fatal to the cause of the Allies.[26]

Although Robertson recognized the need to maintain Britain's industrial base, shipping, and farming, he argued that a rigid commitment to a defensive policy in the west might spell disaster. On October 26 he had written:

If by some miracle we could suddenly pass over the next 18 months and in 1919 resume the war under present conditions, plus the reinforcement in France of, say, a million well-trained American troops, there would be no question as to the best policy. But unfortunately we cannot perform miracles, and therefore we have to consider whether, all things considered, the Entente may not, despite American assistance, be much weaker, and not stronger, in 1919 than in 1918.[27]

These words were written prior to the Bolshevik seizure of power in Russia and the collapse of the Italian Second Army's front. As the strategical initiative passed to Ludendorff and Hindenburg, Robertson continued to reject committing "ourselves irretrievably to the defensive for the next 18 months." Although now at odds with Haig about continuing the Flanders offensive in 1918, Robertson knew that a commitment to a defensive policy in the west would encourage the War Cabinet to concentrate on the outlying theaters, especially Palestine. In a review of future military policy on November 19, he shrewdly noted: "We may prefer to avoid seeking a decision in 1918, but the enemy may, and we must assume that he will, try to force a decision upon us at a time and place most favourable to himself. For example, it is clear that if it would pay us to wait for the Americans and to defer our main effort till 1919, it would equally well pay the enemy to deprive us of the opportunity and try to get a decision in 1918." Robertson's conclusion was very much on the mark. "The Campaign of 1919 may never come, and in any case we shall next year inevitably have to bear the chief brunt of the war."[28]

The Army Council also tried to disabuse civilians of their belief that defensive warfare would reduce British casualties, noting that "there is nothing in the experience of this war or in any other to support the argument that a defensive policy necessarily entails fewer losses than an offensive policy, once fighting begins. . . . The adoption of a defensive policy does not justify making provision for a lower rate of wastage than that estimated by the War Office."[29] Several months later, when Germany began its massive assault on the British front to end the war, the BEF suffered 221,000 casualties from March 21 to April 15, surpassing British losses during any comparable period.

Lloyd George, however, didn't believe that Germany would make a supreme military effort in the west in 1918. If they did, he was confident that Hindenburg would have no more success than Haig and Nivelle had had in 1917. "By all means. Nothing [a German offensive in the west] would suit us better—but unfortunately he has learnt his lesson,"[30] he wrote on one of Robertson's memoranda. When the Army Council requested 615,000 recruits for the army to replace its anticipated losses, the government allocated only 150,000 category A troops (troops considered fit for combat).[31] The navy, air force, shipbuilding, food production, and even timber-felling were given a higher priority than the field forces.

On January 7, Haig unwittingly encouraged the civilians to believe that his front was secure. When he appeared before the War Cabinet, Bonar Law asked him: "If you were a German commander, would you think there was a sufficient chance of a smashing offensive to justify incurring the losses which would be entailed?"[32] The field marshal's reassuring response shocked Robertson who later gave the following explanation. With both the prime minister and the general staff opposed to a continuation of his Flanders offensive, Haig "had to try and convince the Prime Minister that the operations had resulted in serious loss to the enemy, while he also had to prove his need for men, the enemy still being very powerful."[33]

Prompted by Derby and Robertson, Haig immediately tried to correct the impression that he had made, this time on paper,[34] but the damage was done. Lloyd George was "convinced by the figures" that the British were "all right" in the west and nothing would "budge him."[35] When he read Haig's paper "to the Cabinet he contemptuously threw it on the table and asked what could be thought of a man who now expressed an opinion totally different from what he had told them two days before."[36]

A thorough examination of the government's manpower policy is beyond the scope of this study,[37] but it should be noted that the War Office's demand for over 600,000 new recruits was probably an impossible one. Faced with Germany's hammer blows from March to July 1918, the government did everything possible to replace Haig's losses, but only 372,330 category A recruits were found from January through November.[38]

Robertson was partially to blame for Haig's shortage in infantry. Had he stopped the Flanders offensive after it became obvious that its ambitious strategical objectives were unobtainable, there would have been no manpower crisis during the winter of 1917–1918. Moreover, Robertson's refusal to restrain Haig encouraged the civilian leaders to believe that if the army's demands for riflemen were met, there would be further Passchendaeles. Rather than exhaust British manpower, Lloyd George's government resorted to forcing Haig to reduce his divisions from twelve to nine (or thirteen to ten if the pioneer battalions are counted); cutting cavalry from five to three divisions; and emphasizing advanced weaponry, poison gas, tanks, planes, artillery and machine guns, rather than infantry shock tactics.

The ministers also had little faith in the War Office's figures and calculations.[39] Although many of the roughly one and a half million troops quartered in Britain were either underage or considered unfit for combat, the civilians thought that riflemen for Haig could be found from this source. Robertson apparently did not disagree. But, as he notes in his memoirs, "the responsibility for reducing it rested with the Army Council as a whole and not with the General Staff, as each department of the War Office trained men at home on services connected with its own special duties, and the General Staff could do nothing except try to bring about a reduction so as to set free more men for the battle-fronts."[40]

Another limitation for Robertson was plans made by the general staff and Admiralty in 1916 and approved by the government to thwart a German invasion. The Admiralty reckoned that 160,000 Germans might be landed before the navy could interrupt the amphibious assault. To defend the beaches, Sir John French, the commander in chief of the Home Forces, had a force at the beginning of 1917 of roughly 470,000 men divided into two categories: mobile troops (232,459), which included ten infantry divisions, and those assigned to coastal and antiaircraft defense (237,894).[41] By January 1918, the War Cabinet had reduced the Home Defence Forces to 400,979. The "mobile troops," diminished from ten to eight infantry divisions, consisted of 190,045 men, but 16,000 troops were stationed in rebellious Ireland and another approximately 50,000 were under nineteen years of age. With the threat of a German invasion being downgraded, Robertson favored breaking up four infantry divisions to release some 50,000 troops as reinforcements. He saw little savings in breaking up the remaining four infantry divisions "as practically the whole of the infantry in the remaining four would, under the new arrangement, consist of lads under nineteen years of age, who are not available for service abroad."[42]

On March 21, 1918, Haig was down some one hundred thousand infantry and responsible for defending a longer front because of an agreement to take over some of the French line. Who was ultimately responsible for not supplying him with reinforcements prior to the German assault? Was it Lloyd George? Robertson? Seeking an answer to this question, Edmonds in 1935 wrote Sir Robert Whigham, Robertson's Deputy CIGS. "Lloyd George tells me that this was nothing to do with him, that Robertson could have sent more men to France had he wished. On the other hand, Lloyd George claims that after the 21st March mishap, he personally ordered more troops to France. What is the truth?"[43]

If Whigham responded, his letter apparently has not survived. The postwar testimony of Colonel C. Allanson, a staff officer in the War Office in 1917–18, may provide a partial answer as to why Haig's depleted divisions were not strengthened by troops from the Home Defence Forces. Allanson claims that after Haig gave assurances that any German assault could be contained for eighteen days, the general staff recommended that available mobile reserves be retained in Britain to conceal them from German intelligence, "conserve the morale of the nation suffering from the effect of Passchendaele," and help the economy by having the troops spend their wages at home instead of in a foreign country.[44]

According to Allanson, Lloyd George suggested a fourth reason for keeping the mobile reserves in England: "I don't trust Haig with men."[45] Since becoming prime minister, Lloyd George had limited the army's intake of men through conscription. But this was not the same as withholding men already in uniform from Haig.[46] Robertson, who vigorously criticizes Lloyd George's position on conscription, never accuses him of denying Haig reinforcements from the pool of mobilized men in Britain.

Robertson and Lloyd George both apparently believed that retaining the mobile reserves in Britain didn't endanger the BEF. Nor apparently did Haig. Otherwise why would he have sent 88,000 troops home on leave on the eve of the German offensive? When the Germans ruptured the British front in March, the War Cabinet identified 212,000 men as immediate reinforcements, a body composed of 18,000 trained troops available as drafts up to April 20, the 88,000 home on leave, and 106,000 from the mobile reserves.[47]

A recent commentator on British strategy makes the acid comment: "In 1914 the British had intended to fight to the last Frenchman and the last Russian. By late 1917 they had nearly done so. But the Germans were still resisting and it seemed as if the General Staff were now willing to fight to the last Briton."[48] An alternative to the general staff's policy of relying on the BEF to "wear down" and eventually defeat the German army was a compromise peace. During the winter of 1917–18, there was renewed talk of peace in both Britain and the Central Powers. The *Daily Telegraph*'s publication of Lord Lansdowne's letter favoring a compromise peace created a sensation in London. Meanwhile, Count Ottokar Czernin, the spokesman for the Central Powers at the peace negotiations with Bolshevik Russia, appeared ready to accept the Bolshevik formula for a peace without annexations or indemnities. Lloyd George's response to these peace pressures was to soften British war aims in a much-publicized speech on January 5, 1918, designed in large part to convince the nation that the peace he espoused was worth fighting for, but also to weaken the resolve of the enemy peoples. He told the ministers that he wanted to go "to the extreme limit of concession" to demonstrate "to our people and to our Allies, as well as to the peoples of Austria, Turkey, and even Germany, that our object was not to destroy the enemy nations."[49] He even included a hint to Berlin that a negotiated peace with Berlin might be possible, with Germany gaining compensation from Russia for concessions to the western powers.[50]

Robertson had long urged a redefinition of war aims, especially on the part of Britain's allies, in order to detach countries such as Bulgaria and Turkey. But he remained hostile to peace negotiations unless Berlin was forced to renounce its bid to dominate Europe and become a global power. Dominant in southeastern Europe and with such countries as Courland, Lithuania, and Poland in its camp, German military autocracy would dominate the Continent. Overseas, with its colonies restored and in league with Turkey, Berlin could threaten the British in Asia and endanger imperial sea communications with submarine bases. "Peace would then find Germany in a stronger position than ever," he argued, "while the burden of the defence of the British Empire would become almost intolerable."[51]

With Berlin sensing victory and the War Cabinet agreeing with Robertson that a German peace would be intolerable, the war continued with no end in sight. Lloyd George hoped that the Americans could be convinced to do most of the fighting in 1919. In the meantime, he sought to bolster the British sector with Americans, either through amalgamating U.S. troops with British divisions or placing U.S. divisions under Haig's command.[52]

U.S. mobilization, however, proceeded at a snail's pace. After nine months of war, only 175,000 American soldiers were in France, most of them unprepared for combat. Prodded by Lloyd George, Robertson sought to persuade John J. Pershing, the commander in chief of the American Expeditionary Force, to place newly arriving U.S. regiments (or three battalions) with British divisions for training. (This, of course, would allow Haig to maintain twelve-battalion divisions.) Robertson, however, met his match in Pershing, who was determined to create an independent U.S. Army with its own front and strategic objectives. After frustrating and unsuccessful negotiations, Robertson reported to the War Cabinet: "America's power to help us to win the war—that is to help us to defeat the Germans in battle—is a very weak reed to lean upon at present, and will continue to be so for a very long time to come unless she follows up her words with actions much more practical and energetic than she has yet taken."[53]

One view is that Robertson's personality cost him his position as CIGS. According to the British official history:

His disability—in that he does not stand alone among great soldiers, who deal with crude force and not with rhetoric—lay in his lack of outward grace; the total absence of any power of persuasion, save a blunt and often rough statement of opinion; and a complete inability either to understand the minds of civilian statesmen, his masters, or to make clear to them what he considered the mere elements of sound strategy, with which every educated man, he thought, must be familiar.[54]

This is very much a distortion. Robertson had been chosen CIGS in large part to end the haphazard deployment of British military resources that had characterized the Kitchener era. Even after Lloyd George became prime minister, the ministers usually supported his steady and pragmatic approach over the Welshman's propensity to jump from one strategic expedient to another. The government's 1918 manpower policy, however, represented a decisive repudiation of Robertson's position that a British peace depended upon the BEF's playing the leading role in the western theater.

Hoping to avoid a public controversy because of the press and political support the high command enjoyed, Lloyd George sought to make Robertson irrelevant through the creation of an inter-Allied body to coordinate the Allied military effort in 1918. One can detect grudging admiration in Robertson's assessment of the prime minister's cunning: "The preparation of the ground, the division of opponents, the isolation of the victim, the swift changes of front which tended to obscure the main issue, and the handling of the Press, were all brought into play in the usual skilful manner."[55]

NOTES

1. War Cabinet (282), November 26, 1917, CAB 23/4.
2. *Military Operations: Italy, 1915–1919*, 56; and Cabinet Paper G.T. 2438 of October 27, 1917, CAB 24/30.
3. Robertson, "The Situation in Italy," November 14, 1917, WO 158/24.
4. Robertson, "Future Military Policy," November 19, 1917, WO 158/24.
5. Hankey, "FUTURE MILITARY POLICY," November 24, 1917, Hankey MSS, CAB 63/23.
6. Diary entry of November 23, 1917, Hankey MSS 1/3.
7. Roskill, *Hankey*, 449.
8. Robertson, "Future Military Policy," November 19, 1917, WO 158/24.
9. Haig to Robertson, November 15, 1917, WO 158/24.
10. Cabinet Paper G.T. 2243 of October 8, 1917, CAB 24/28.
11. Robertson to Haig, October 18, 1917, WO 158/24.
12. Haig to Derby, December 10, 1917, 920 Derby MSS (17).

13. Diary entry of November 13, 1917, Haig MSS No. 119.

14. "Private. 1st Cavalry Division. Cavalry Operations November 20–26th, 1917," n.d., Haig MSS No. 119.

15. It has recently been argued by Griffith, who emphasizes the weakness of the German defenses at the point of the attack (fewer than two enemy divisions with weak artillery support), that the "the success at Cambrai should not be attributed entirely, or perhaps even primarily, to the tank." Griffith, *Battle Tactics of Western Front*, 164–65. For a debunking of the role of the tank, see J. P. Harris, "The Rise of Armour," in *British Fighting Methods in the Great War*, ed. Paddy Griffith (London, 1996), 113–37.

16. For a revisionist view of the utility of cavalry on the western front, see Stephen Badsey, "Cavalry and the Development of Breakthrough Doctrine," in *British Fighting Methods in the Great War*, ed. Paddy Griffith (London, 1996), 138–74.

17. This was Sir Edward Carson's report to the War Cabinet, War Cabinet (292), December 5, 1917, CAB 23/4.

18. Diary entry of November 10, 1917, Haig MSS No. 119.

19. Robertson to Edmonds ["Observations on the First Seven Chapters of the 1918 Volume"], December 1, 1932, CAB 45/193.

20. Northcliffe to Sassoon, December 13, 1917, Northcliffe MSS, vol. VIII.

21. Derby to Haig, December 12, 1917, enclosed in Derby to Lloyd George, December 13, 1917, Lloyd George MSS F/14/4/85.

22. Ibid.

23. Robertson to Wilson, December 16, 1917, Woodword, MCWR, 268.

24. Robertson to Haig, August 17, 1917, Woodward, MCWR, 217–18.

25. These were the figures provided by Hankey. War Cabinet (300), December 17, 1917, CAB 23/4. See also Woodward, *Lloyd George and the Generals*, 174–75, 232–38.

26. Hankey, "Note by the Secretary," December 8, 1917, M.P.C.2, CAB 27/14.

27. Robertson to Hankey, October 26, 1917, WO 106/313.

28. Robertson, "Future Military Policy," November 19, 1917, WO 158/24.

29. Cabinet Paper G.T. 3265 of January 7, 1917, CAB 24/38.

30. "Extracts from Sir W. Robertson's Memo," November 19, 1917, Lloyd George MSS F/162/3.

31. The draft Report of the Man-Power Committee, dated January 7, recommended only 100,000 men. Following a protest by the Army Council, however, the final report of the committee, dated January 9, 1918, raised the number of new recruits to 150,000. This was exclusive of 120,000 young men already in uniform who would become nineteen and eligible to fight overseas and other combat soldiers who could be combed out from the home divisions. See Keith Grieves, *Politics of Manpower, 1914–18* (Manchester, 1988), 174; and Cabinet Paper G.T. 3265 of January 7, 1918, CAB 24/38.

32. War Cabinet (316 A), January 7, 1918, CAB 23/13.

33. Robertson to Edmonds ["Observations. . ."], December 1, 1932, CAB 45/193.

34. Cabinet Paper G.T. 3268 of January 8, 1918, CAB 24/38.

35. Amery to Wilson, January 12, 1918, Wilson MSS file 8.

36. Robertson to Edmonds ["Observations. . ."], December 1, 1932, CAB 45/193.

37. For a comprehensive account, see Grieves, *The Politics of Manpower*.

38. *Statistics of the Military Effort of the British Empire*, 371–74.

39. In Hankey's view, the War Office's figures and statements were "utterly unreliable, and their facts are twisted to support their arguments." Entry of December 6, 1917, Hankey MSS 1/3.

40. Robertson, *Private to Field-Marshal*, 343.

41. Robertson, "Number of Divisions Which Can Be Sent to France during the Next Few Months," January 29, 1917, WO 106/311.

42. Robertson, "Troops Required for Home Defence," January 3, 1918, WO 106/314.

43. Edmonds to Whigham, January 2, 1935, CAB 45/185.

44. "Talk with Colonel C. Allanson," August 19, 1937, Liddell Hart MSS 11/1937/69.

45. Ibid.

46. David R. Woodward, "Did Lloyd George Starve the British Army of Men Prior to the German Offensive of 21 March 1918?" *Historical Journal* 27 (March 1984):241–52.

47. War Cabinet (372), March 25, 1918, CAB 23/5. By May 5, 1918, Haig had received 133,092 reinforcements: 26,384 from March 27–31; 102,698 from April 1–30; and 4,010 from May 1–5. When the 88,000 on leave are added, the total sent out was 221,092. Entry of May 6, Haig MSS No. 127.

48. French, *Strategy of Lloyd George Coalition*, 184.

49. War Cabinet (312), January 3, 1918, CAB 23/5.

50. For an examination of Lloyd George's consideration of a separate peace with Germany at Russia's expense, see David R. Woodward, "David Lloyd George, a Negotiated Peace with Germany and the Kühlmann Peace Kite of September 1917," *Canadian Journal of History* 6 (March 1971):75–92.

51. Robertson, "The Present Military Situation, with Reference to the Peace Proposals by the Central Powers," December 29, 1917, WO 106/313.

52. See Woodward, *Trial by Friendship*, 130–48.

53. Robertson, "American Battalions for British Divisions," January 12, 1918, Lloyd George MSS F/163/4/1.

54. Sir James E. Edmonds and A. F. Becke, *Military Operations: France and Belgium, 1918* (London, 1935), vol. 1, 90.

55. Robertson to Edmonds ["Observations. . ."], December 1, 1932, CAB 45/193.

Chapter 11

Robertson's Downfall

Unity of command is an important maxim of warfare. Prior to 1918, Germany, as the dominant member of the Central Powers, enjoyed a measure of strategical unity and central direction that the Allies couldn't match. Divergent war aims, differing strategic perspectives, and national sentiment probably made the creation of an Allied supreme commander impossible until Germany was on the verge of winning the war in the spring of 1918.[1] Initially limited to the western front, the new generalissimo's authority was extended piecemeal. In May, during the fifth session of the Supreme War Council, Ferdinand Foch was allowed to coordinate military operations on the Italian front, and shortly before the Armistice, he gained the control of all operations against Germany, including a plan to invade Germany through Bavaria.[2]

Foch's appointment as generalissimo represented a clear improvement over earlier efforts to coordinate Anglo-French operations. The unity that previously existed was due to France's dominant military role. Joffre had assumed the role of de facto Allied commander, with British arms relegated to a supporting role. This didn't change until Nivelle's failure in the spring of 1917 made the BEF the dominant Allied army.

Foch played an important role in the Allied victories of 1918, but his control of operations should not be overstated. He was more of a persuader in chief than a commander in chief. Unlike Dwight Eisenhower, who had an Allied Joint Chiefs of Staff and a Supreme Headquarters Allied Expeditionary Force (SHAEF), Foch lacked the machinery for efficient inter-Allied military coordination. He could have (as the British suggested) relied on the PMRs at Versailles for his general staff, but instead he looked to his own staff officers. His essentially personal command fostered mistrust in London. When the BEF appeared endangered in May and July 1918 by his handling of reserves, the War Cabinet was prepared to challenge his authority. On July 11, the ministers instructed Lloyd George to remind Foch that he was "an Allied and not merely a French Commander-in-Chief, and that he must treat the Allied interests as a whole, making his dispositions on this basis and not mainly from the point of view of French interests."[3]

Foch was also hampered by divisions among the Allies about both the deployment of Allied resources and the peace to be obtained. With their Continental allies placing a low priority on the defense of the eastern realms of the British Empire, British and Dominion imperialists, desiring a strategical reserve, hesitated to commit their remaining resources to Foch's command. Sir Henry Wilson, an advocate of unity of command, accused the French in May of wanting to absorb "us, our Army, our Bases, our Merchant Marine, our Food, Italy, Salonica, etc."[4] What Allied politicians failed to reach a consensus on couldn't easily be delegated to an Allied generalissimo.

An unexpected consequence of the new unity of command was that Haig was shielded from civilian intervention during the BEF's nine successive victories over the German army from August 8 to November 11. Having marched under the banner of unity of command to destroy Robertson, Lloyd George discovered that the British civilians had less influence than before on military operations in the principal theater.

With some justification, Robertson has been pictured as being on the wrong side of the vital issue of unity of command. Lloyd George accuses him of having "a profound and disturbing suspicion of all foreigners,"[5] with his deepest distrust reserved for the French. France and Britain were allies for only the second time in history, and like many senior British officers Wully privately expressed contempt for many French practices. He, however, consistently argued that Anglo-French cooperation was essential to victory and played a key role in late 1915 in instigating the first of many conferences of Allied commanders and their chiefs of staff to plan future campaigns. His commitment to Anglo-French unity was put to a severe test when the French conspired with Lloyd George to place the BEF under Nivelle's command at the Calais Conference. Having protected Haig from some of the most objectionable elements of Nivelle's scheme, Robertson took the lead in restoring peace. He told Nivelle that "no two allies in any war have ever worked so well together as the French and the English," and assured the headstrong French commander in chief that his sole aim "is, as it has been throughout the war, to work to the best advantage with the French Army and its Commander-in-Chief."[6] After Nivelle's offensive failed, Robertson visited Pétain, took his hand, and "promised to tell him the truth and help him in every way." When informed that Pétain had been much affected by this gesture, he remarked, "Yes, I can do the right thing sometimes, can't I?"[7]

Pétain proved to be a more competent general than Nivelle, but his priorities (not unlike the British) were much influenced by national self-interest. While waiting for the Americans, he sought to limit French losses, leave most of the fighting to the British, and shift the focus of French military activity to Alsace-Lorraine, France's major war objective.[8]

The French, who hoped to retain their dominance of military policy in the west, found an accomplice in Lloyd George, who had a history of using the French and Italians to undermine his general staff's advice. When Foch in August 1917 lobbied for a central Allied body, Lloyd George talked with Painlevé about appointing a French supreme commander.[9] With Haig's offensive just getting underway in Flanders, however, the Welshman had to be content with laying the groundwork for unity of command at an inter-Allied conference meeting in London on August 7–8. "Had we really worked as one Government and one General Staff it was his belief that we should already have won the war," he asserted.[10]

Lloyd George's deviousness, of course, magnified Robertson's suspicions of his motives in advocating a "one front" approach. "Unfortunately," he wrote Haig on August 9,

Lloyd George has got the French with him as well as the Italians. Foch is hopeless. . . . As the French keep rubbing in that it is necessary to have a Central Staff at Paris, I can see Lloyd George in the future wanting to agree to some such organisation so as to put the matter in French hands and to take it out of mine. However, we shall see all about this. His game will be to put up (the useless) Foch against me as he did Nivelle against you in the Spring. He is a real bad 'un.[11]

Lloyd George found an ally in Sir Henry Wilson, who had recently resigned as head of the British mission at French headquarters. Glib, irreverent, and amusing, Wilson was temperamentally better suited than Wully to get along with Lloyd George. Once when Lloyd George, Wilson, and a British admiral were examining an involved marine chart, the admiral noted that they had it upside down. "That's how the Prime Minister likes it," remarked Wilson, to Lloyd George's great amusement.

A brilliant advocate, especially when his self-interest was involved, Wilson told his political masters what they wanted to hear. At a country house in Sussex on August 23, the lanky Irishman lobbied the prime minister to create a committee of the British, Italian, and French premiers and three soldiers "to be over all C.I.G.S. & to draw up plans for the whole theatre from Nieuport to Baghdad." It went without saying, of course, that Wilson saw himself as the Welshman's "soldier" on the proposed committee. On behalf of Lloyd George, Wilson subsequently lobbied members of the War Cabinet for such an inter-Allied body.[12]

Believing that the time wasn't right for a rupture with the high command, Lloyd George held his hand for the moment. The French also required delicate handling. On September 25, at a meeting at Boulogne, Lloyd George privately discussed with Painlevé a two-step plan that promised eventually to make Foch supreme commander. First, an inter-Allied body with its own general staff would be established, with Sir Henry Wilson as the British military representative. After the British public became accustomed to the concept of unity of command, Foch could be selected as generalissimo.[13]

Three weeks later, at a Sunday morning gathering with Hankey, Smuts, Balfour, Foch, and Henri Franklin-Bouillon, the French minister of propaganda, Lloyd George raised the question of an inter-Allied council and general staff. Hankey, who had a good sense of what was politically possible, was stupefied. "Why is he so blind sometimes?," he recorded in his diary. Franklin-Bouillon was unrestrained in his enthusiasm, wanting to establish an inter-Allied general staff within the week. Lloyd George, however, refused to act so precipitously, explaining that he was not making a formal proposal, only seeking to discover how the French would react to such a suggestion.[14]

Robertson had just warned the ministers that the principal of "unity of command" must be "cautiously applied," reminding the ministers of the Nivelle fiasco and the dispatch of heavy guns to Italy whereupon Cadorna abandoned his offensive. Rather than magnify the influence of her allies, Robertson wanted Britain to dominate next year's operations, "as we are entitled to do by our successes this year, the efficiency and spirit of our Armies, and the stability of our Government as compared with that of practically all our European Allies."[15]

Lloyd George's maneuvers to wrest control of the war from Robertson and Haig are pictured in a very bad light by Hankey, who accuses him of allowing the Flanders operations to continue, "knowing that the bad weather was preventing a big success," in order to strengthen his arguments against a continuation of the offensive in 1918.[16] Meanwhile, Lloyd George in October went over Robertson's head, seeking the professional advice of Wilson and Sir John French.

When the War Cabinet agreed to include Wilson and French in an extraordinary war council, compared by Lloyd George to the one that had decided to commit the BEF to the Continental war in August 1914, Robertson was enraged.[17] "It is a very weak-kneed craven-hearted Cabinet," he wrote Haig, "and L. G. hypnotises them and is allowed to run riot."[18] Robertson feared the worst when he and Haig were brought before Lloyd George's rigged jury. This showdown never occurred. Haig was unable to come to London, and Derby stressed that Robertson was still the constitutional strategical adviser to the War Cabinet. The War Cabinet accepted Derby's point, and Wilson and French set to work preparing memoranda for the CIGS's perusal. Wilson went so far as to involve the prime minister, rewriting his paper according to the Welshman's strategic views.[19]

The finished appreciations, although they mirrored Lloyd George's views on delaying a war-winning offensive until 1919 and the necessity of greater Allied coordination, were not utilized to overrule the general staff. The crafty Welshman seized upon a better opportunity to undermine Robertson: the Caporetto disaster. As he told Hankey, he "meant to take advantage of the present position" to gain "control of the War."[20] His weapon of the moment was an inter-Allied general staff.

With Robertson dispatched to assess the Italian setback, Lloyd George told the War Cabinet that the practice of having periodic summit meetings had proven ineffective, for they represented "a 'tailoring' operation at which different plans were stitched together." As an alternative, he proposed an inter-Allied war council with its own general staff, not to give orders, but "to examine the military situation of the Allies and of ourselves as a whole." For obvious reasons, Lloyd George insisted that the inter-Allied general staff be independent of the national general staffs.[21] Robertson was given the choice of remaining CIGS or of becoming the British representative on the proposed inter-Allied general staff.[22] He apparently declined the latter position, for Wilson was chosen as the Allied staff officer when the War Cabinet accepted "in principle" Lloyd George's formula for Allied coordination of the war effort.[23]

On November 6–7, at Rapallo, Italy, the French, British, and Italian statesmen worked on the details of the Supreme War Council (SWC). Robertson was present, but he had been told by Hankey that Lloyd George had the War Cabinet's backing and "that it was useless for him to kick against it." The rugged north countryman uttered not a word, but he refused to be a party to its formal inauguration. He rose and walked out, stopping to tell Hankey, "I wash my hands of this business."[24]

The discussion that Robertson boycotted didn't bode particularly well for effective coordination of the Allied war effort. The Italians and the French, the latter with particular concerns in Salonika, wanted the SWC to limit its role to the western front. Major powers such as Japan and Russia were apparently not going to be included, and there was uncertainty about the U.S. role.[25] As constituted, the SWC was limited to the political leadership of France, Britain, and Italy. Meeting at least once a month, its mission was to "watch over the general conduct of the War" and coordinate "military action." Technical advice would come from the inter-Allied general staff.[26]

Although the premise behind the SWC was good, the devil was in the details, and Robertson had legitimate concerns. The creation of an inter-Allied general staff at Versailles without an inter-Allied commander was, in his words, "a misnomer."[27] The SWC, a committee of political leaders, was a civil rather than a military body and wasn't designed to plan and coordinate military operations. Moreover, Lloyd George's selection of Sir Henry Wilson and his insistence that the British PMR be independent of the War Office created a system of dual military advice, pitting the CIGS against Lloyd George's man at Versailles. Robertson argued that Wilson was in the position "of the man who can say, 'Heads I win, tails you lose.'" He bluntly wrote Wilson, "You have your responsibility, & I have mine, and more than you have because you are free of execution which I am not."[28]

Wilson, who resisted efforts by the Army Council to restrict his freedom of action, not very convincingly retorted that "duality of advice" was not a problem because "I give no advice—as Wilson. The advice put up by the Military Representatives is signed by the soldiers of four countries. It is not the individual advice of any one man."[29] Wilson's true motives were revealed when he became CIGS, because he immediately emasculated his successor at Versailles.

Lloyd George overplayed his hand by linking the new SWC to criticism of the British high command's conduct of the war. Having set in motion a press campaign against the general staff, he made one of the most controversial speeches of his premiership in Paris on November 12. Dramatic enemy successes in Italy and elsewhere were compared to the modest victories of the BEF. "When I look at the appalling casualty list, I sometimes wish it had not been necessary to win so many," he sarcastically exclaimed.[30]

When the prime minister returned to London the next day, he found his government in jeopardy. Unlike the earlier crisis over Haig's subordination to Nivelle, his differences with the general staff were being ventilated in public. Asquith rose in Parliament to cheers on both sides of the chamber to demand an explanation of the new SWC, especially its military staff; Austen Chamberlain and other conservatives threatened to withdraw their support; and the pro-Robertson press was unsparing in its criticism, with the *Daily News* accusing Lloyd George of trying to become a "military dictator." "HANDS OFF THE BRITISH ARMY!" demanded the *Star*. "THE GENESIS OF AN UNWORKABLE SCHEME. THE DISESTAB-LISHMENT OF THE GENERAL STAFF!" thundered the *Globe*.[31]

This violent reaction forced Lloyd George to retreat. He praised the generals in an exchange with Asquith in Parliament on November 19, and insisted that his motive in promoting the SWC was the "co-ordination" of Allied plans and that he had no intention of diminishing Robertson's powers.

Meanwhile, Lloyd George assured Derby that no proposals would be put before the SWC until "the War Cabinet has had it in front of them, and heard the opinion of the C.I.G.S. on the proposal." Robertson, he promised, would also attend all SWC meetings. Derby was satisfied, telling Haig that he had erected "a sufficient safeguard against any wild cat scheme."[32]

But Derby was no match for Lloyd George's cunning. Encouraged by his successful, though misleading, Parliamentary defense of his actions at Rapallo and Paris, Lloyd George remained determined to bypass Robertson in favor of Wilson. As it turned out, the other PMRs at Versailles didn't develop into independent military advisers. Foch, who had been prevented from being PMR because he was chief of the French general staff, appointed a loyal subordinate, General Maxime Weygand, to do his bidding. The Italian representative, Cadorna, in disgrace after Caporetto, had little standing. President Wilson, although he refused to select a permanent political representative for the SWC, appointed General Tasker H. Bliss, a former American chief of general staff, as the American PMR. But Bliss deferred to Pershing, who dominated the U.S. military role in Europe.

Despite his promise that Robertson would be allowed to vet the views of the PMRs, Lloyd George now took the position that "whether any particular matter is first mooted at the Council or at the War Cabinet is really an unimportant detail, so long as it is clear that the C.I.G.S. will have his say and the War Cabinet the final decision. In fact, if the C.I.G.S.

accompanies the Prime Minister to the meetings of the Council, he will have his say in both places, and the question of where a matter is initiated becomes immaterial."[33] The catch, of course, was that Lloyd George expected Robertson not to disagree with him publicly during meetings of the SWC. When Wully dared raise objections to a major British offensive in Palestine, Lloyd George was furious. Despite apologizing for confronting the prime minister in a meeting with Britain's allies, Robertson was apprehensive, writing Derby that Lloyd George probably contemplated "'taking action' against me before long."[34]

Robertson's contempt for Lloyd George's brainchild, the inter-Allied general staff at Versailles, was in no way lessened when it began its work in late November. "Wilson's large staff, with Milner, have been at Versailles all the week," he sarcastically observed, "opening their shop & waiting for customers! And no one taking any notice of them!"[35] That Wilson would be ignored was wishful thinking, for the Irishman was now, if not in name, the new CIGS. Amery was attached to his staff at Versailles to act as the personal representative of Lloyd George and Milner and liaison officer with the War Cabinet.[36] Lloyd George contemplated ending this charade in December by making Wilson CIGS, but Wilson advised the continuation of the policy of reducing Robertson "from the position of a master to that of a servant."[37]

Wilson pleased the War Cabinet with his apparent flexibility. "Wilson is going strong, & as full of ideas as an egg is full of meat. One may not always agree with him," Milner wrote Lloyd George from Paris, "but I always feel personally, that I get more help from him in considering any of our big war problems than from any other 'expert.'"[38]

When the prime minister questioned Versailles on Germany's next move, Wilson promised to give an answer after he got "inside the Boche mind."[39] He set his staff to work on war games, with some officers reversing their caps to assume the role of German strategists. The results were not impressive. Wilson got both the time and focus of the German offensive wrong when he finally submitted a report.[40] Robertson viewed these war games as an example of Nero fiddling while Rome burned, telling Wilson and his staff that "there was not much doubt as to what the enemy can do and may do, but there is a good deal of difficulty in providing the means we need to defeat the enemy, and that is the direction in which they should put their energies chiefly."[41]

As German troops massed on the western front, an effective means of quickly deploying Anglo-French reserves in the event of a German break-through became a military imperative. France might be expected to place its first priority on the defense of Paris, and the British were equally determined to protect their lifeline to Britain, the Channel ports. Faced with these differing strategic priorities, the PMRS at Versailles, with advisory powers only, would be of little use in dealing with a military catastrophe.

The obvious need for the central direction of Allied reserves encouraged the French to intensify their pressure for a supreme Allied commander. Alexandre Millerand, a former French minister of war, visited Esher, who reported the contents of his discussion to Lloyd George on December 12. Having just talked with Clemenceau, Millerand emphasized that "the enemy is not likely to permit us to 'wait for America.'" There was only one solution: "Joffre as Generalissimo." The SWC with its inter-Allied general staff was "a fifth wheel to a coach, and a further complication."[42] Meanwhile, General Eugéne Debeney, Pétain's chief of staff, approached Lieutenant-General Sidney Clive, the chief of the British mission at French general headquarters, with a plan for making Joffre generalissimo.[43]

Clive immediately left for London to talk with the British war leaders. Robertson "quite agreed with the logic of the idea, and with the general lines of the particular scheme. He even went so far as to say it would have his support on the understanding that its adoption will cause the disappearance of the Versailles body."[44] Robertson's general acceptance of a generalissimo was no doubt partly prompted by his distaste for the inter-Allied general staff at Versailles. Conversely, the War Cabinet, which had launched this flawed experiment in unity of command, would have difficulty in abandoning it. A further complication was that Lloyd George in Parliament had denied any interest in creating an Allied commander in chief.[45]

Alive to the many difficulties of creating a powerful French generalissimo, Clemenceau pushed a limited version, an Allied commander whose powers would be confined to directing "a joint reserve, composed of both French and British elements, for use at any point where the Germans made a big attack."[46] To make this system more palatable to the British high command, Maurice then asked the prime minister to consider appointing Robertson as Joffre's chief of staff. When consulted, Sir Henry Wilson responded: "No, believe me a Generalissimo is impossible, nor is such an appointment rendered more practicable by giving him a foreigner as Chief of the Staff. . . . I suggest that a Central Reserve be placed under Versailles." Amery was equally negative about Maurice's "absurd" proposal, viewing it as a desperate attempt by Robertson to salvage his position.[47]

The differences between the CIGS and the prime minister were now quite personal and damaged the higher direction of the war effort. If not for a campaign waged by the Northcliffe press against the general staff, Lloyd George probably would have gotten Wully out of the way by sending him to India as commander in chief.[48] On January 21, Lovat Fraser of the *Daily Mail* attacked "the ridiculous 'theory of attrition'" and accused the general staff of resorting to the "strategy of the Stone Age" in the west while in the east its operations were formulated "from the point of view of a sergeant-major." Britain was "being outmatched in brain power," Fraser concluded.

Lloyd George could have written Fraser's piece. With great bitterness he told Lord Stamfordham on January 22 that Robertson was "no strategist & had no experience in fighting, never commanded a battalion, knows nothing of the fighting of this war and yet comes to the War Cabinet with all the airs of a great general." It was his view that Robertson "never originated any strategic plan" and was "almost always wrong in his forecasts."[49]

Yet Lloyd George regretted Fraser's blast, especially under the imprimatur of the controversial Northcliffe, the most hated press lord in Britain. "I could have taken him [Northcliffe] out and shot him,"[50] he told Stamfordham, who recognized that the press attacks frustrated the Welshman's plan to change Britain's military leadership. The Unionist War Committee, which spoke for Conservative backbenchers, reacted angrily, suggesting that the country's confidence in the government depended on official condemnation of the intrigue against Robertson and other soldiers. Bonar Law, the leader of the House of Commons, subsequently condemned the press attacks.

A beleaguered Robertson believed that the press attacks were inspired by Lloyd George who now "hated him." "What a d____d disgraceful position for a Government to be in," he wrote Gwynne, "to have to resort to such vile and unmanly tactics to get rid of those they don't like!"[51] The divide between Robertson and Lloyd George was now unbridgeable. Even so devoted a friend as Maurice was on the verge of concluding that "either L. G. or Wully must go. They can't pull together & the conduct of the war suffers accordingly."[52]

Prior to the third session the SWC, Robertson tried unsuccessfully to work with Haig and Pétain to achieve a common Anglo-French military policy. He hoped to bypass Wilson and the other PMRs,[53] but he also wanted a general reserve to be used on the western front and in Italy. "No doubt you and Pétain have talked this over but I know nothing about it," he wrote Haig.[54]

The SWC had a chaotic beginning on January 30. Three sets of military advisers, the CIGSs, the PMRs, and the commanders in chief sat at the same table. "They all gave different advice," Hankey wrote his wife, "and the meeting got into a worse state of chaos than I have ever known in all my wide experience!"[55]

Control of the general reserve was one of several issues that divided Lloyd George and Robertson. Robertson, who wanted authority vested in the chiefs of the general staff, was opposed by Wilson who lobbied for Versailles having executive authority. When Foch proposed a board in Paris made up of the French and British chiefs of general staffs and generals representing Italy, America, and Belgium, Lloyd George demurred. With Wilson busily passing him notes across the table, he suggested that Robertson would be too preoccupied with his work in the War Office.[56]

Following the meeting, Wilson gave Lloyd George a new formula that eliminated any role by Robertson. Foch, who would replace Weygand, would chair a committee composed of the PMRs. Robertson immediately wrote the prime minister: "I do not quite see how a British Commander-in-Chief can be made, constitutionally, to obey the orders of an Allied body, or indeed of anyone except the Army Council and the Secretary of State for War—a Minister of the Crown. If the C.I.G.S. were made a member of the Versailles body, as is proposed in the case of General Foch, this difficulty could be more easily surmounted perhaps."[57]

Haig supported Robertson and demanded to know how a foreign general under the British constitution could order British troops around. Foch, however, accepted the new arrangement without a murmur. And why not? "It conferred upon him a considerable degree of control over the British armies without in any way impinging upon his control over the French armies,"[58] Robertson later wrote. Backed by the French and Italians, Lloyd George easily carried the day. The new body, known as the Executive War Board, had broad powers to determine the size of a general reserve for the western, Italian, and Balkan fronts. Orders to deploy this force went directly to the commanders in chief.

As the meeting broke up, Robertson sat "motionless, his head resting on his hand, glaring silently in front of him."[59] But it was not Robertson's nature to remain silent. He succinctly summarized his objections to the "Versailles Soviet" in a letter to Plumer: "It is impossible to have Chiefs of the General Staffs dealing with operations in all respects except reserves and to have people with no other responsibilities dealing with reserves and nothing else. In fact the decision is unsound, and [neither] do I see how it is to be worked either legally or constitutionally."[60]

Robertson also told Derby that "the Army, the Army Council, the C.I.G.S., and Commanders-in-Chief will look to you, their Minister, to see that they are not placed in an impossible, unfair, and unpractical position." Derby took up the cudgels, suggesting to the War Cabinet that in the event of a military disaster, he would have to tell Parliament that he had "abnegated all power and all responsibility and that that has been conferred on a Committee composed of a single representative from this country, not chosen by the Secretary of State, and over which a French General presides." An especially ominous note was sounded by the Secretary of State for War: "It is absolutely impossible for anybody in my position to accept such a situation. I am perfectly certain the Country would not accept it."[61]

That the country might have to decide between Robertson and Lloyd George became a real possibility when the press took up the issue. Repington, who now wrote for the *Morning Post* after being fired by Northcliffe, asserted that the prime minister had approved "a decision which deprives our Commander in France of his full command" and has "clearly and finally proved his incapacity to govern England in a great war. This is the situation which Parliament must clear up in such a manner it thinks best."[62] Robertson seemed to welcome a public confrontation, writing Gwynne: "The country always claims that the soldier should 'stand up' to the politician. I have stood up. What will the country do?"[63]

As yet another civil-military crisis loomed, Haig's position became critical to Robertson's survival. The enigmatic Scotsman had opposed unity of command, including the version that would have made Robertson Joffre's chief of staff. Yet after the creation of the Executive War Board, Esher found him "perfectly placid, having accepted the Versailles decisions without further ado."[64] He may have believed that he and Pétain could prevent the cumbersome Versailles machinery from interfering with their commands, and that the creation of a general reserve might require the transfer of British divisions from Italy, Salonika, and elsewhere to his front. Whatever his motives, he showed little inclination to become embroiled in a fight to save Robertson, whom he believed had compromised strategic principles that had hitherto served as their common bond. Wully had "not resolutely adhered to the policy of 'concentration on the Western front,'" he wrote his wife. "He has said that is his policy, but has allowed all kinds of resources to be diverted to distant theatres at the bidding of his political masters."[65]

Haig, however, couldn't keep his distance from the crisis brewing in London. Derby requested his presence in London and joined Robertson in asking for his views. His response was to take Robertson's position that a general reserve was "desirable" but that he didn't "concur in system set up for commanding it."[66]

With Robertson at Eastbourne recuperating from a severe attack of bronchitis, Haig arrived in London on February 9 and was driven from Victoria Station to Downing Street by Derby.[67] Having changed his mind several times, Lloyd George had another scheme up his sleeve. Why not, he artfully proposed, have Robertson and Wilson exchange positions? If Robertson refused, he told Milner, "he would put himself in the wrong and nobody would have any sympathy with him."[68] If he accepted, Lloyd George and Wilson would plot strategy in London while Robertson cooled his heels at Versailles.

Although Haig thought that the army would be "very shocked" by Wilson's appointment as CIGS, he made no difficulties.[69] Robertson's fate seemed sealed when Derby also accepted this arrangement. Informed of what had happened, Robertson rushed back from the coast. The government sought to buy him off with the promise of raising his salary from four thousand to five thousand pounds and providing him a house in Paris or Versailles.[70] Abandoned by many of his former allies, he nonetheless insisted that he would only go to Versailles as CIGS. "I imagine it means the end of my military career, after over 40 years' hardish work, and it lands me once more into poverty," he wrote Derby. "But these considerations must be ignored."[71]

With the press discussing his differences with the CIGS, Lloyd George's resolve began to waver. Derby also began to backtrack, although Haig, who believed that Robertson meant "to embarrass the Government" and lectured him on his "duty" to go to Versailles, did not.[72] Milner, who had had enough of both Robertson's obstinacy and the prime minister's gyrations, bluntly informed the Welshman, "We are on absolutely strong ground, & if there is to be a fight, wh. I don't feel sure of, we can win. But let us at least make sure that at the end of the fight we are free men & not still saddled with our Old Man of the Sea!"[73]

Although Milner threatened resignation over what he considered a question of who was in charge, the government or Robertson, Lloyd George wanted to assess Parliament's mood before acting decisively. On February 12 he had one of his worst days in Commons. Already agitated by the government's manipulation of the press, the MPs were in no mood for Lloyd George's rhetorical flourishes. Challenged by Asquith, the Welshman sought to escape discussing the specifics of the SWC's recent decisions on grounds of state secrecy. When Asquith rose to his feet, "a great storm of applauding cheers broke out, which went on with constant renewal for the space of a minute or two," reported the *Daily Telegraph*, which described the incident as "a violent personal demonstration against the Prime Minister."

Lloyd George concluded his speech with fighting words: If Parliament thought that another government could conduct the war better, "then it is their business, in God's name, to put that other Government in!" But he was clearly put on the defensive. The War Cabinet was divided, with Curzon threatening resignation if Robertson were removed, and Milner and George N. Barnes, who had replaced Henderson as the Labour representative in the War Cabinet, suggesting that they would go if he emerged triumphant. Another obstacle to sacking Robertson, as Lloyd George told Hankey, was that "all the world would say it was done at Northcliffe's dictation."[74]

With Robertson's fate still undecided, Derby revived a plan that had been discussed earlier: Make Wilson the CIGS's deputy when the CIGS wasn't available to sit on the Executive War Board. This satisfied the Army Council's constitutional questions, and Robertson immediately accepted. Lloyd George and Milner just as quickly rejected it because it preserved Robertson's position.

When Robertson was brought before the War Cabinet on February 14, he came right to the point. The real issue was not the Executive War Board's machinery. Rather, it was whether the War Cabinet wished to retain him as the government's strategical adviser. He then calmly talked about his concerns if the CIGS's powers were divided. Derby's most recent proposal solved this problem by allowing Robertson to use Wilson as his deputy if he were unable to attend a meeting of the Executive War Board. With Robertson speaking in favor of making the British PMR a deputy CIGS to overcome any constitutional or practical difficulties, Lloyd George saw an opening that he could exploit. Would Robertson, he wanted to know, agree to go to Versailles as deputy CIGS? Caught off guard, Wully asked for a moment to collect his thoughts. His answer, but Wilson was "only a temporary general," made him appear more interested in protecting his status than the army's.[75] Nonetheless, the War Cabinet gave him another chance to trade places with Wilson or stay on as CIGS without the special powers he had been granted when he took the office. What Milner called "the game of deliberation, negotiation, and reconsideration"[76] thus continued a little longer.

Robertson's refusal to budge an inch united the government against him. The prevailing sentiment, according to Milner, who had talked with Balfour and Bonar Law, was that "the Government could not afford to give in and that, if the Prime Minister decided to fight the matter out, we must all stand by him."[77]

The king had also been neutralized when Lloyd George took a firm stand. "If His Majesty insisted upon his (Sir W. R.) remaining in office on the terms he laid down the Government could not carry on," he said, "and the King would have to find other Ministers. The Government *must* govern, whereas this was practically military dictation."[78] Given one last chance to accept the government's terms, Robertson sent a letter of refusal.[79] Although he never officially resigned—a formality really because he had turned down his last chance to remain CIGS.

Robertson later told Repington that "he had found that he had more friends than he knew, but fewer on whom he could count than he expected. Everybody had told him to stand firm, but few, except Gwynne and I, had stood by him when he did so."[80] Robertson apparently expected Haig to stand with him. As the field marshal's protector, who had won far more battles with the civilians than he had lost, he pointedly warned him that the prime minister planned to argue in Parliament that Haig had no objections to the Versailles machinery. But Haig, when he talked with Lloyd George on February 17, made it clear that he wouldn't defend Robertson. "We discussed the whole position for hours," Lloyd George writes. "Haig put up no fight for Robertson.[81] And he shouldn't have, not when the issue was civilian supremacy. When Haig refused to accept Robertson as one of his army commanders, the government announced on February 18 that Wully had accepted the lackluster Eastern Command, one of the seven "commands" of the army in Great Britain.[82]

Lloyd George triumphed over Wully when he shifted their differences to a favorable battleground. Another CIGS could be found. But a new prime minister? If the choice were portrayed in this way, Robertson was certain to lose. Asquith was the obvious alternative to the Welshman, but as a headline in the *Daily Mail* put it, "WHICH WOULD YOU GO TIGER HUNTING WITH? ASQUITH OR LLOYD GEORGE?"

NOTES

1. What follows on Foch's position is largely taken from French, *Strategy of the Lloyd George Coalition*, 225–28, and Woodward, *Trial by Friendship*, 165, 185–205. See also Jehuda L. Wallach, *Uneasy Coalition: The Entente Experience in World War I* (Westport, Conn., 1993).

2. Woodward, *Lloyd George and the Generals*, 334, n. 111.

3. War Cabinet (444 A), July 11, 1918, CAB 23/14.

4. Woodward, *Trial by Friendship*, 165–66.

5. Lloyd George, *War Memoirs*, vol. 1, 467.

6. Robertson to Nivelle, March 13, 1917, Woodward, MCWR, 162–63.

7. Repington, *First World War*, vol. 1, 560.

8. Porch, "The French Army in the First World War," in Millett and Murray, *Military Effectiveness*, vol. 1, 201.

9. Paul Painlevé, *Comment J'ai Nommé Foch et Pétain* (Paris, 1923), 241.

10. Allied Conference, August 7–8, 1917, CAB 28/2/I.C.-25 (c).

11. Blake, *Papers of Haig*, 251.

12. Woodward, *Lloyd George and the Generals*, 195–96.

13. Painlevé, *Foch et Pétain*, 244–46.

14. Roskill, *Hankey*, 443; and "Secretary's notes of a conversation at Chequers Court on Sunday, October 14, 1917," CAB 28/I.C.-28.

15. Robertson, "Future Military Policy," October 9, 1917, WO 106/313.

16. Diary entry of October 21, 1917, Hankey MSS 1/3.

17. War Cabinet (247b), October 11, 1917, CAB 23/13.

18. Robertson to Haig, October 11, 1917, Woodward, MCWR, 236.

19. As it happened, French's criticism of Robertson and Haig was so violent that the War Cabinet read both memoranda before deciding what to do with them. French was persuaded to tone down his criticism. Hence the War Cabinet actually saw these memoranda before they were given to the CIGS. Derby to Lloyd George, October 12, 1917, Lloyd George MSS F/14/4/72; and Brock Millman, "Henry Wilson's Mischief: Field Marshal Sir Henry Wilson's Rise to Power, 1917–18" *Canadian Journal of History* 30 (December 1995): 483.

20. Diary entry of October 29, 1917, Hankey MSS 1/3.

21. War Cabinet (259 A), October 30, 1917, CAB 23/13.

22. Maurice to Delmé Radcliffe [following for Robertson], October 31, 1917, Woodward, MCWR, 249.

23. War Cabinet (263), November 2, 1917, CAB 23/4.

24. Hankey, *Supreme Command*, vol. 2, 720–21; and Lloyd George, *War Memoirs*, vol. 2, 1441.

25. PROCES-VERBAL OF A CONFERENCE OF THE BRITISH, FRENCH, AND ITALIAN GOVERNMENTS, HELD AT THE "NEW CASINO HOTEL," RAPALLO, ON WEDNESDAY, NOVEMBER 7, 1917, AT 11 A.M., I.C.-30 (c), CAB 28/2.

26. "Amended Draft Approved by British and French Governments," November 7, 1917, in Appendix of ibid.

27. Robertson to Derby, November 15, 1917, Woodward, MCWR, 252–53.

28. Robertson, *Soldiers and Statesmen*, vol. 1, 216; and Robertson to Wilson, December 6, 1917, Woodward, MCWR, 261.

29. Wilson to Robertson, December 10, 1917, Woodward, MCWR, 263–64.

30. *Times* (London), November 13, 1917.

31. Woodward, *Lloyd George and the Generals*, 225–26.

32. Derby to Lloyd George, November 18, 1917, Lloyd George MSS F/14/4/77; and Derby to Haig, November 26, 1917, 920 Derby MSS (17).

33. Italics are author's. Lloyd George to Derby, November 26, 1917, Lloyd George MSS F/14/4/80.

34. Robertson to Derby, February 2, 1918, Woodward, MCWR, 280.

35. Robertson to Maurice, November 30, 1917, Woodward, MCWR, 259.

36. L. S. Amery, *My Political Life*, vol. 1: *War and Peace, 1914–1929* (London, 1953), 129.

37. Diary entry of December 30, 1917, Wilson MSS.

38. Milner (Paris) to Lloyd George, December 23, 1917, Lloyd George MSS F/38/2/27.

39. Hankey to Lloyd George (Wilson to Hankey, December 27, 1917, enclosed), December 29, 1917, Lloyd George MSS F/23/1/37.

40. *Military Operations, France and Belgium, 1918*, vol. 1, 79–80.

41. Robertson to Haig, January 12, 1918, Woodward, MCWR, 270–71.

42. Esher to Lloyd George, December 12, 1917, Lloyd George MSS F/16/1/22.

43. There apparently exists no copy of the plan that Debeny gave Clive. Diary entry of December 10, 1917, Clive MSS, CAB 45/201.

44. Clive to Maurice, December 18, 1917, Maurice MSS 3/5/63; and entries of December 12–17, Clive MSS, CAB 45/201.

45. These concerns were expressed by Milner and Hankey when Clive talked with them. Diary entry of December 14, 1917, Clive MSS, CAB 45/201.

46. "Notes of a Conversation Held at the Quai d'Orsay," Paris, December 23, 1917, CAB 28/3/I.C.-37, and War Cabinet (306), December 26, 1917, CAB 23/4.

47. Diary entry of January 10, 1918, Maurice MSS 4/3; Wilson to Milner, January 14, 1918 [enclosed in Milner to Lloyd George, n.d.], Lloyd George MSS F/38/3/2; and Barnes and Nicholson, *Amery Diaries*, vol. 1, 199.

48. Diary entry of January 19, 1918, Hankey MSS 1/3.

49. Stamfordham, "Record of a Conversation with the Prime Minister," January 22, 1918, RA Geo. V F. 1259/4.

50. Ibid.

51. Robertson to Gwynne, January 22, 1918, Woodward, MCWR, 273–74; and Robertson's comment to Stamfordham in the latter's account of the crisis, February 13–18, 1918, RA Geo. V F. 1259/32.

52. Maurice to his wife, February 6, 1918, Maurice MSS 3/1/4.

53. Woodward, *Lloyd George and the Generals*, 253; and Robertson to Stamfordham, January 22, 1918, Woodward, MCWR, 273.

54. Robertson to Haig, January 21, 1918, Woodward, MCWR, 271–72.

55. Hankey to Lady Hankey, January 31, 1918, Hankey MSS 3/23.

56. Supreme War Council, February 1, 1918, CAB 28/3/I.C.-42.

57. Robertson to Lloyd George, February 1, 1918, Woodward, MCWR, 276.

58. Robertson, *Soldiers and Statesmen*, vol. 1, 231.

59. Peter E. Wright, *At the Supreme War Council* (London, 1921), 65.

60. Robertson to Plumer, February 4, 1918, Woodward, MCWR, 283.

61. Robertson to Derby, February 2, 1918, Woodward, MCWR, 281; and Derby, "Memorandum," February 4, 1918, 920 Derby MSS (17).

62. *Morning Post*, February 11, 1918.

63. Robertson to Gwynne, February 7, 1918, Woodward, MCWR, 287.

64. Esher to Milner, February 9, 1918, Milner MSS dep. 355.

65. Haig to his wife, February 5, 1918, Haig MSS No. 149.

66. Haig to Derby, February 8, 1918, 920 Derby MSS (17).

67. The following account of the crisis draws extensively on the author's day-by-day account in *Lloyd George and the Generals*, 262–75.

68. Milner's account of the crisis, misdated February 14, 1918, Milner MSS, dep. 374.

69. Lloyd George to Milner, February 9, 1918, Lloyd George MSS F/38/3/11.

70. Gwynne to Asquith, February 11, 1918, K. Wilson, *Rasp of War*, 243–44; Maurice to Edmonds, November 29, 1932, CAB 45/193.

71. Robertson to Derby, February 11, 1918, 920 Derby MSS (17).

72. Diary entry of February 11, 1918, Haig MSS No. 123.

73. Milner to Lloyd George, February 11, 1918, Lloyd George MSS F/38/3/12.

74. Diary entry of February 13, 1918, Hankey MSS 1/3.

75. "Statement by Sir William Robertson," War Cabinet (345 A), February 14, 1918, CAB 23/13.

76. Derby, "Memorandum," February 4, 1918, 920 Derby MSS (17).

77. Ibid.

78. Stamfordham's account of the crisis, February 13–18, 1918, RA Geo. V F.1259/32.

79. Robertson to Lloyd George, February 16, 1918, Woodward, MCWR, 304.

80. Repington, *First World War*, vol. 2, 246.

81. Lloyd George, *War Memoirs*, vol. 2, 1689. Haig did, however, resist being used to justify Robertson's removal. Lloyd George was permitted only to say that Haig would "work under it" [Versailles machinery] but not that it was "workable." Davidson to Hankey, February 18, 1918, Bonar Law MSS 84/7/3.

82. J. M. McEwen, ed., *The Riddell Diaries 1908–1923* (London, 1986), 218.

Epilogue

Before vacating the War Office on February 18, Wully wrote touching notes to the three officers closest to him: Maurice, Macdonogh, and Whigram. He thanked them for their loyalty and concluded with a typical admonition: "Now get on with the war."[1]

Approximately five weeks after Robertson's fall, the British confronted their greatest crisis of the war.[2] The German high command, as Robertson had predicted, staked everything on a battle of annihilation against the French and British before the Americans arrived in force. By March 21, 192 German divisions (with more on the way) faced 98 French, 57 British, and a handful of Belgian and Portuguese divisions. When the four double-strength U.S. divisions ready for deployment were added, the anti-German alignment could count on 169 divisions.[3] But the Americans had no tanks, planes, or artillery; the British divisions were understrength; and the French lacked reserves.

A proper coordination of Allied defenses had been undermined by civil-military strife. Lloyd George's cunning and his determination to undermine Robertson at almost any price led to the creation of the controversial Executive War Board, which never really functioned.[4] Foch commanded a phantom army when Haig and Pétain refused to place any of their divisions under his command. To salvage the principle of a general reserve, the politicians gave Foch control over the British and French divisions in Italy, but this was an empty gesture. When the German offensive began on March 21, General Sir Charles J. Sackville-West, Wilson's friend in the British section at Versailles, exclaimed: "The Executive War Board is dead, dead as a doornail."[5] In its place was a personal understanding between Haig and Pétain, and it was by no means certain that either commander would weaken his front to help the other.

The German blow fell on the part of the British front defended by the British Third and Fifth armies. German superiority in numbers was overwhelming: some 750,000 against 300,000. The Fifth Army, which had just occupied French trenches in a bad state of repair and had to defend a forty-two-mile front with only twelve infantry and three cavalry divisions, bore the brunt of the attack. With its defenses breached in two places and unable to plug the gaps, the Fifth Army began to break up. In one day the Germans captured as much territory as the British had in 140 days of fighting on the Somme in 1916.[6]

The magnitude of the British defeat was apparent in London on March 23, when the deputy director of military operations on the general staff, Kirke, arrived by plane from GHQ and told the anxious War Cabinet that the British had been thrown back twelve miles, suffered heavy casualties, and lost as many as six hundred guns. News from the front only got worse. Wilson reported on March 27 that Gough's retreating force could "no longer be regarded as a fighting unit." He even questioned whether any of the corps in this army retained their cohesion.[7] Before the German offensive was halted at the key rail center of Amiens on April 4–5, the Germans inflicted upon the British 160,000 casualties, including 90,000 taken prisoner.

The Fifth Army's destruction, the greatest British defeat of the war, put paid to the War Cabinet's manpower policy, which was designed to limit British losses and preserve the country's staying power. If the BEF survived the present crisis, Milner bluntly informed Lloyd George, "it is simply deluding ourselves to think that the Germans... will not continue to press us for all they are worth. They are certain to keep on pushing, &, if they do not break us now, they will break us later, unless we can keep on sending substantial reinforcements."[8]

That Haig's divisions were understrength may not have been the critical factor in the stunning British defeat. There was blame to be assigned as well to the British high command. This did not, however, stop Haig from looking in Whitehall's direction and proclaiming that the BEF was the victim of an "Organizer of Defeat."[9]

This was also the view of Robertson's supporters. When Wully had been forced out, Leo Maxse's National Review issued a blunt warning: "Those who have at last succeeded in getting rid of Sir William Robertson must at least have the courage of their opinions. They will assuredly be held responsible for anything that goes wrong."[10] On April 8–9, some London newspapers began to do exactly that: blame the government for the British defeat. Repington in the *Morning Post* (April 8, 1918) demanded answers. "Why have the reiterated demands of the Army for men remained unanswered? Who but Mr. Lloyd George is responsible for the failure to supply the Army's needs?" The *Daily News* (April 9, 1918) emphasized Lloyd George's differences with the general staff, especially over peripheral operations, and asked if it were "a coincidence that it [destruction of the Fifth Army] occurred immediately after Sir William Robertson's dismissal because of a disagreement between him and Mr. Lloyd George on military policies." The *Star* (April 8, 1918) suggested that Parliament bring back Robertson as secretary of state for war.

Lloyd George immediately responded to the deadly charge that he had let the army down. Repington had facetiously suggested that the government "stand in white sheets when they face the Parliament," and Lloyd George was in a combative mood. Attempting to silence his critics, he made two statements that he would later regret: The BEF was stronger in January 1918 than it had been in January 1917, and Allenby had only three "white" infantry divisions under his command. The latter statement was clearly wrong (Allenby commanded seven infantry divisions on March 21, which included few native troops) and the former statement was misleading. Haig's ration strength (which included noncombatants such as labor battalions) was greater in January 1918, but this did not answer the charge that Haig was down in infantry.

Lloyd George went out of his way to praise Robertson's successor. Not surprisingly he failed to mention that Wilson originally informed the War Cabinet that the March 21 attack "might only develop into a big raid or demonstration." As the Fifth Army's defenses were being breached, the War Cabinet under Wilson's strategic guidance had focused on Germany's potential threat to Asia.[11] What Lloyd George did say was untrue. Calling it "one of the most remarkable forecasts of enemy intentions that has ever been made," he claimed that Wilson had predicted exactly where and when the Germans would attack.

Lloyd George's speech didn't silence his press critics. The *Star* on April 10 questioned the consequences of Lloyd George's efforts at "coordinating" Allied war policy. The Fifth Army, it asserted, "was asked to hold a bad front with a thin line of depleted divisions. Who is responsible? The War Cabinet, surely, which set Versailles and its nondescript strategists over Haig and Robertson and their staffs." The *Morning Post*, with its intimate connections with the War Office, remained the government's most dangerous opponent. On April 17, Repington accused Lloyd George of mis-representing the number of white divisions under Allenby's command, and Gwynne attacked his use of "fancy figures." "For our part," he asserted, "we believe it to be true from all we can gather of the position that our soldiers are facing a substantial superiority, both in men and guns, on the western front."

The *Globe* wanted Robertson's influence over strategy restored. "There is no member of the War Cabinet who is indispensable, no, not even our revered Premier himself. Sir William Robertson is."[12] Confronted with headlines such as the *Morning Post*'s "BRING ROBERTSON BACK,"[13] Lloyd George seized upon Haig's suggestion that Wully be sent to France as his second in command. Robertson, however, refused, writing Haig that "my job is C.I.G.S. or nothing."[14] Repington, in close touch with Robertson, then chimed in. "Every endeavour to get rid of Robertson by sending him abroad the public may regard as a pretext for getting him out of the way of the imbeciles who are trying to conduct war in London."[15]

With questions being raised in Parliament and the *Morning Post* arguing that with "LLOYD GEORGE as Prime Minister the country cannot win the war,"[16] the Welshman not unnaturally suspected a military conspiracy. In opposition to Lloyd George's statement to Parliament on March 20 that the Allies had a slight superiority in riflemen on the western front, the general staff in its weekly summary on April 18 gave the Germans, who continued to transfer divisions to the west, a superiority of some 333,000 infantry.[17] Lloyd George saw the new estimates as "part of Robertson's campaign,"[18] and fired off an angry letter to Lord Derby. "From any point of view this document is extraordinarily slipshod," he wrote, "and I suggest that a thorough investigation be made as to how it came to be prepared and who is responsible for editing and issuing it."[19]

An internal investigation in the War Office subsequently lowered Allied inferiority in rifle strength to 262,000. Emphasis on infantry, of course, ignored Allied superiority in cavalry and the strengthening of the BEF in areas such as artillerymen, tankers, pilots, and machine gunners. But the fact remained that Germany now enjoyed an advantage in infantry and (as Wilson told the War Cabinet) was employing approximately 75 percent of its divisions against the BEF.[20]

The bickering over numbers and the role played by the civilians in the destruction of the Fifth Army came to a head when Robertson's alter ego, Maurice, who had recently been removed as director of military operations by Wilson, published on May 7 a potentially explosive letter in several newspapers, including the *Morning Post*. Violating the king's regulations,

Maurice publicly accused the government of misrepresenting facts about the BEF's fighting strength, the extension of its front, and the number of white divisions in the Egyptian Expeditionary Force. Maurice emphasized that his letter was "not the result of a military conspiracy. It has been seen by no soldier. . . . and the last thing I want is to see the Government of our country in the hands of soldiers."[21]

Maurice may have been literally correct, but he had taken Robertson into his confidence before giving his letter to the press. Robertson made no effort to discourage him, despite the certainty that Maurice's military career would be destroyed. Quite the contrary. "You are contemplating a great thing—to your undying credit,"[22] he wrote Maurice.

Because of Robertson's bitterness over his removal and his history of using the press, he has been linked to an effort to drive Lloyd George from office. Lloyd George then and later believed that Robertson and his supporters "had every hope of being able to build up a Parliamentary combination drawn from all parties which would reverse the Versailles decision, supplant the Government, and substitute for it one which would make Robertson virtual dictator for the rest of the War, as Hindenburg was in Germany and by the same means."[23] Lloyd George labels Maurice the military-political cabal's "fizzling cracker" chosen "to blow up the Government."[24]

What can one make of these charges? Robertson had certainly resorted to brinkmanship over the control of the general reserve in February, leading Lloyd George to remark that "either Wully is Prime Minister or I am."[25] Intransigent to the end, Wully had fed information to Asquith and leaned on the press for support.[26] Gwynne's quixotic response had been to conspire to make him prime minister. "If we can find nobody in the ranks of our political leaders," he wrote Mrs. Asquith, "we shall have to look elsewhere."[27] Maxse, another right-winger, also demanded a "War Government" or military leadership in his column in the National Review.[28] But Britain was no Germany, and it is absurd really to think that Parliament would tolerate a military dictator or that Robertson wanted to become one. The best that Robertson apparently hoped for in February was that he remain CIGS. This would have been a temporary humiliation for the War Cabinet, but it would not really have altered Robertson's position in the government.

Robertson certainly never underestimated the Welshman's political skills or staying power, telling Maurice before he wrote his letter in May that he doubted if "the days of Lloyd George are numbered."[29] He may, however, have believed that public pressure after the defeat of the Fifth

Army would restore him to the War Office. But as always, he refused to be used by any political faction. Even the most fantastic and wildly inaccurate rumors surrounding Maurice's challenge to the government had Robertson distancing himself from any military-political cabal. On May 8, Hankey recorded the following in his diary:

Mark Sykes called before the War Cabinet and told me in confidence "from one Chinovnik to another" that Robertson had lunched with Asquith on the previous day. Later I learned from Davies, who got it from Ll. G's valet (!) that a few days ago Robertson gave a dinner to Trenchard [the chief of air staff who had created a stir in mid-April when he had resigned], Repington & Gwynne . . . & Maurice, & that after dinner the party were joined by Asquith & Jellicoe; that the Maurice letter was discussed, and that at the end Robertson said he would have nothing to do with it.[30]

Lloyd George's stunning performance in the Commons quickly reduced what the *Star* had termed "GEN. MAURICE'S BOMBSHELL" to a dud. Lloyd George disarmed his critics with statistics furnished by Maurice's own department. This was effective but dishonest, because Lloyd George had been given corrected figures before his speech. "While he had figures from the D.M.O.'s Dept. showing that the fighting strength of the army had increased from 1 Jan. 1917 to 1918," Hankey noted in his diary, "he had the Adjutant General's figures saying the precise contrary, but was discreetly silent about them."[31]

Although Lloyd George emerged from the Maurice episode stronger than ever, there were many more anxious days ahead on the battlefields of France. After thwarting the last German offensive in July at the Second Battle of the Marne, the Allies regained the strategic initiative. For its part, the BEF inflicted nine successive defeats upon the German army from August 8, the Battle of Amiens, to the last British drive of the war, the Battle of Sambre, November 1–11. During the Hundred Days' Campaign, Haig's forces captured 188,700 prisoners and breached the final defenses of the Hindenburg Line.

Allied success hinged upon many factors. The German high command had exhausted its reserves in a desperate gamble to win total victory before the Americans arrived in force. By July an exhausted and demoralized German army found itself beyond its formidable Hindenburg Line defending vulnerable salients. The war's last year was also the most costly one for the BEF, whose casualties may have approached nine hundred thousand.[32] Although almost every available man was sent to Haig, the government couldn't replace these enormous losses. The United States became the Allied reserve, with approximately two million troops in Europe by the end of the year.

Robertson, ignored by the government as the war turned in favor of the Allies, believed that "fresh Allied troops in France between March and October" constituted the critical factor in the Allied victory. And he wondered, "Would the public and would history ever understand these elementary facts?"[33] Robertson, an early advocate of methodical preparations, limited objectives, and the dominance of the high-explosive shell, could also have emphasized the increasingly sophisticated British methods. Rather than prolonged battles with distant objectives, the BEF attacked different parts of the German front and suspended the assault when German resistance stiffened. As Foch explained to Milner, "Instead of hammering away at a single point, we [the BEF] had made a series of successive attacks, all more or less surprises & all profitable."[34] British artillery superiority was now effectively exploited through improved tactics that included silent registration, creeping barrages, and the neutralization of the enemy artillery by counter-battery fire. Mechanical warfare played a role, too, but modern scholarship is inclined to assign tanks a supporting rather than a decisive role in the British drive to victory.[35]

Success in Palestine and the Balkans, viewed as "side shows" by Robertson, also played a role in Berlin's desire for peace as her allies cracked under military pressure in the autumn. A successful Allied offensive put the Bulgarians to flight on September 15. The Turks were also routed. Despite the transfer of many of the EEF's troops to France, Allenby's army was approximately what it had been prior to the German offensives on the western front, seven infantry and four cavalry divisions. Two Indian divisions had been sent from Mesopotamia, and Indians filled up his other infantry divisions save one, the 54th Division, which after much agonizing, the War Cabinet had left in Allenby's command.[36] His cavalry, which was vastly superior in number and quality to the Turks, constituted his greatest strength.

On September 19 Allenby launched an attack with overwhelming superiority, the Battle of Megiddo. The British had an advantage of perhaps two to one in infantry, eight to one in cavalry, and three to two in guns. Employing surprise, Allenby's infantry ruptured the enemy front. Massed cavalry poured through the gap, one division covering seventy miles in thirty-four hours. Damascus and Aleppo were captured, and on October 30 the Turks surrendered. Within a few weeks the Turkish forces facing Allenby had been destroyed in a rapid and distant advance. British forces, suffering only 5,666 casualties, had taken 75,000 prisoners.[37]

Lloyd George rejoiced at Allenby's triumph at Megiddo, and he made certain that the spokesman for the War Office emphasized the "far-reaching military and political results" of this "eastern" triumph when he talked to the press.[38] But did Allenby's overwhelming victory over the Turks really discredit Robertson's earlier strategic advice? Not really. It would be wrong to suggest that Allenby could have achieved after his capture of Jerusalem what he accomplished in September-October 1918. The weather would have prevented him from immediately following up his victory. "Rains such as octogenarian Arabs with wagging white beards," writes Cyril Falls, "asserted they had never seen before flooded the land and swept away bridges and culverts."[39] Sir Henry Wilson might talk glibly of military operations in Palestine during the "mud months" of northern Europe, but the normal rainfall in Palestine was twenty-eight inches, with most of this precipitation between the end of October and March.[40]

In 1931 there was a fascinating exchange of letters between Murray and Allenby, who both had been invited to give lectures at Aldershot about their campaigns. Murray went right to the heart of the matter, asking Allenby, "Were the enormous successes in Palestine and the successes in Macedonia a justification for the risk in the main theatres?"[41]

Allenby equivocated. The results had justified the risk, but he wasn't sure that he would have "risked making the detachment from the Western Theatre, as I don't know the political & strategical views of the Allies or the existing possibilities when the decision was taken." He then mirrored almost exactly the views of Britain's political leadership during the winter of 1917–18:

Concentration of force is a sound general rule; but high politics & high strategy must see widely and think forward. War's strain exhausted our ally Russia. France's moral fibre was weakening towards the end; and it is not impossible that an offer by Germany to evacuate occupied territory in Belgium & Northern France; perhaps to surrender Alsace-Lorraine to France & Trentino to Italy; in return for cessation of hostilities; might have sent France & Italy the same way as Russia. Germany might then have ended the war supreme from the North Sea to the Persian Gulf; winner in fact, if not in theory. With Turkey & Bulgaria out, Germany's road to the East was cut irreparably. That's how I look at it.[42]

The War Cabinet had been convinced that the western front was secure and that risks could be taken in the imperial war against Turkey as an insurance policy in the event that the Continental war had an unsatisfactory conclusion. Robertson's focus on the west and his opposition to peripheral operations isolated him in the inner councils of war. The destruction of the Fifth Army, however, gave Robertson the better of the argument.

The Armistice didn't end Robertson's service to his country. In April 1919 he took command of the British Army of the Rhine. After relinquishing this command in March 1920, he was promoted to field marshal. When he returned to London, there was no official greeting party at Victoria Station. "Having secured a broken-down taxi I drove to my residence in Eccleston Square, and thereupon joined the long list of unemployed officers on half-pay,"[43] he notes in his memoirs. He died on the morning of February 12, 1933, of a thrombosis. It is alleged that his last words were, "Where's the damn tea?"[44]

NOTES

1. Robertson to DMO, DMI, and Deputy CIGS, n.d., Maurice MSS 3/1/4.

2. For accounts of the domestic turmoil generated by the German offensive, see Turner, *British Politics and the Great War*, 286–307; and Woodward, *Lloyd George and the Generals*, 282–305.

3. T. Wilson, *Myriad Faces of War*, 556; the day after the attack, Wilson informed the War Cabinet that the Germans had 191 divisions as opposed to 165 Allied divisions exclusive of the American divisions. This represented an increase of 14 German divisions since February 12. On the other hand, Wilson claimed that the Allies enjoyed a slight superiority in rifle strength, 1,418,000 to 1,402,000. These figures, of course, were meaningless to the greatly outmanned British divisions under attack. Memorandum by general staff, February 12, 1918, WO 106/314; and War Cabinet (370), March 22, 1918, CAB 23/5.

4. See Woodward, *Lloyd George and the Generals*, 275–78.

5. Sackville-West to Wilson, March 21, 1918, Wilson MSS file 12 B.

6. Martin Middlebrook, *The Kaiser's Battle 21 March 1918: The First Day of the German Spring Offensive* (London, 1978), 309.

7. War Cabinet (371 and 374), March 23 and 27, CAB 23/5.

8. Milner to Lloyd George, March 28, 1918, Lloyd George MSS F/38/3/22.

9. *Military Operations: France and Belgium, 1918*, vol. 1, vii.

10. "Episodes of the Month," *The National Review* 71 (March 1918):31–32.

11. War Cabinet (369), March 21, 1918, CAB 23/5; and Woodward, *Lloyd George and the Generals*, 292–93.

12. *Globe*, April 20, 1918.

13. *Morning Post*, April 18, 1918.

14. Robertson to Haig, April 19, 1918, Haig MSS No. 126.

15. *Morning Post*, April 20, 1918.

16. *Morning Post*, April 22, 1918.

17. See War Cabinet (396), April 22, 1918, CAB 23/6.

18. Diary entry of April 22, 1918, Wilson MSS.

19. Lloyd George to Milner, April 24, 1917, Lloyd George MSS F/38/3/25.

20. War Cabinet (396), April 22, 1918, CAB 23/6.

21. A copy of this letter is in Lloyd George, *War Memoirs*, vol. 2, 1784–86.

22. Robertson to Maurice, May 4, 1918, Maurice MSS 4/5/24.

23. Lloyd George, *War Memoirs*, vol. 2, 1673.

24. Ibid., 1778.

25. Brett, *Journals and Letters of Esher*, 181.

26. Robertson to Asquith, February 16, 1918, Woodward, MCWR, 305. When the government prosecuted the *Morning Post* under the Defence of the Realm Act for revealing facts about the command of the general reserve, Gwynne wrote Lady Bathurst, his employer, on February 20, 1918: "Between ourselves, all I have done was with the warmest approval of Sir W[illiam] R[obertson] and the whole of the General Staff." K. Wilson, *Rasp of War*, 250.

27. Gwynne to Mrs. Asquith, February 18, 1918, Gwynne MSS 14.

28. Maxse, "The Tragedy of It," *National Review* 71 (May 1918): 322–32.

29. Robertson to Maurice, May 4, 1918, Maurice MSS 4/5/24.

30. Diary entry of May 8, 1918, Hankey MSS 1/3. These rumors were so prevalent that Robertson had to write Milner, assuring him that they were false. Robertson to Milner, May 17, 1918, Lloyd George MSS F/38/3/33.

31. Diary entry of May 9, 1918, Hankey MSS 1/3. For an account of the Maurice Debate, see Woodward, *Lloyd George and the Generals*, 298–304.

32. One source puts the losses as high as 876,250. *Statistics of the Military Effort of the British Empire*, 167.

33. Repington, *First World War*, vol. 2, 467.

34. Milner to Lloyd George, September 17, 1918, Lloyd George MSS F/38/4/17.

35. See, for example, Harris, "Rise of Armour," in Griffith, *British Fighting Methods*, 113–37; Prior and Wilson, *Passchendaele*, 16–17; and Jonathan Bailey, *Strategic and Combat Studies Institute Occasional Paper No. 22—The First World War and the Birth of the Modern Style of Warfare* (London, 1996), 11–21.

36. The decision to leave the 54th with Allenby had been made when the outcome of the war in the west was still uncertain. War Cabinet (446), July 16, 1918, CAB 23/7.

37. Falls, *The Great War*, 402.

38. See, for example, J. T. Davies to Sir Henry Wilson, September 24, 1918, Lloyd George MSS F/47/7/44.

39. Falls, *Armageddon*, 15.

40. See Major-General Downay, "Memorandum regarding certain factors to be taken into account in considering future operations in Palestine," December 13, 1917, WO 106/718.

41. Murray to Allenby, December 21, 1931, Murray MSS 79/48/3.

42. Allenby to Murray, December 23, 1931, Murray MSS 79/48/3.

43. Robertson, *Private to Field-Marshal*, 377.

44. Bonham-Carter, *Soldier True*, 382.

Bibliography

MANUSCRIPT COLLECTIONS

Bodleian Library, Oxford
        Asquith MSS
        Dawson MSS
        Gwynne MSS
        Milner MSS
British Library, London
        Northcliffe MSS
Churchill College, Cambridge
        Esher MSS
        Hankey MSS
        Rawlinson MSS
House of Lords Record Office, London
        Bonar Law MSS
        Lloyd George MSS
        Selborne MSS
Imperial War Museum, London
        Fitzgerald MSS
        Gwynne MSS
        Kirke MSS
        Lynden-Bell MSS
        Murray MSS
        Wilson MSS
Liddell Hart Military Archives, King's College, London
        Clive MSS
        Kiggell MSS
        Liddell Hart MSS
        Maurice MSS

Robertson MSS
Spears MSS
Liverpool Record Office, Liverpool City Library, Liverpool
Derby MSS
National Library of Scotland, Edinburgh
Haig MSS
National Army Museum, London
Rawlinson MSS
Oriental and India Office and Records, London
Curzon MSS
Public Record Office, Kew
Clive MSS
Grey MSS
Hankey MSS
Kitchener MSS
Macdonogh MSS
Royal Archives, Windsor
George V MSS
War Office Library, London
Isaac MSS

OFFICIAL DOCUMENTS (PUBLIC RECORD OFFICE, LONDON)

Files of the Cabinet Office, including
Cabinet Memoranda
Committee of Prime Ministers
Dardanelles Committee
International Conferences
Man-Power Committee
Supreme War Council
War Cabinet
War Committee
War Policy Committee
Files of the Foreign Office
Files of the War Office

NEWSPAPERS

Daily Chronicle
Daily Mail
Daily News
Daily Telegraph
Globe
Manchester Guardian
Morning Post
National Review
Star
Times

OFFICIAL SOURCES

Edmonds, J. E. (general editor and compiler). *History of the Great War: Military Operations: Egypt and Palestine,* 2 vols., London, 1928–30; *France and Belgium,* 14 vols., London, 1922–48; *Italy, 1915–1918,* 1949; *Macedonia,* 2 vols,. London, 1933–35; *Campaigns in Mesopotamia,* 4 vols., London, 1923–27.

Mitchell, T. J. and G. M. Smith. *History of the Great War. Medical Services: Casualties and Medical Statistics of the Great War.* London, 1931.

War Office. *Statistics of the Military Effort of the British Empire during the Great War 1914–1920.* London, 1922.

PUBLISHED PRIMARY SOURCES

Amery, L. S. *My Political Life,* vol. 1: *War and Peace, 1914–1929.* London, 1953.

Barnes, J., and D. Nicholson, eds. *The Leo Amery Diaries:* vol. 1, *1896–1929.* London, 1980.

Barrow, G. de S. *The Fire of Life.* London, c. 1942.

Beckett, I.F.W., ed. *The Army and the Curragh Incident.* 1986.

Blake, R., ed. *The Private Papers of Douglas Haig 1914–1919.* London, 1952.

Boraston, J. H., ed. *Sir Douglas Haig's Despatches: December 1915–April 1918.* London and Toronto, 1919.

Brett, M. V., ed. *Journals and Letters of Reginald Viscount Esher,* vol. 4: *1916–1930.* London, 1938.

Callwell, E. E. *Field-Marshal Sir Henry Wilson: His Life and Diaries.* 2 vols. London, 1927.

Charteris, J. *At G.H.Q.* London, 1931.

Fay, S. *The War Office at War.* East Ardsley, England, 1973 ed.

Gibbs, P. *Now It Can Be Told.* New York, 1920.

Gilbert, M., ed. *Winston S. Churchill, Vol. 3 Companion Part 1 Documents July 1914–April 1915.* London, 1972.

Hankey, Lord. *The Supreme Command 1914–1918.* 2 vols. 1962.

Lloyd George, D. *War Memoirs of David Lloyd George.* 2 vols. London, 1938.

McEwen, J. M., ed. *The Riddell Diaries 1908–1923.* London, 1986.

Painlevé, P. *Comment J'ai Nommé Foch et Pétain.* Paris, 1923.

Repington, C. à Court. *The First World War 1914–1918.* 2 vols. London, 1921.

Riddell, G. *Lord Riddell's War Diary 1914–1918.* London, 1933.

Robertson, W. *From Private to Field-Marshal.* London, 1921.

_____ . *Soldiers and Statesmen 1914–1918.* 2 vols. London, 1926.

Roskill, S. *Hankey: Man of Secrets,* vol. 1: *1877–1918.* London, 1970.

Spears, E. L. *Prelude to Victory.* London, 1939.

Taylor, A.J.P., ed. *Lloyd George: A Diary by Frances Stevenson.* New York, 1971.

Terraine, J. *The Road to Passchendaele: The Flanders Offensive of 1917: A Study in Inevitability.* London, 1977.

Wilson, K., ed. *The Rasp of War: The Letters of H. A. Gwynne to the Countess Bathurst 1914–1918.* London, 1988.

Wilson, T., ed. *The Political Diaries of C. P. Scott, 1911–1928.* London, 1970.

Woodward, D. R., ed. *The Military Correspondence of Field-Marshal Sir William Robertson, Chief of the Imperial General Staff, December 1915–February 1918.* London, 1989.

Wright, P. E. *At the Supreme War Council.* London, 1921.

SECONDARY SOURCES

Adams, R.J.Q., and P. P. Poirier. *The Conscription Controversy in Great Britain 1900–18.* Columbus, 1987.

Aspery, R. B. *The German High Command at War: Hindenburg and Ludendorff Conduct World War One.* Asprey, N.Y., 1991.

Badsey, S. "Cavalry and the Development of the Breakthrough Doctrine." In P. Griffith, ed. *British Fighting Methods in the Great War.* London, 1996.

Bailey, J. "British Artillery in the Great War." In P. Griffith, ed. *British Fighting Methods in the Great War.* London, 1996.

_____. *Strategic and Combat Studies Institute Occasional Paper No. 22—The First World War and the Birth of Modern Style of Warfare.* London, 1996.

Barker, A. J. *The Neglected War: Mesopotamia 1914–1918.* London, 1967.

Bassford, C. *Clausewitz in English: The Reception of Clausewitz in Britain and America 1815–1945.* New York and Oxford, 1994.

Beaverbrook, Lord. *Politicians and the War 1914–1916.* London, 1960.

Beckett, I.F.W. "Frocks and Brasshats." In B. Bond, ed. *The First World War and British Military History.* Oxford, 1991.

_____. "Revisiting the Old Front Line: The Historiography of the Great War Since 1984." *Stand To! The Journal of the Western Front Association* 43 (April 1995).

Bidwell, S., and D. Graham. *Fire-Power: British Army Weapons and Theories of War 1904–1945.* Boston, 1985.

Bonham-Carter, V. *Soldier True: The Life and Times of Field-Marshal Sir William Robertson.* London, 1963.

Bourne, J. M. *Britain and the Great War 1914–1918.* London, 1989.

Cassar, G.H. *Kitchener: Architect of Victory.* London, 1977.

_____. *Asquith as War Leader.* London and Rio Grande, 1994.

Churchill, R. *Lord Derby, "King" of Lancashire: The Official Life of Edward Earl Derby, 1865–1948.* London, 1959.

Clausewitz, C. von. *On War.* ed. Anatol Rapoport. Middlesex, England, 1968.

Clayton, Anthony. "Robert Nivelle and the French Spring Offensive of 1917." In B. Bond, ed. *Fallen Stars: Eleven Studies of Twentieth-Century Military Disasters.* London, 1991.

Corum, J. S. *The Roots of Blitzkrieg: Hans Von Seeckt and German Military Reform.* Lawrence, Kansas, 1992.

Cruttwell, C.R.M.F. *A History of the Great War 1914–1918.* Oxford, 1934.

_____. *The Role of British Strategy in the Great War.* London, 1936.

De Groot, G. J. *Douglas Haig, 1861–1928.* London, 1988.

Dupuy, T. N. *A Genius for War: The German Army and General Staff, 1807–1945.* Englewood Cliffs, 1977.

Dutton, D. "The 'Robertson Dictatorship' and the Balkan Campaign of 1916." *Journal of Strategic Studies* 9 (March 1986).

Edmonds, J. E. "Field-Marshal Sir William Robertson, Reminiscences and an Appreciation." *The Army Quarterly* 26 (April 1933).

Erickson, J. *The Road to Berlin: Continuing the History of Stalin's War with Germany.* Boulder, 1983.

Esher, Lord. *The Tragedy of Lord Kitchener.* London, 1921.

Falls, C. *The Great War.* New York, 1961.

_____ . *Armageddon 1918*. Philadelphia and New York, 1964.

Fischer, F. *Germany's Aims in the First World War*. New York, 1967.

Frandale, M. *History of the Royal Regiment of Artillery: Western Front 1914–18*. Dorchester, 1986.

Fraser, P. *Lord Esher: A Political Biography*. London, 1973.

French, D. *British Strategy and War Aims, 1914–1916*. London, 1986.

_____ . "The Meaning of Attrition, 1914–1916." *English Historical Review* 103 (April 1988).

_____ . "Who Knew What and When? The French Army Mutinies and the British Decision to Launch the Third Battle of Ypres." In L. Freedman, P. Hayes, and R. O'Neill, eds. *War, Strategy, and International Politics: Essays in Honour of Sir Michael Howard*. Oxford, 1992.

_____ . *The Strategy of the Lloyd George Coalition, 1916–1918*. Oxford, 1995.

Gilbert, B. B. *David Lloyd George A Political Life: Organizer of Victory, 1912–1916*. Columbus, Ohio, 1992.

Gollin, A. M. *Proconsul in Politics: A Study of Lord Milner in Opposition and in Power*. New York, 1964.

Gooch, J. "The Maurice Debate 1918." *Journal of Contemporary History* 3 (October 1968).

_____ . *The Plans of War: The General Staff and British Military Strategy c. 1900–1916*. New York, 1974.

_____ . "Soldiers, Strategy and War Aims in Britain 1914–1918." In B. Hunt and A. Preston, eds. *War Aims and Strategic Policy in the Great War 1914–1918*. London, 1977.

Graham, D., and S. Bidwell. *Coalitions, Politicians and Generals: Some Aspects of Command in Two World Wars*. London, 1993.

Grieves, K. "'Total War'?: The Quest for a British Manpower Policy, 1917–19." Journal of Strategic Studies 9 (March 1986): 79–95.

_____ . *Politics of Manpower, 1914–18*. Manchester, 1988.

Griffith, P. *Battle Tactics of the Western Front: The British Army's Art of Attack 1916–18*. New Haven, 1994.

_____ , ed. *British Fighting Methods in the Great War*. London, 1996.

Grigg, J. *Lloyd George: From Peace to War 1912–1916*. Berkeley, 1985.

Guinn, P. *British Strategy and Politics, 1914–1918*. Oxford, 1965.

Harris, J. P. "The Rise of Armour." In P. Griffith, ed. *British Fighting Methods in the Great War*. London, 1996.

Heenan, L. E. *Russian Democracy's Fatal Blunder: The Summer Offensive of 1917*. New York, 1987.

Herwig, H. H. "The Dynamics of Necessity: German Military Policy during the First World War." In A. R. Millett and W. Murray, ed. *Military Effectiveness*: vol. 1, *The First World War*. Boston, 1988.

_____ . *The First World War: Germany and Austria-Hungary 1914–1918*. London, 1997.

Holmes, R. *The Little Field-Marshal Sir John French*. London, 1981.

Howard, M. *Studies in War and Peace*. New York, 1970.

_____ . *The Continental Commitment: The Dilemma of British Defence Policy in the Era of the Two World Wars. The Ford Lectures in the University of Oxford*. London, 1972.

Hughes, M. D. "General Allenby and the Campaign of the Egyptian Expeditionary Force, June 1917–November 1919." Ph.D. thesis, King's College, University of London. 1995.

Hussey, J. "Defeating the Weak to Bring Down the Strong: The Palestine Argument, 1917–18." Unpublished paper.

Jackson, W., and Lord Bramall. *The Chiefs: The Story of the United Kingdom Chiefs of Staff.* London, 1992.

Johnson, H. C. *Break-through! Tactics, Technology, and the Search for Victory on the Western Front in World War I.* Novato, Calif., 1994.

Johnson, J. H. *Stalemate! The Great Trench Warfare Battles of 1915–1917.* London, 1995.

Jomini, Baron de. *The Art of War.* Westport, Conn., 1962.

Keegan, J. *Face of Battle: A Study of Agincourt, Waterloo and the Somme.* New York, 1977.

Kennedy, P. "Military Effectiveness in the First World War." In A. R. Millett and W. Murray, eds. *Military Effectiveness,* vol. 1: *The First World War.* Boston, 1989.

Leask, G. A. *Sir William Robertson: The Life Story of the Chief of the Imperial General Staff.* London, 1917.

Liddell Hart, B. H. "The Basic Truths of Passchendaele." *Journal of the Royal United Service Institution* 104 (November 1959).

———. *The Real War 1914–1918.* Boston and Toronto, 1930.

Lupfer, T. T. *The Dynamics of Doctrine: The Changes in German Tactical Doctrine during the First World War.* Washington, D.C., 1981.

McEwen, J. M. "Brass-Hats and the British Press during the First World War." *Canadian Journal of History* 18 (April 1983).

Magnus, P. *Kitchener: Portrait of an Imperialist.* London, 1958.

Maurice, F. *British Strategy: A Study of the Application of the Principles of War.* London, 1929.

Maurice, N., ed. *The Maurice Case: From the Papers of Major-General Sir Frederick Maurice.* London, 1972.

Middlebrook, M. *The First Day on the Somme 1 July 1916.* New York, 1972.

———. *The Kaiser's Battle 21 March 1918: The First Day of the German Spring Offensive.* London, 1978.

Millman, B. "Henry Wilson's Mischief: Field Marshal Sir Henry Wilson's Rise to Power, 1917–18." *Canadian Journal of History* 30 (December 1995).

Neilson, K. "Kitchener: A Reputation Refurbished?" *Canadian Journal of History* 15 (August 1980).

———. *Strategy and Supply: The Anglo-Russian Alliance, 1914–17.* London, 1984.

Newell, J. Q. C. "Learning the Hard Way: Allenby in Egypt and Palestine 1917–1919." *Journal of Strategic Studies* 14 (September 1991).

Nicholls, Jonathan. *Cheerful Sacrifice: The Battle of Arras, 1917.* London, 1990.

Philpott, W. J. "British Military Strategy on the Western Front: Independence or Alliance, 1904–1918." Ph. D. thesis. Oxford, 1991.

Porch, D. "The French Army in the First World War." in A. R. Millett and W. Murray, eds. *Military Effectiveness,* vol. 1: *The First World War.* Boston, 1988.

Prior, R., and T. Wilson. *Command on the Western Front: The Military Career of Sir Henry Rawlinson 1914–1918.* Oxford, 1992.

———. *Passchendaele: The Untold Story.* New Haven, 1996.

Rothwell, V. H. *British War Aims and Peace Diplomacy, 1914–1918.* Oxford, 1971.

Samuels, M. *Command or Control? Command, Training and Tactics in the British and German Armies 1888–1918.* London, 1995.

Stevenson, D. *French War Aims against Germany 1914–1919.* Oxford, 1982.

Taylor, A.J.P. *English History 1914–1945.* New York, 1965.

Terraine, J. *Ordeal of Victory.* Philadelphia and New York, 1963.

_____. *The U-Boat Wars 1916–1945*. New York, 1989.

Travers, T. "A Particular Style of Command: Haig and GHQ, 1916–18." *Journal of Strategic Studies* 10 (September 1987).

_____. *The Killing Ground: The British Army, the Western Front and the Emergence of Modern Warfare 1900–1918*. London, 1987.

_____. *How the War Was Won: Command and Technology in the British Army on the Western Front, 1917–1918*. New York, 1992.

_____. "The Somme: July 1, 1916, The Reason Why." *MHQ: The Quarterly Journal of Military History* 7 (Summer 1995).

Turner, J. *British Politics and the Great War: Coalition and Conflict 1915–1918*. New Haven, 1992.

Wallach, J. L. *Uneasy Coalition: The Entente Experience in World War I*. Westport, Conn., 1993.

Wiest, A. A. *Passchendaele and the Royal Navy*. Westport, Conn., 1995.

Williams, M. J. "Thirty Per Cent: A Study in Casualty Statistics." *Journal of the Royal United Service Institution* 109 (February 1964).

Wilson, K. M. *A Study in the History and Politics of the Morning Post 1905–1926*. Lewiston, 1990.

_____. "Over the Top? The Question of Political Aspirations on the Part of the British High Command in the Course of the First World War." *Journal of the Society for Army Historical Research* 74 (Summer 1996).

Wilson, T. *The Myriad Faces of War: Britain and the Great War, 1914–1918*. Cambridge, 1986.

Winter, D. *Haig's Command: A Reassessment*. London, 1991.

Winter, J. M. *The Great War and the British People*. Cambridge, 1986.

Woodward, D. R. "David Lloyd George, a Negotiated Peace with Germany and the Kühlmann Peace Kite of September 1917." *Canadian Journal of History* 6 (March 1971).

_____. "The Imperial Strategist: Jan Christiaan Smuts and British Military Policy, 1917–1918." *Military History Journal* 5 (December 1981).

_____. *Lloyd George and the Generals*. Newark, 1983.

_____. "Did Lloyd George Starve the British Army of Men Prior to the German Offensive of 21 March 1918?" *Historical Journal* 27 (March 1984).

_____. *Trial by Friendship: Anglo-American Relations, 1917–1918*. Lexington, 1993.

Wynne, G. C. "The Development of the German Defensive Battle in 1917, and Its Influence on British Defence Tactics, Part 1." *The Army Quarterly* 34 (April 1937).

_____. *If Germany Attacks: The Battle in Depth in the West*. London, 1940.

Index

Sir William Robertson is referred to as R throughout this index. Subentries are listed in ascending page order.

About the Author

DAVID R. WOODWARD is Professor of History at Marshall University. He has been a student of the First World War for over thirty years. His previous publications include a volume of the military correspondence of Sir William Robertson.

ISBN 0-275-95422-6